I0812506

IMAGES
of America

MILLINOCKET

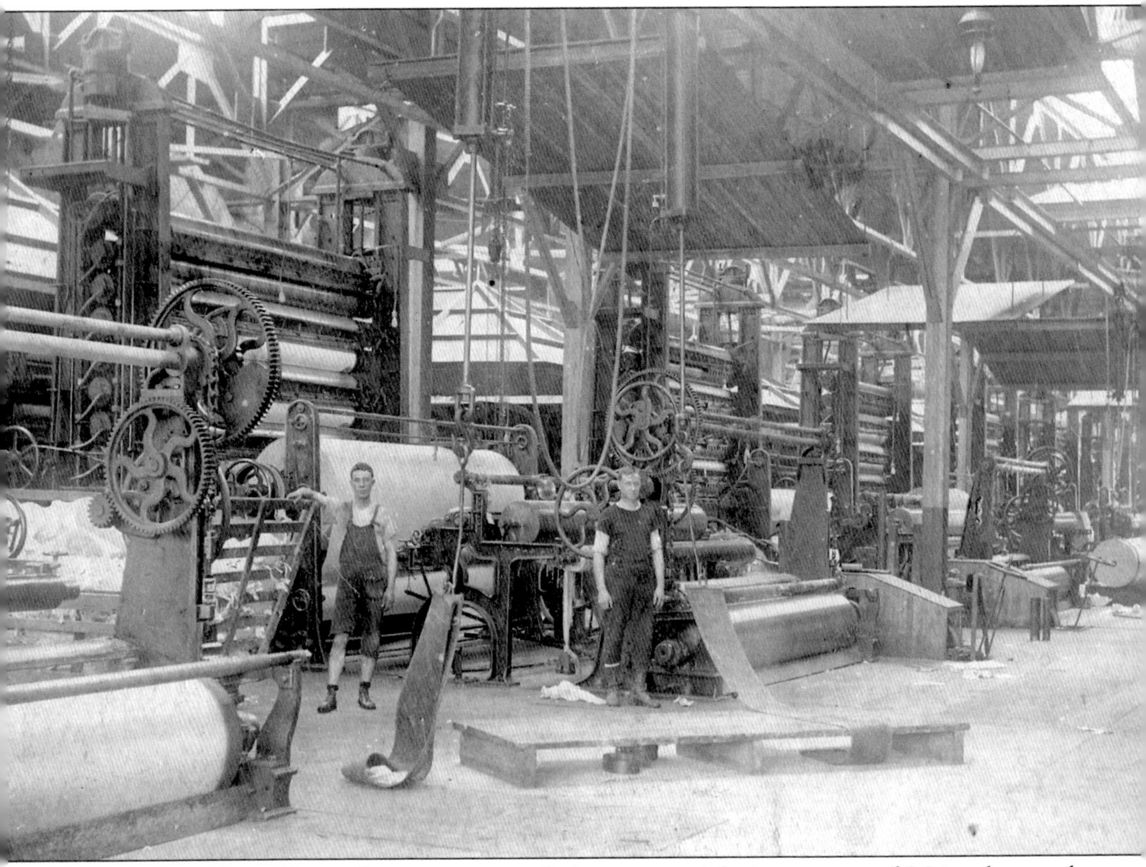

Great Northern Paper Company sprouted almost overnight in an area of Maine known by the Native Americans as Millinocket. There was nothing here except for a few early settlers that braved the wilds to set up small farms. Within a few short years of hurried construction, a mill sprang up and a town appeared beside it. Great Northern Paper Company grew to be the largest mill in the world at the time, and the town became known as "the magic city in Maine's wilderness." Harnessing the water of the West Branch of the Penobscot River, power was generated to drive the mill and turn out paper that was exported throughout the world. Churning out newsprint at the rate of 240 tons a day kept the mill operating 24 hours a day seven days a week. Great Northern Paper Company was a leader in the industry and set the trend for the making of paper.

On the cover: Please see above. (Courtesy of the Millinocket Historical Society.)

IMAGES
of America

MILLINOCKET

David R. Duplisea

ARCADIA
PUBLISHING

ISBN 978-0-7385-5654-3

Published by Arcadia Publishing
Charleston, South Carolina

Printed in the United States of America

Library of Congress Catalog Card Number: 2007941863

For all general information contact Arcadia Publishing at:
Telephone 843-853-2070
Fax 843-853-0044
E-mail sales@arcadiapublishing.com
For customer service and orders:
Toll-Free 1-888-313-2665

Visit us on the Internet at www.arcadiapublishing.com

Dedicated to the people who made this town what it is today.

Contents

ACKNOWLEDGMENTS

I have always enjoyed history. As a young child I remember wondering about how it used to be in the old days. How did people live? What were their everyday lives like? Did they have the same ups and downs in life that we have today? I listened to the stories my grandfather told me as he reminisced about when he was growing up. I was totally engrossed in his memories of when he was a child. I was fascinated. My parents fostered that fascination that I had with the past and encouraged me to find out more. I had a hunger to learn where my family came from and what they went through that finally resulted in my existence. History allows one to have a true sense of being, a feeling of completeness.

A picture snapped by an individual who witnessed an event unfold is about as basic as it can get. Viewing the picture is like looking through the photographer's eyes. It provides the feeling of being part of the event.

This book has been a pleasure to work on; I have learned a lot. I thank the Millinocket Historical Society for the opportunity to use the pictures that appear in this book. The historical society is made up of a dedicated group of people who care enough to preserve the local history. They put long hours in to caring and preserving the artifacts entrusted to them by fellow town citizens.

I would like to thank my parents, Leroy and Theodora (Dody) Duplisea, for encouraging the young boy they raised to explore and find out things to learn by.

Most of all, I thank my wife, Kimberly Duplisea, for being here for me in loving support of all that I endeavor to do.

Unless otherwise noted, all the pictures used in this book are from the collection of the Millinocket Historical Society.

INTRODUCTION

The Penobscot River watershed is the largest in the state of Maine and the second largest river system in New England. For over 5,000 years, Native Americans used the many waterways to travel around to their hunting lands. Mount Katahdin, the highest peak in Maine, sits between the West and East Branches of the Penobscot River as if keeping guard over the land. According to legend, the mountain, with its unique peak, was thought to be the "council place of the Gods." Pamola was one of the gods thought to live on the mountain.

Early in Maine history, the vast, uncut forests were viewed as a resource to feed the world's hunger for lumber. The city of Bangor, which sits on the lower reaches of the Penobscot River, was the lumber capital of the world. Bangor was a bustle of activity with many sawmills in the area churning out lumber to load onto the ships that carried Maine wood products all over the world. The Penobscot River was used as a transportation system to get the timber to the mills by floating the logs downriver.

It was in 1829 that Thomas Fowler of Pittsfield packed up two teams of oxen with his worldly possessions and headed north. Initially he settled in an area known as Grand Falls, which is at the head of Shad Pond. It was around 1837 or 1838 that he relocated his family to the area where the Penobscot River and Millinocket Stream meet. The Fowler homestead was their home until 1899, when the Great Northern Paper Company began construction of the mill.

Charles Mullen came to the Mount Katahdin area during the construction of the Bangor and Aroostook Railroad line to Houlton, which opened in 1894. The railroad line crossed the area somewhere between Quakish Lake and Shad Pond. Mullen could see a lot of potential in the area, with the vast timberlands and the fall of the water in the Penobscot River. He formed a small group of speculators from the Bangor area known as the syndicate, including James Rice, Millard E. Mudgett, Clarence S. Lunt, Joseph P. Bass, and Thomas F. Hegarty. During the negotiations that followed, Garret Schenck entered into the arrangement. At the time, Schenck was the manager and director of the Rumford Falls Paper Company. It was in 1897 that the Maine legislature issued a charter to the syndicate, and the Northern Development Company was born. In the original charter, it was the intent of Mullen to harness the power of the Penobscot River to provide power to lumbering operations that were to appear in the area. In 1899, with Schenck as the new president of the Northern Development Company, the Maine legislature was petitioned for an amendment to its charter. There had been ongoing discussions about obtaining timberland and going into the lumbering business. The amendment to the charter was approved, and in 1899, the Great Northern Paper Company was born.

Great Northern Paper Company was a leader in the industry and set the standard for the other mills in the world. If it was not for the Great Northern Paper Company coming to the area, Millinocket would not be here. Millinocket owes its existence to the company. There may have been a town built here someday, but not the one that exists today. Millinocket will always be synonymous with the Great Northern Paper Company. The company no longer exists, as it has slowly melted away through downsizing and the selling of assets. The mill is still here though, and so are the people.

This book is not intended to be the definitive history of Millinocket or the Great Northern Paper Company; there are other good books out there that have done that. I have strived for accuracy through research and speaking with longtime residents. This is a book of memories and of how life used to be when the Great Northern Paper Company ruled the north woods of Maine, and I hope that it will help people remember back to a particular moment in their lives that they had forgotten.

Millinocket has been called the "magic city in the Maine wilderness" because it is special and unique, and we have a lot to be proud of. Please enjoy this book.

One

Great Northern Paper

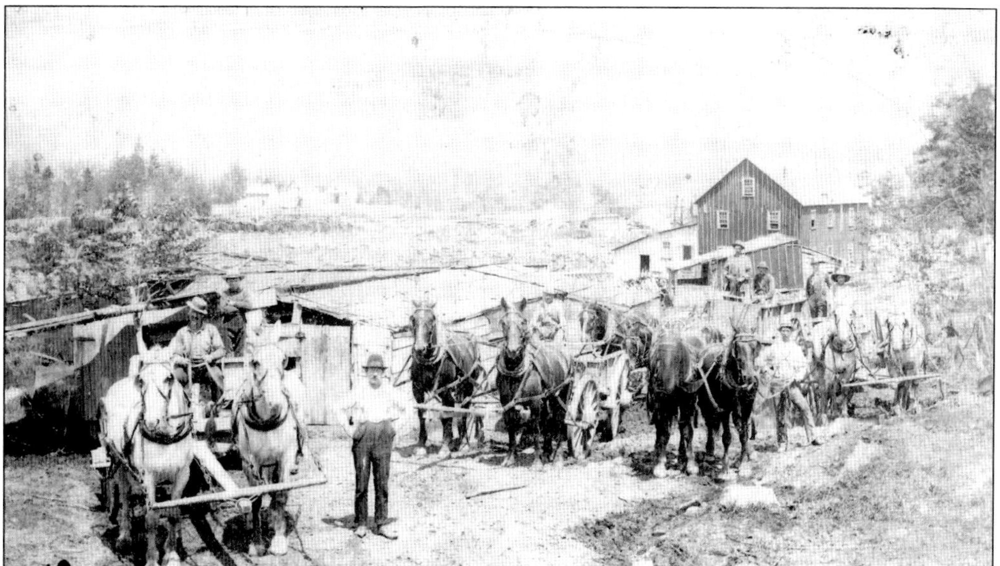

J. B. Mullen and Company was awarded a contract on May 3, 1899, to begin work on the excavation, masonry, and brickwork for the mill known as the Great Northern Paper Company. Just opening up a new consulting business in Lewiston, Hardy S. Ferguson was contracted to design the mill, and his expertise with designing paper mills influenced other mill construction projects throughout the world. Its not known exactly how many men were used to construct the mill, but a figure as high as 1,500 is probably accurate. Immigrants were coming from countries such as Poland, Lithuania, Finland, Hungary, Estonia, and many other countries. Italians made up the biggest part of the unskilled labor force that was adept at stonemasonry. Despite the hard working conditions, there was only one injury logged while the mill was under construction—a worker had his foot crushed by a large stone.

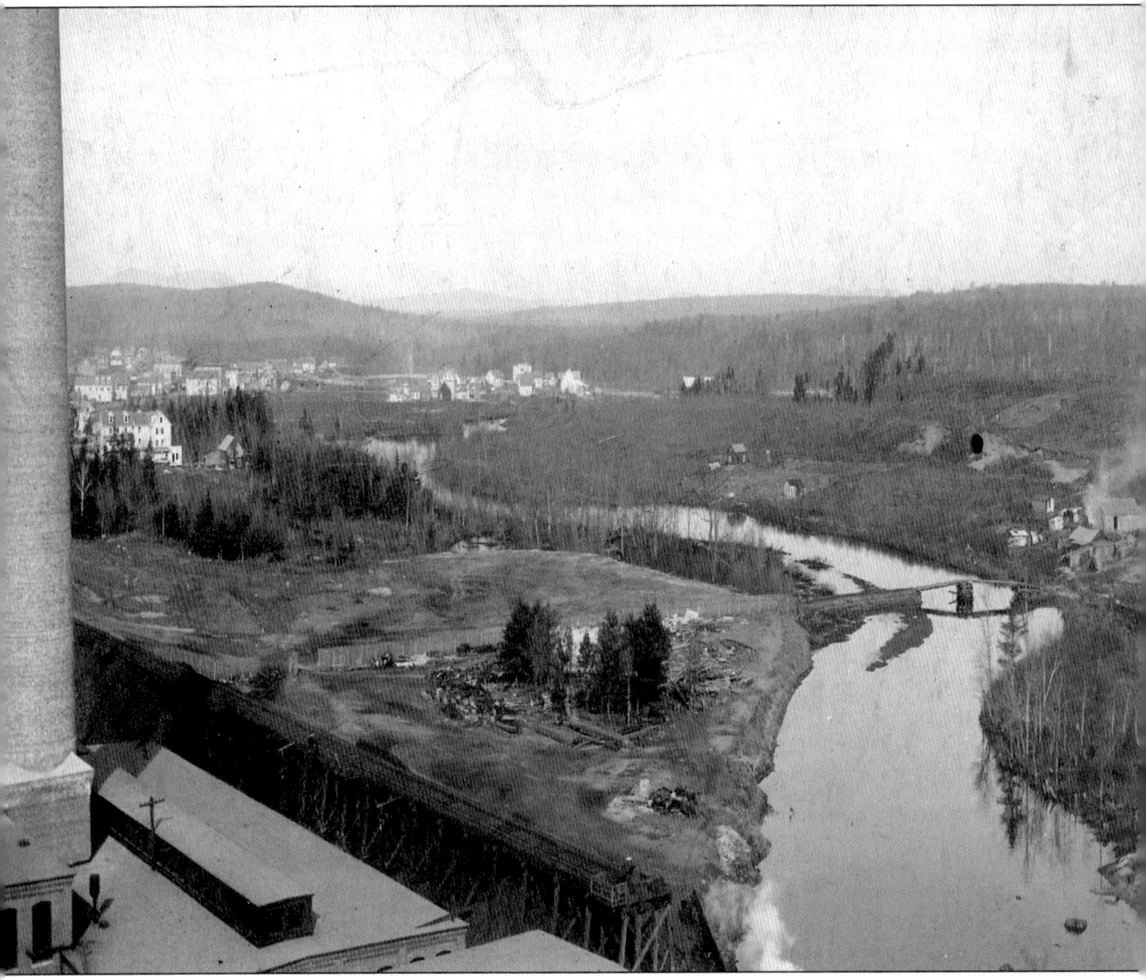

Italian immigrants coming to the area were unfamiliar with the land and the language. Fred Peluso was working as a clerk for John Merrill, and he was appointed to watch over the new workers. Peluso saw to their every need by placing them in jobs, providing them with food, acting as translator, and helping them start their homes. Peluso built a substantial home with some outbuildings that become known as Peluso's Square, and it was complete with cobblestones. He started a store that catered to the homesick Italian immigrants and provided traditional Italian foodstuffs that could be purchased on credit. As more immigrants arrived, they settled in an area that ran along the Millinocket Stream just across from the mill. The small settlement was to become known as Little Italy, and Peluso was called the *padrone* or king of Little Italy.

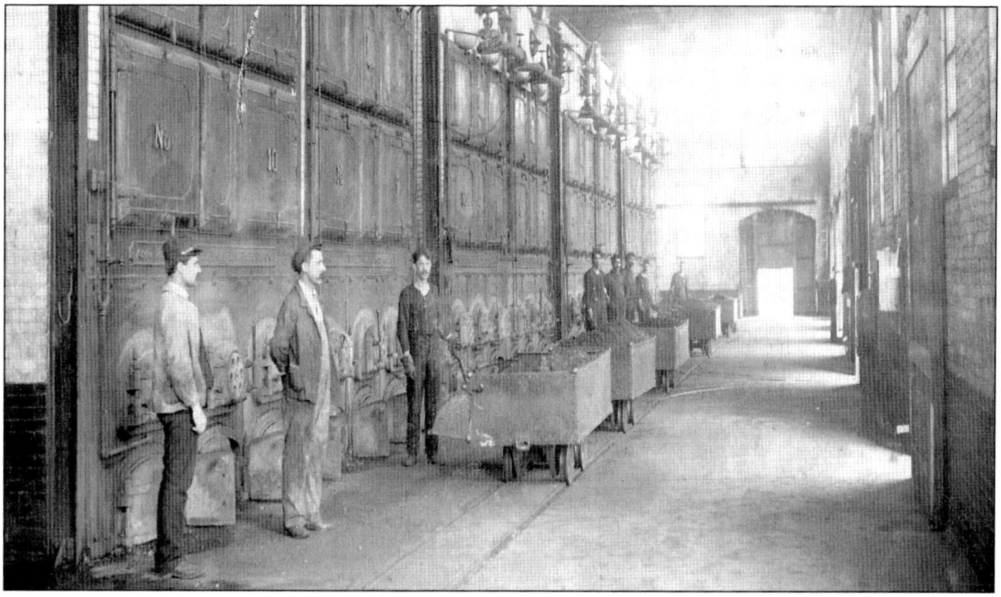

The work was hot and dirty; men had to shovel by hand the coal needed to feed the boilers for the mill. At a common labor pay of about $1.50 a day, men worked the long hours to keep the mill going. The paper machines needed steam to power them and that was provided by rows of coal-fired boilers. The coal was carted in by hand from a 30,000-ton storage pile outside. The ash was also carted out the same way to be disposed of. In later years when the airport was constructed, ash from the mill was used as fill for the runway.

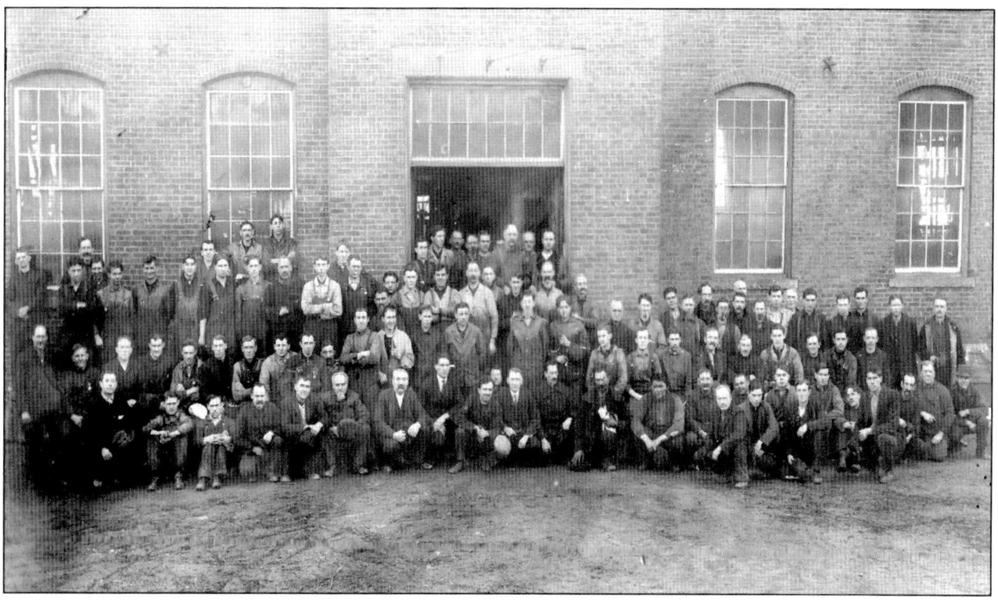

Heeding the call of promised employment, men came from all corners to work either on the construction of the mill, work in the mill, or provide services for those that were employed by the Great Northern Paper Company. With such a mixture of names and the ever-present language barrier, communication was a challenge. For pay purposes, names were usually not used. Instead each worker was provided with a small, numbered, metal disk that was used to identify him so he could get paid.

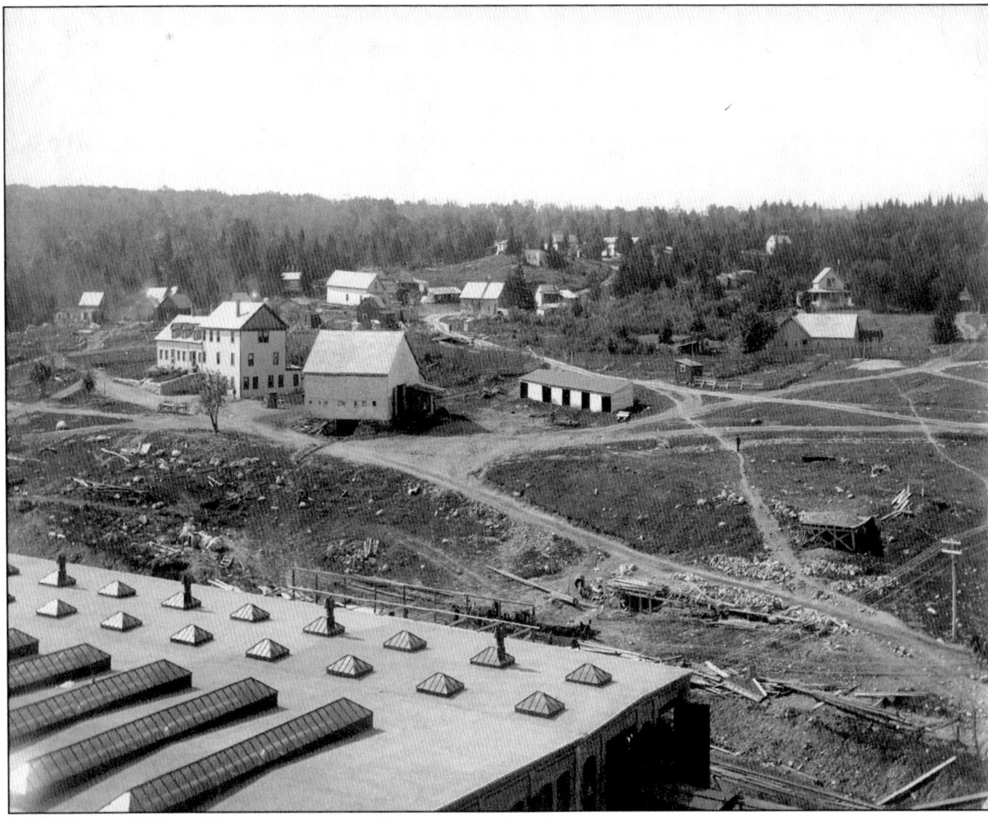

Around 1837 or 1838, Thomas Fowler Sr. was the first settler to the area and took advantage of a tract of land beside Millinocket Stream to build his farm. In 1846, he was visited by Henry David Thoreau and was asked to guide Thoreau on his journey to Mount Katahdin. Great Northern Paper Company purchased the Fowler farm in 1899 and began work on the mill. The company moved in between the Fowler farm and Millinocket Stream and filled the once quiet and tranquil valley with modern industry. Today there are no farms in Millinocket to remind anybody of its early settlers.

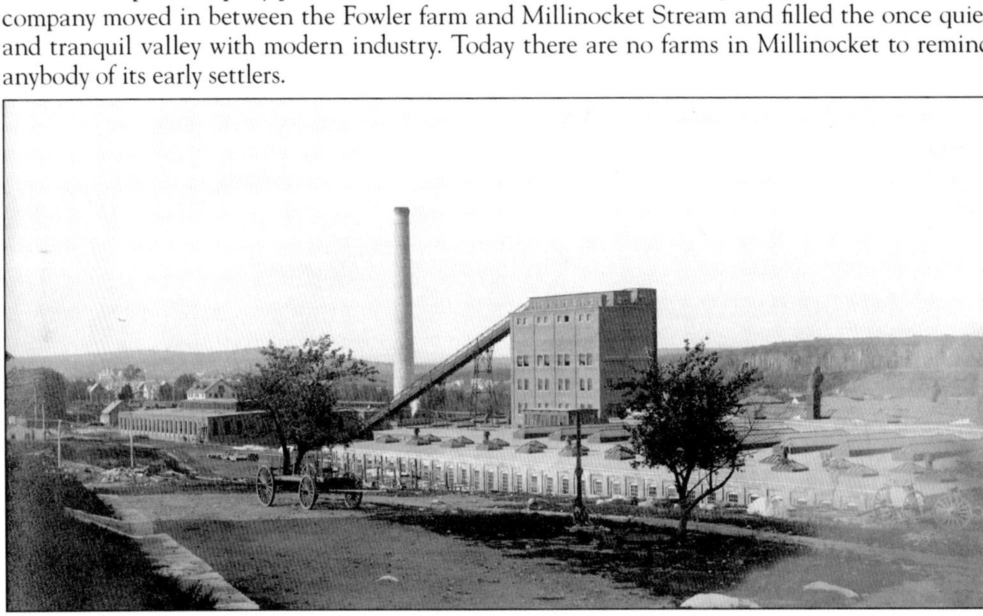

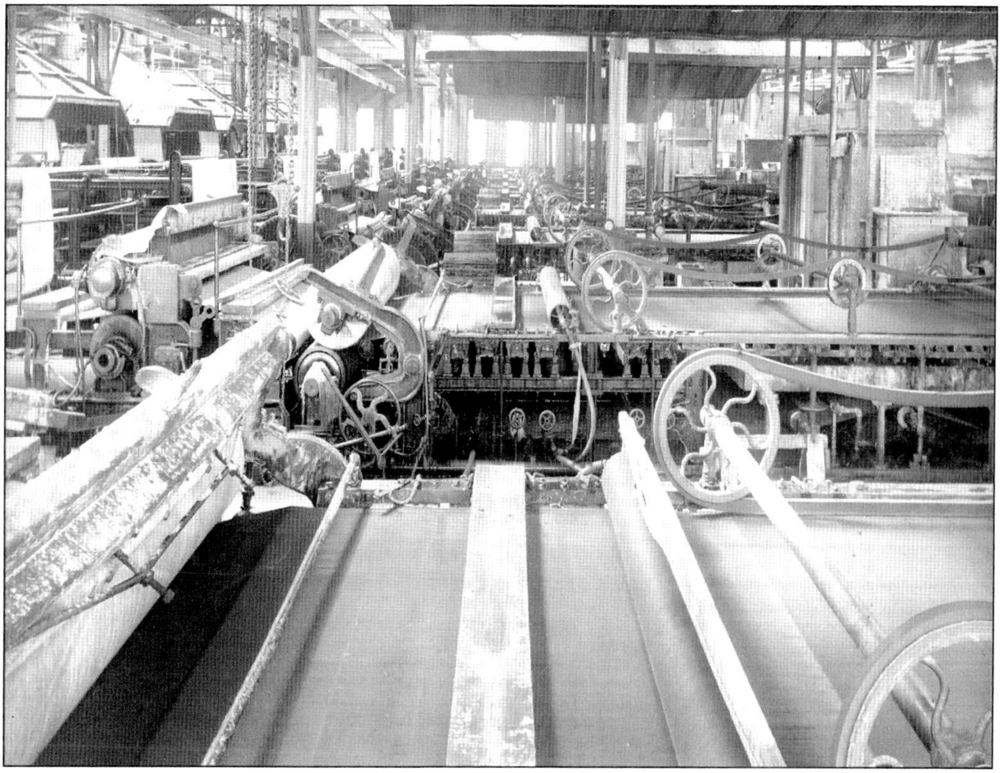

John A. Decker came to Millinocket from Rumford to be the first superintendent of the mill. With an output of 240 tons of newsprint a day, it earned the title of the largest mill in the world at the time. Garret Schenck officially started up the mill on the evening of November 1, 1900. The Great Northern Paper Company was in business.

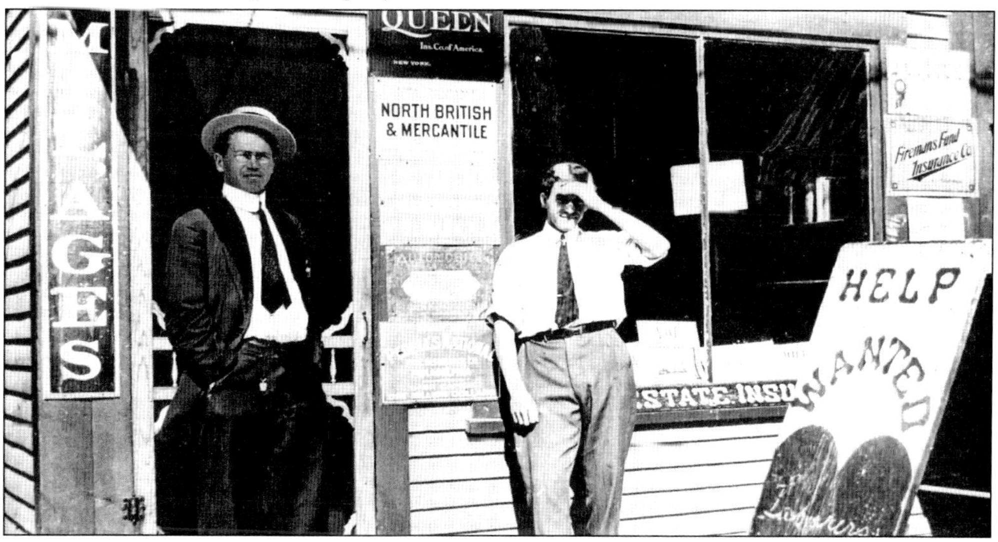

Frank Speed opened an employment office, and it was a bustle of activity trying to keep up with laborers arriving around the clock looking for work. The work force consisted of people from all around the world, as construction continued at a hectic pace. Insurance could also be purchased at the Speed office.

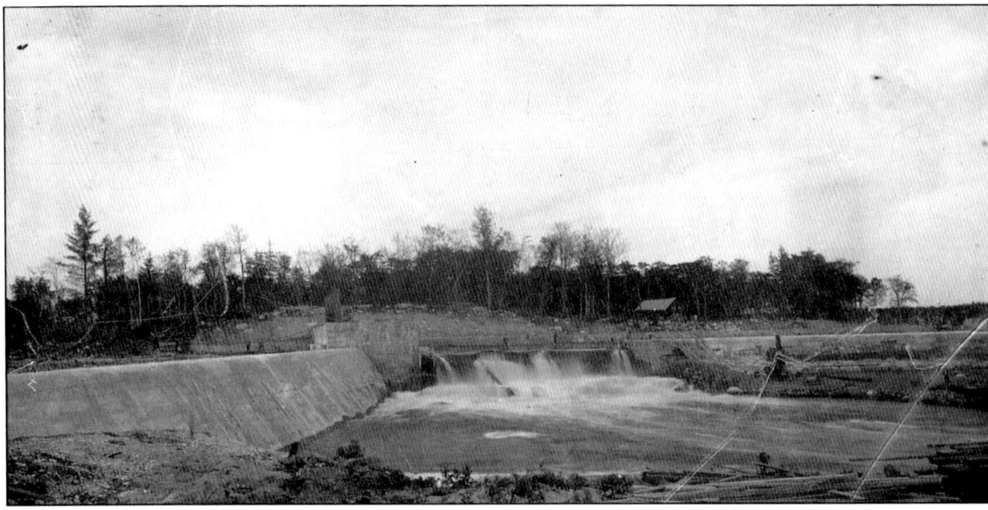

In order to control the water coming to the mill, Stone Dam was built at Rines Pitch at the outlet of Quakish Lake. Ferguson Pond was created by a series of dikes and Wards Dam to allow for the storage of water and pulpwood for the mill. A canal was dug out of the rocky ground to direct water to the penstocks of the mill where power was generated. Millinocket drew its drinking water from Ferguson Pond, and in early times, it was gravity-fed to the town. The gravity feed proved unreliable, as some homes enjoyed good water pressure, and other homes had almost none.

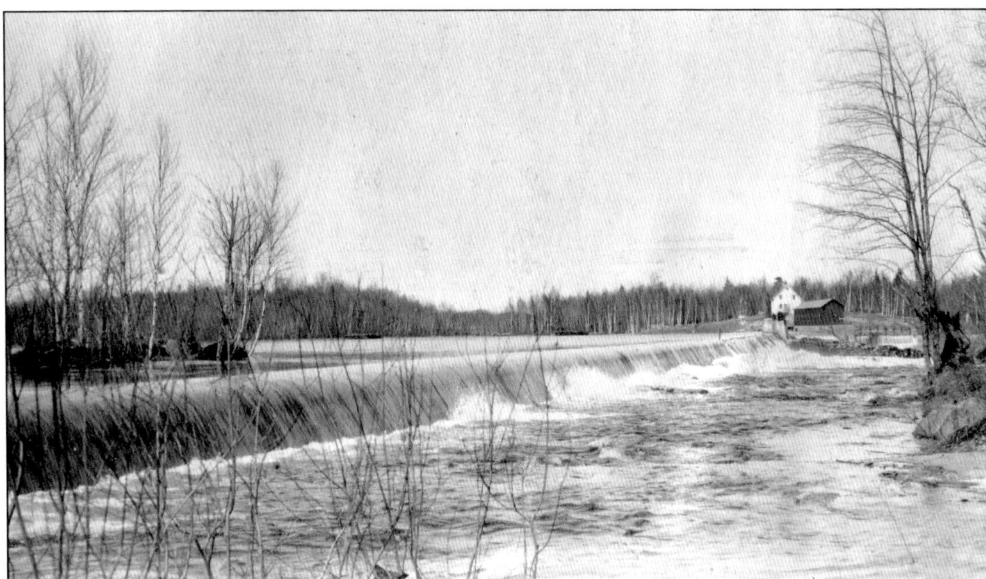

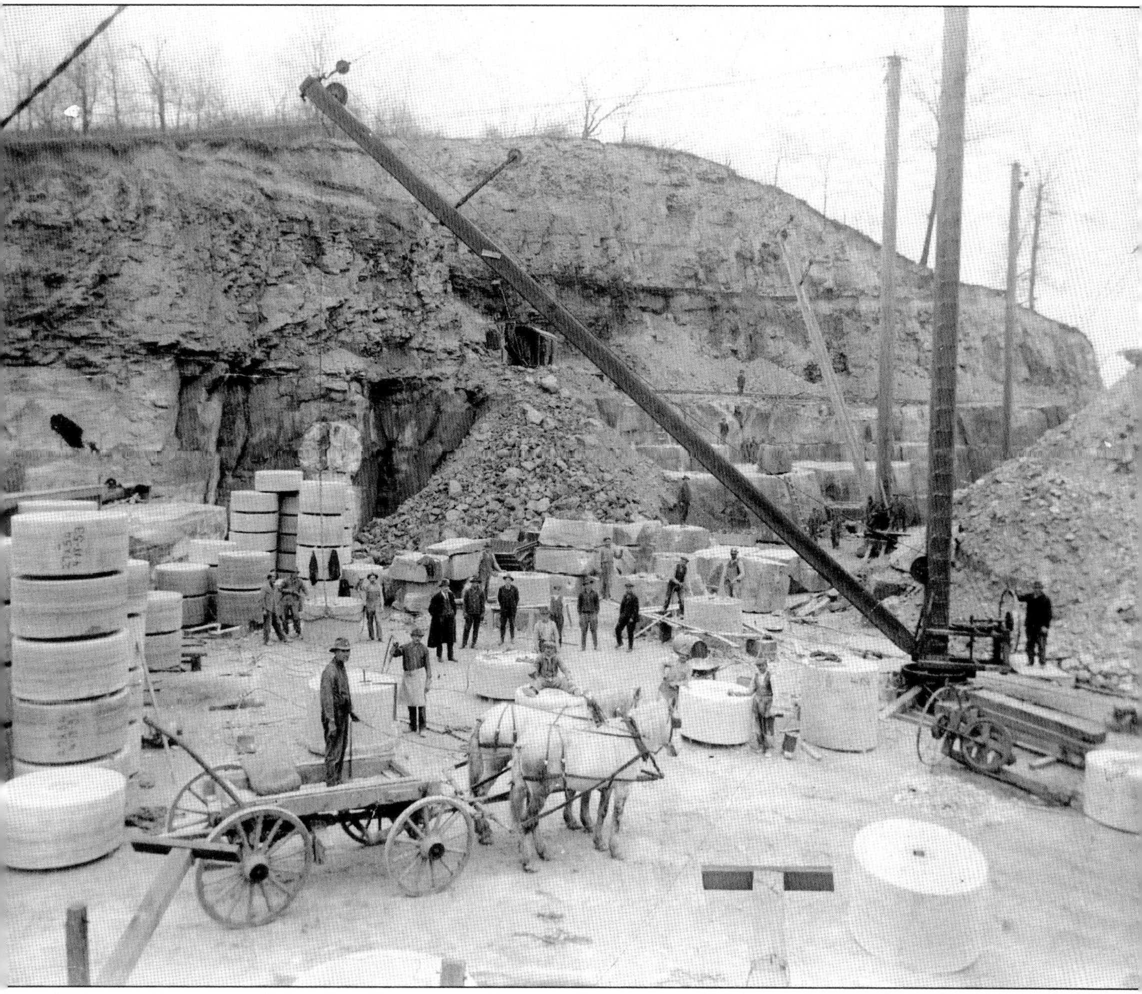

Taking advantage of the abundant natural stone that was available, stonemasons carve out the grinding stones from a hillside. Although considered unskilled labor, the Italians proved to be invaluable stone carvers that plied their trade with a great deal of skill. From the foundation of the mill to the brick in the walls, there was a need for talented laborers that could put the stones and brickwork together. Today many of the homes in Millinocket have fireplaces that were placed together by an Italian craftsman, which will serve the homeowner many more years of good, warm, comfort.

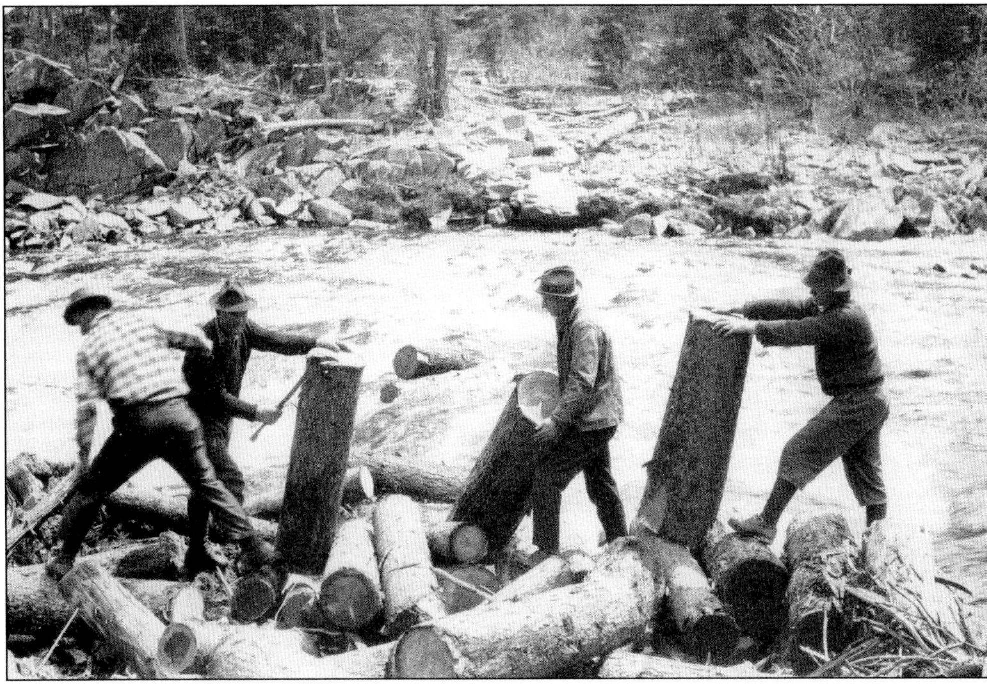

In order to facilitate the floating of the logs down river, the logs were cut into four-foot lengths called pulpwood. Even at that length, the pulpwood was still labor intensive to get down the river. The pulpwood that washed ashore had to be manhandled back into the water to continue its trip down the river.

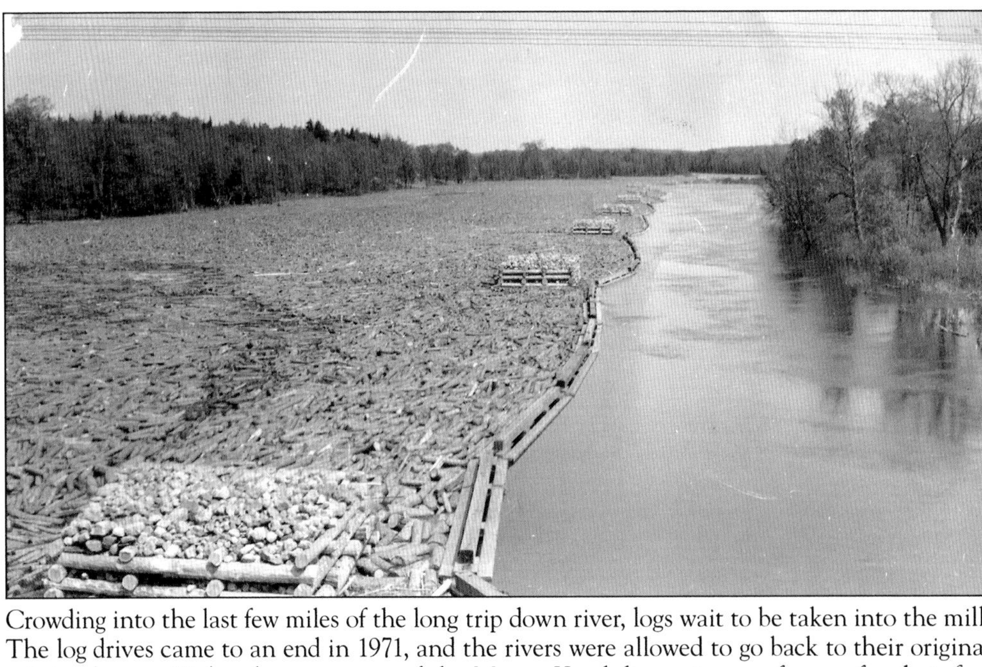

Crowding into the last few miles of the long trip down river, logs wait to be taken into the mill. The log drives came to an end in 1971, and the rivers were allowed to go back to their original pristine beauty. Today the waterways of the Mount Katahdin region are famous for their fine salmon and trout fishing.

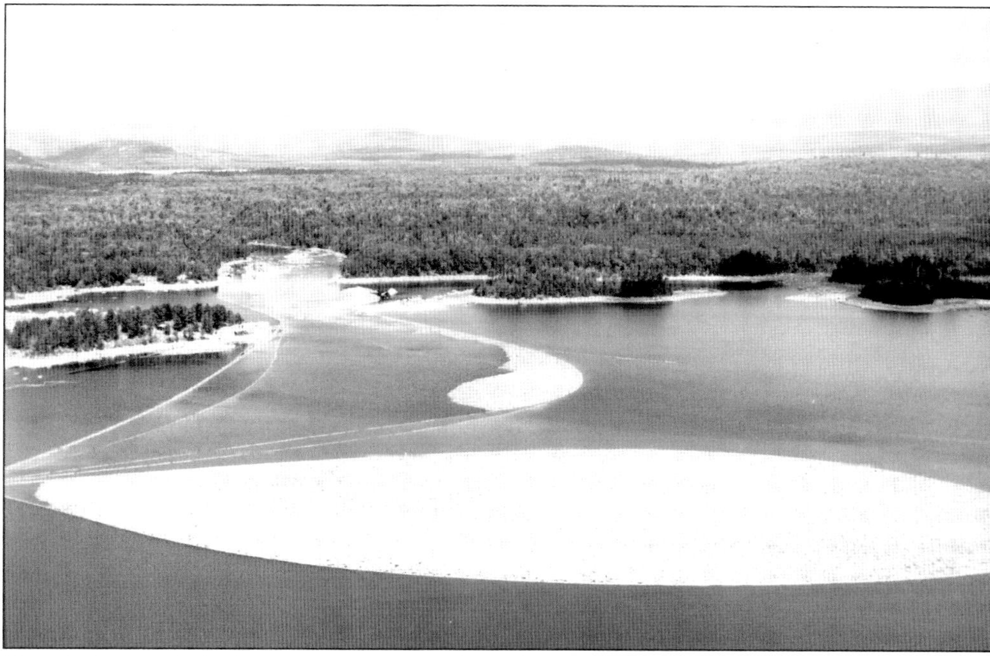

The Ambajejus Lake boom house awaits the pulpwood as it floats out into Ambajejus Lake. Large log booms were chained together and corralled the pulpwood into the enclosed booms. Today the boom house is a museum that is open to the public. Entering the boom house truly takes the visitor back in time.

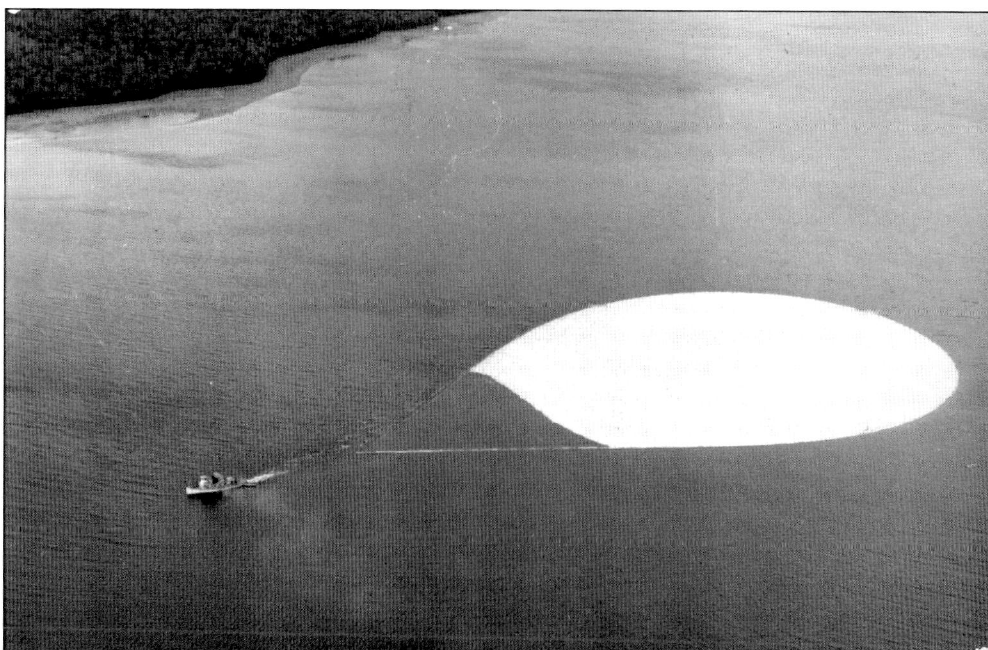

Once the pulpwood was in the booms, a tugboat connected on to the boom and towed the whole thing across the lake. This was a laborsaving move meant to get the pulpwood from the inlet to the outlet without having the logs float freely all over the lake.

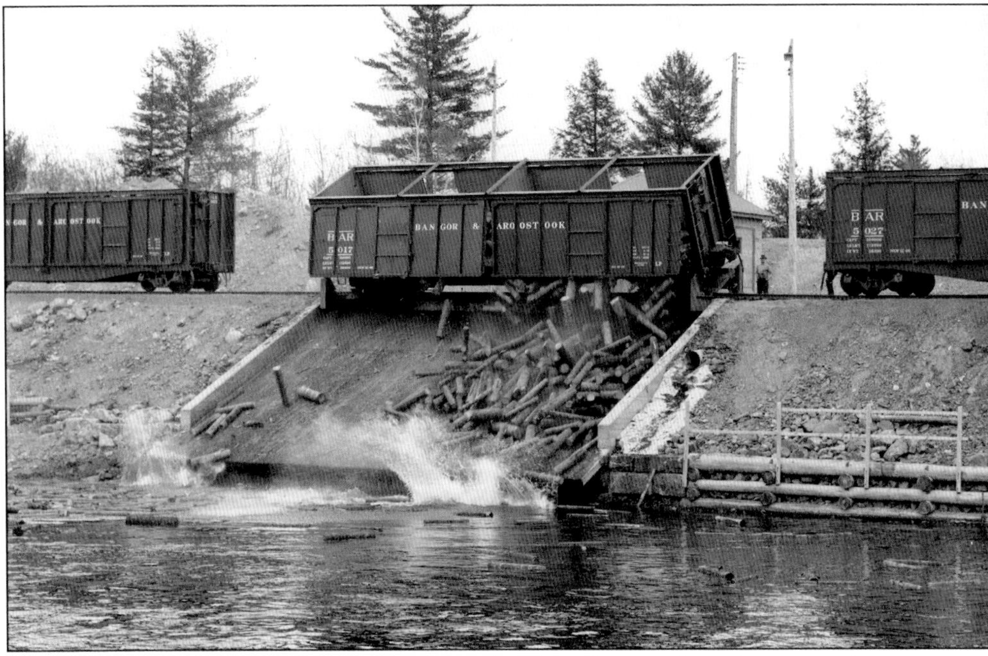

Just down river from South Twin Dam, the railroad tracks ran along the river. The trains were loaded down with pulpwood that was dumped down the chutes into the river. The route went from there to Quakish Lake and then on through Ferguson Lake where the mill sat ready for the logs.

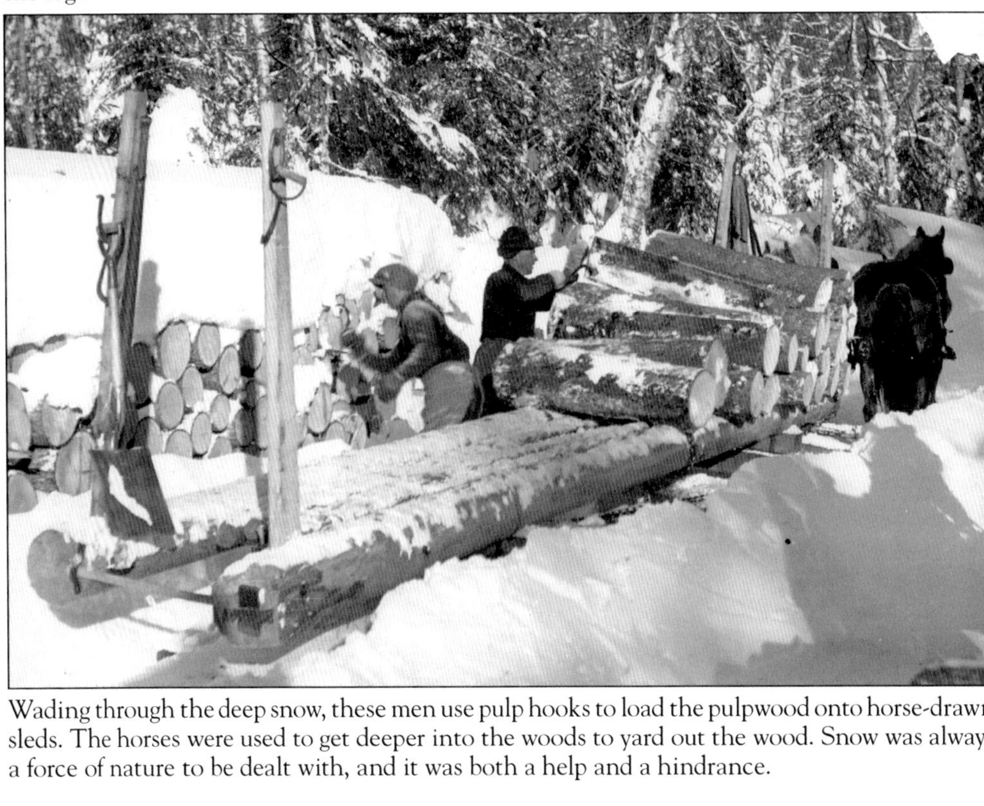

Wading through the deep snow, these men use pulp hooks to load the pulpwood onto horse-drawn sleds. The horses were used to get deeper into the woods to yard out the wood. Snow was always a force of nature to be dealt with, and it was both a help and a hindrance.

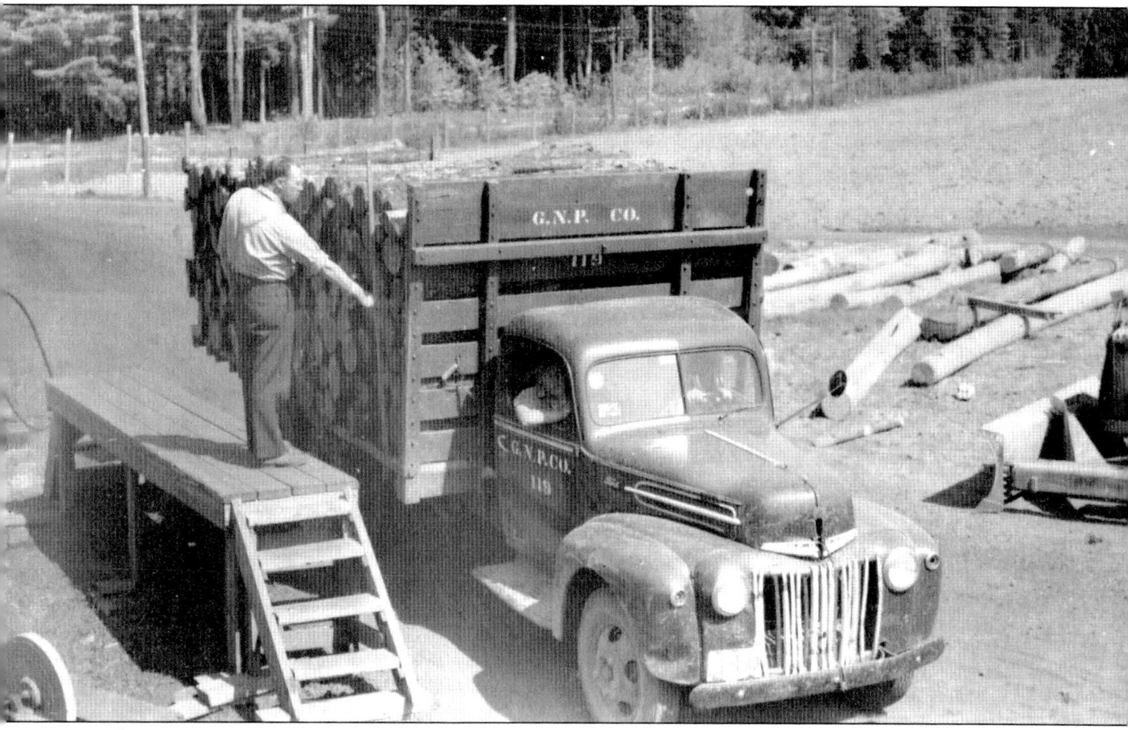

In order to maintain proper accounting of how much wood was delivered to the mill, the trucks were scaled to determine the size of the load. As more trucks were used to transport the pulpwood, more roads were built. Transporting by truck was less costly than hiring men as river drivers to ensure the logs floated all the way down river. A road was built reaching far into the woods that led from the entrance of the mill all the way to the Canadian border. The road was called the Golden Road and was used as the main artery for all the other offshoot roads to connect into it. With more roads being built, it allowed for more selective cutting, and traveling from place to place was done with more ease.

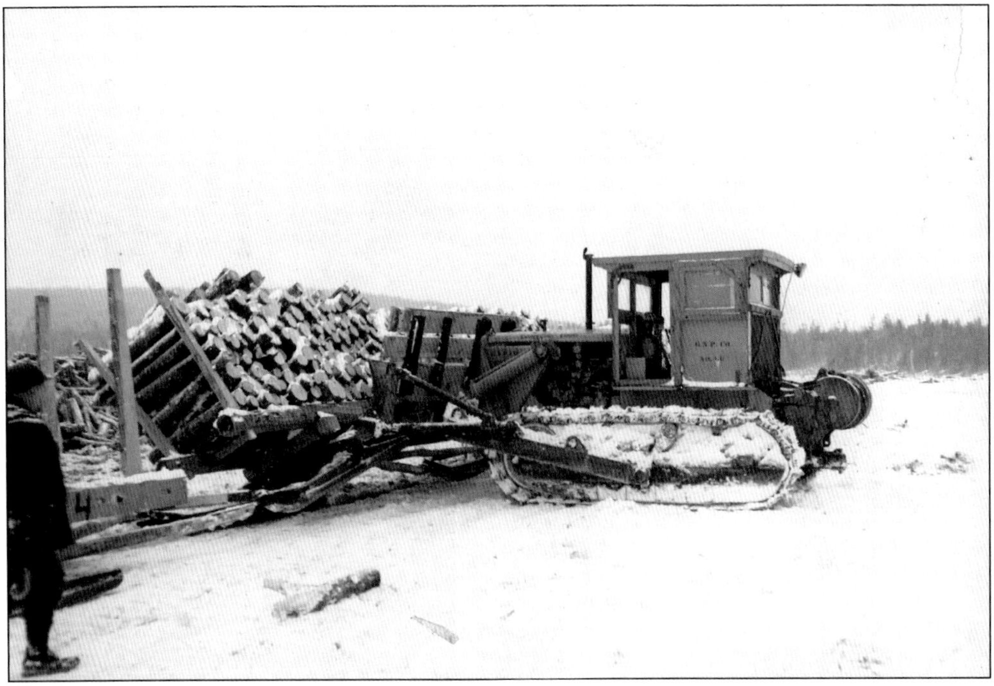

When the pulpwood was yarded out to the frozen stream, a bulldozer tipped the sleds over for a quick job at unloading. Bulldozers were a welcome asset to the north woods operations since they could go anywhere, including the deep snow or the spring-season mud.

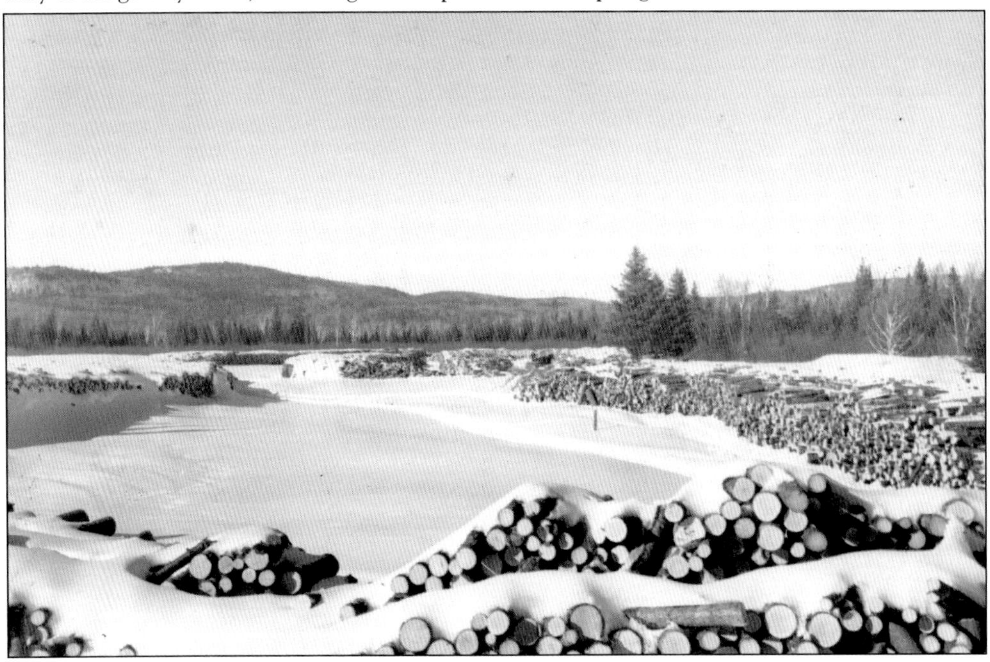

Pulpwood sits on the ice of Russell Stream. Such was the scene all over the Mount Katahdin region in the winter. The cut wood was staged on the edge of waterways or often right on the frozen ice. In the spring thaw as the ice melted, the logs were allowed to start their journey downriver to the mill.

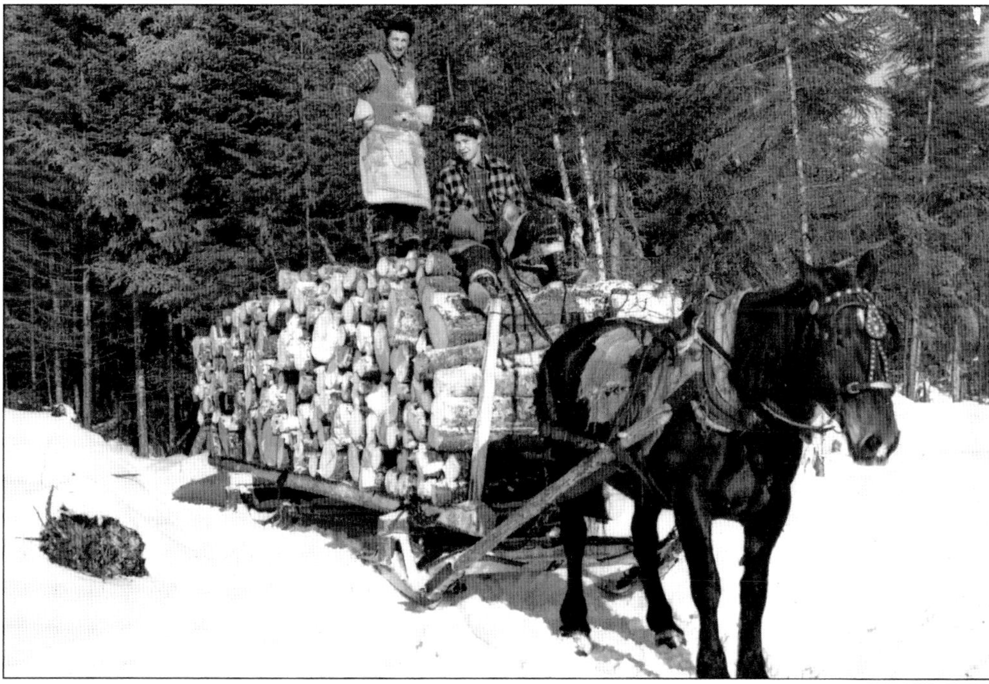

Catching a ride out of the woods on top of a loaded sled, these men are on their way to the yard. Men who worked in the woods were rough and rugged, as the work was hard. Men were housed in lumber camps that were spread throughout the region.

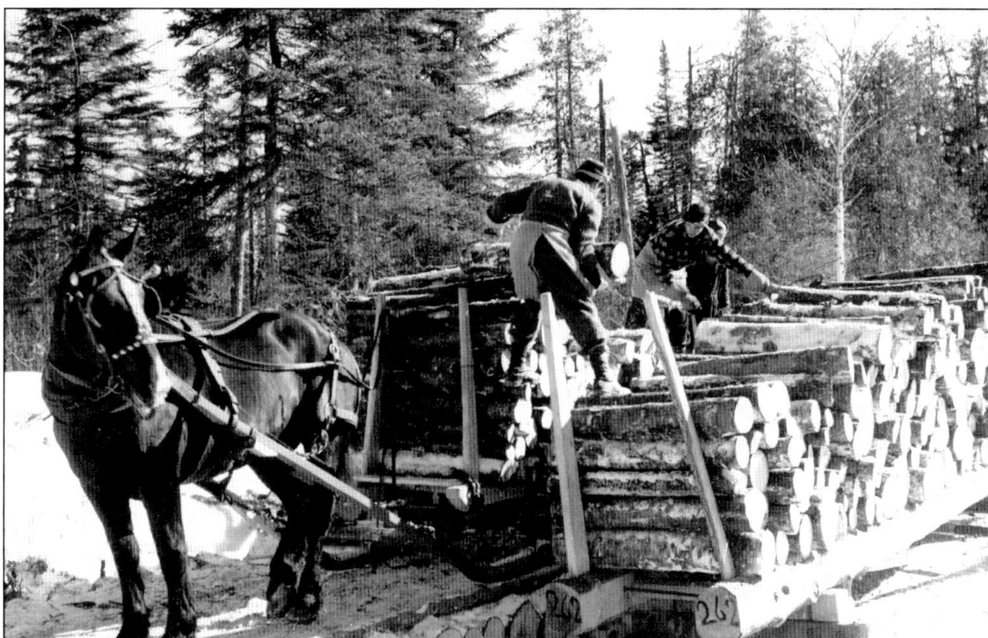

One stick at a time is how all the wood started on its way to the mill. The trees were cut by hand using axes and buck saws, then loaded onto horse-drawn sleds to be taken out of the woods to the log yards. With Sunday being the only day to rest, the men of the lumber camps worked long hours six days a week.

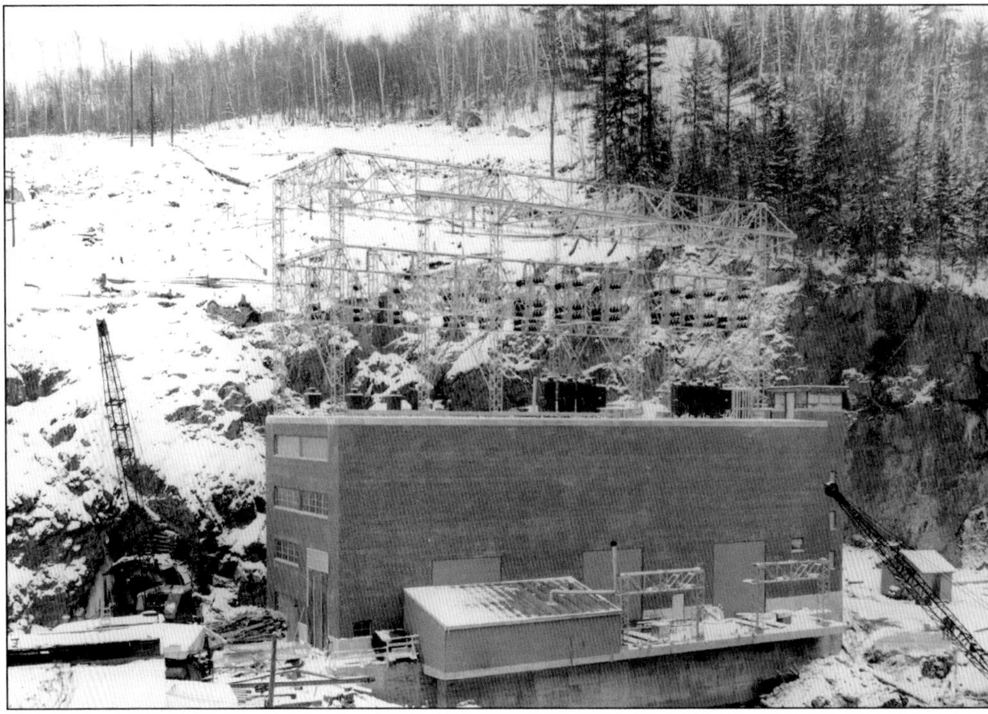

The West Branch of the Penobscot River was harnessed in many locations for use as a generator for power for the mill. The McKay station was built in the early 1950s below the Ripogenus Gorge and was powered by the water at the large Ripogenus Dam. The Abol bridge was built over the Penobscot River at that time to allow for easier access to the station from Millinocket.

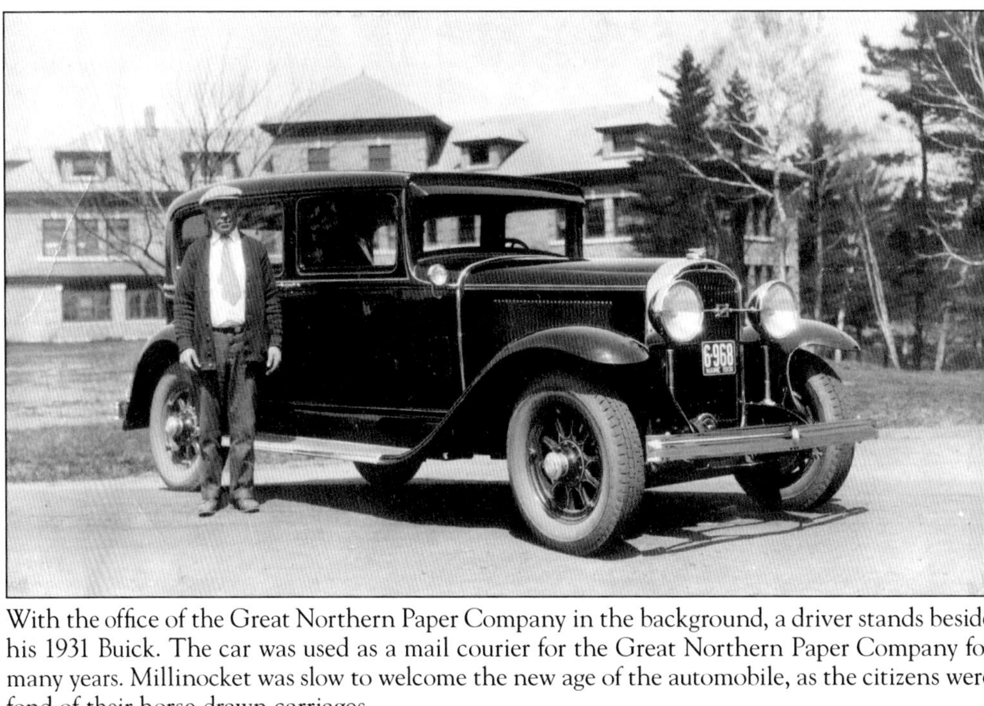

With the office of the Great Northern Paper Company in the background, a driver stands beside his 1931 Buick. The car was used as a mail courier for the Great Northern Paper Company for many years. Millinocket was slow to welcome the new age of the automobile, as the citizens were fond of their horse-drawn carriages.

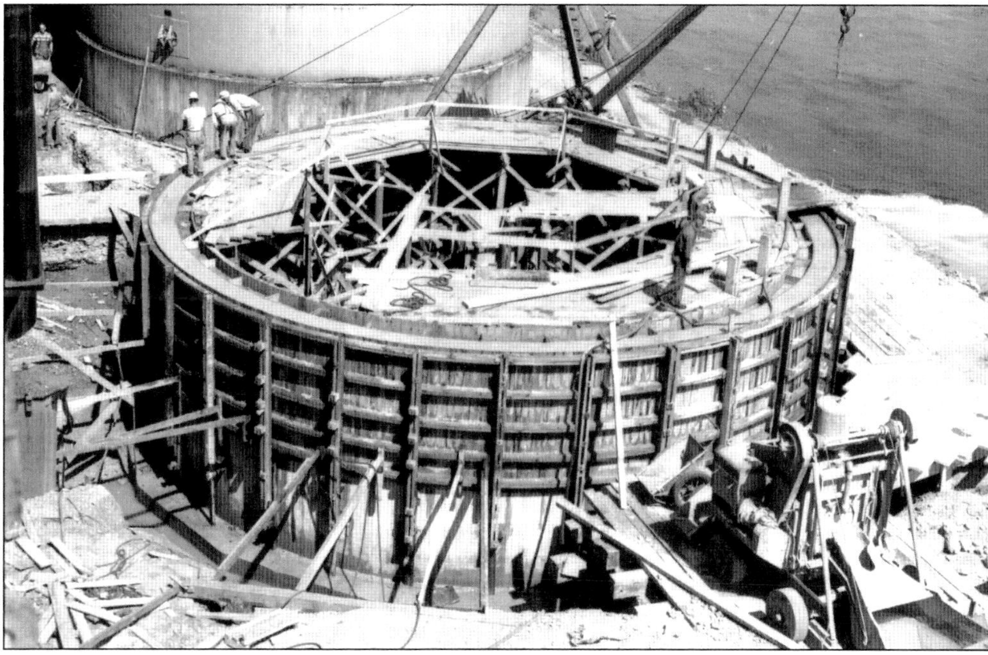

A group of men can be seen here constructing one of the many storage tanks used at the mill. The tank sits beside another one that was placed on the banks of Millinocket Stream. The Great Northern Paper Company was always investing heavily in expanding and upgrading to ensure a steady growth in business.

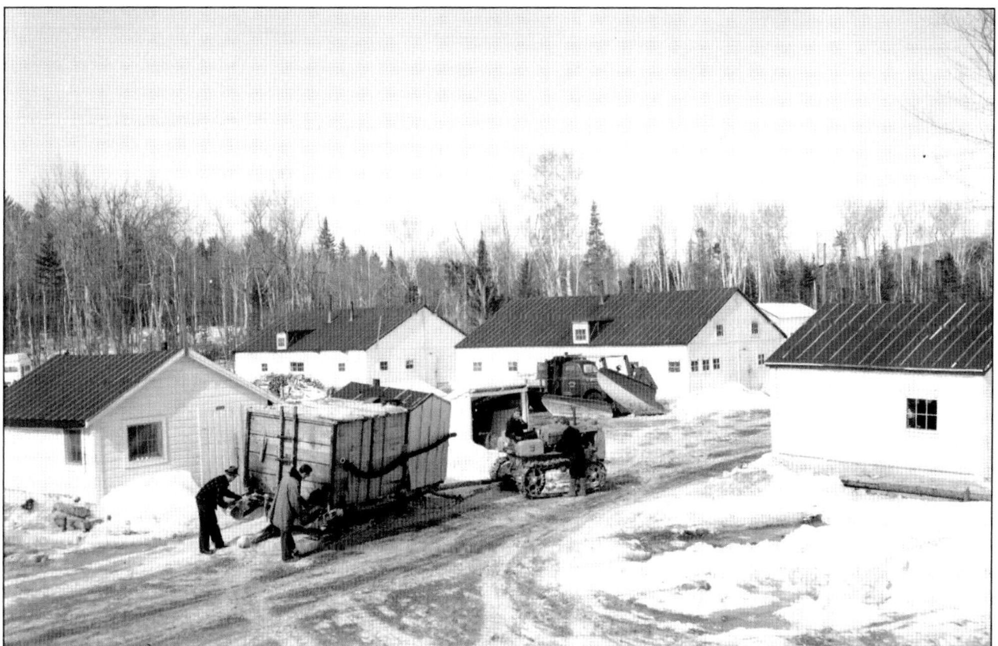

In the winter, crews pulled a water sled over the roads and sprayed the road with water. By doing so, the water froze and strengthened the road. Men are shown here preparing a 2,500-gallon sled-mounted water tank to head out to the logging roads.

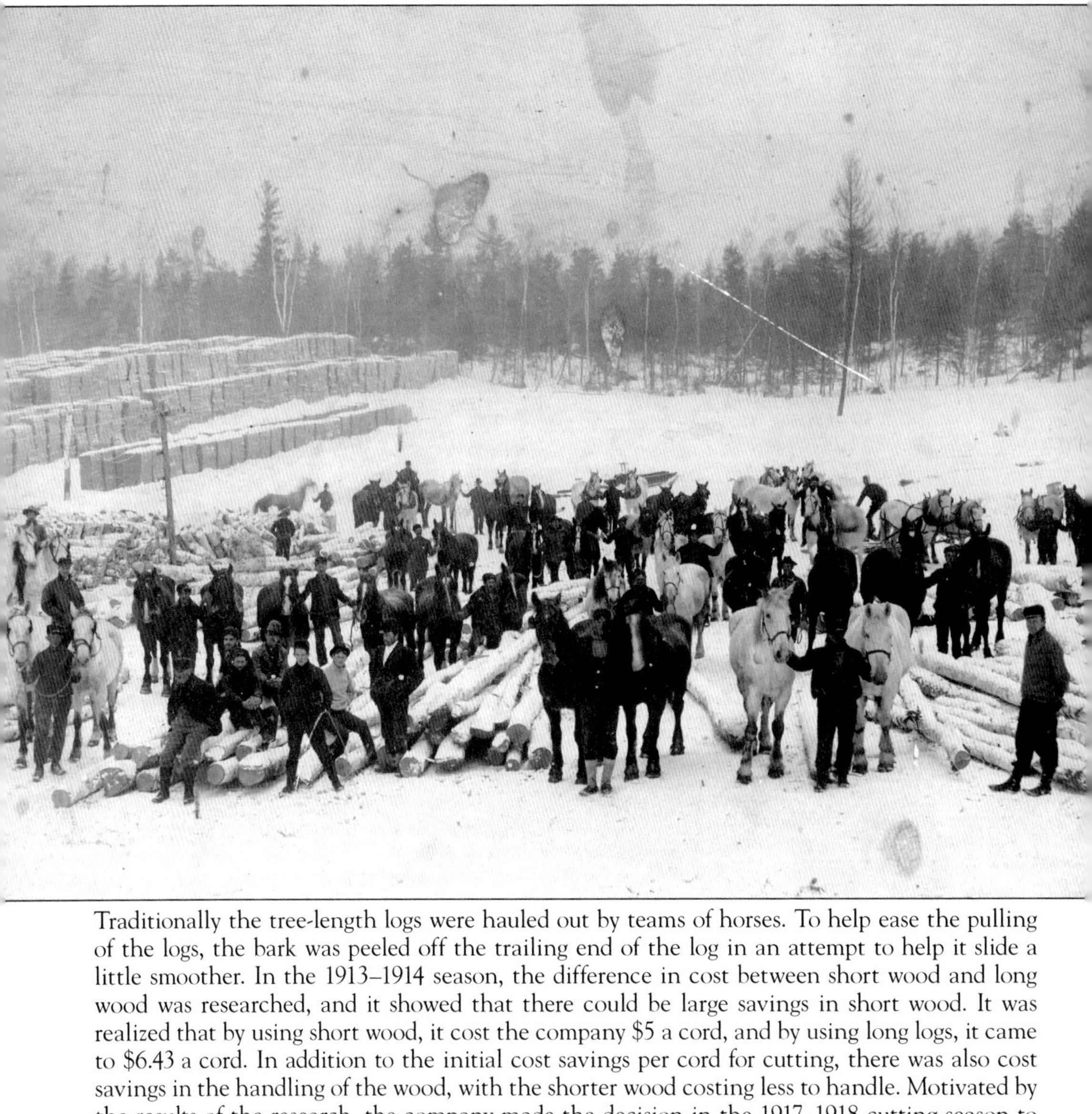

Traditionally the tree-length logs were hauled out by teams of horses. To help ease the pulling of the logs, the bark was peeled off the trailing end of the log in an attempt to help it slide a little smoother. In the 1913–1914 season, the difference in cost between short wood and long wood was researched, and it showed that there could be large savings in short wood. It was realized that by using short wood, it cost the company $5 a cord, and by using long logs, it came to $6.43 a cord. In addition to the initial cost savings per cord for cutting, there was also cost savings in the handling of the wood, with the shorter wood costing less to handle. Motivated by the results of the research, the company made the decision in the 1917–1918 cutting season to switch to the short wood.

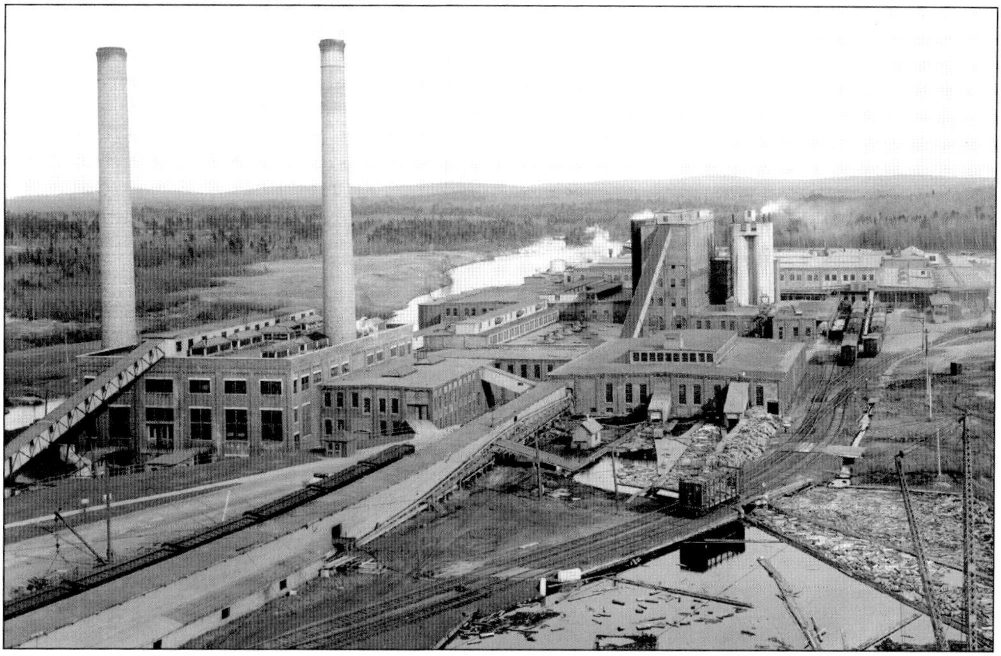

When the brick chimney was constructed in June 1900, it was the tallest in the state of Maine. As construction of the mill progressed, it attracted sightseers from around the state. The Bangor and Aroostook Railroad actually scheduled train rides for the tourists to come to Millinocket to view the progress on the mill.

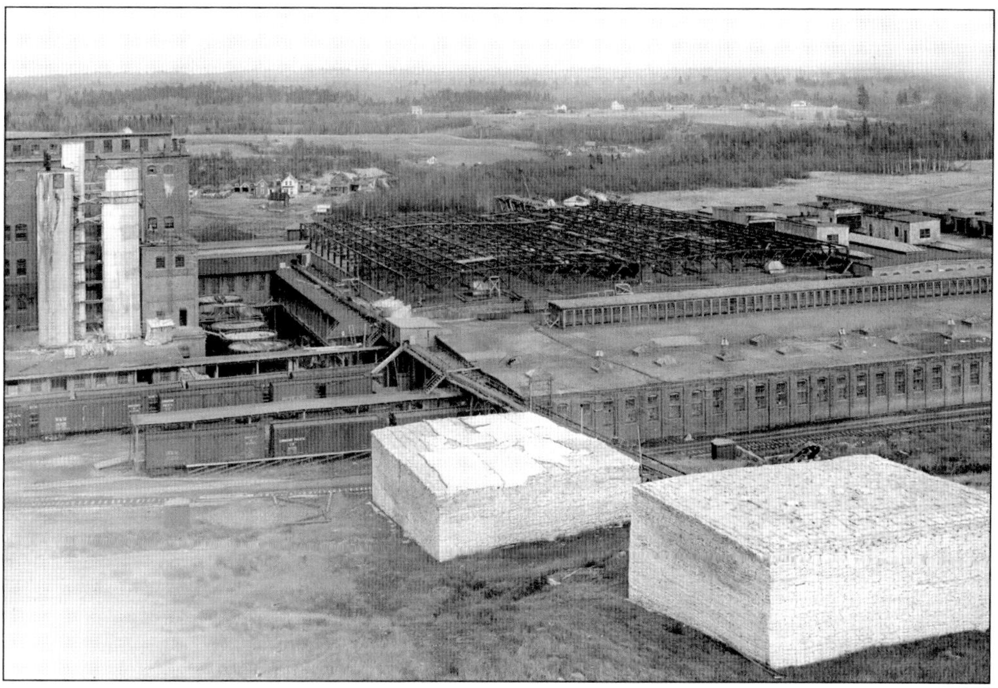

In 1929, work was started on the roof of the machine room and on the Jensson acid tower. Almost the entire mill was constructed out of brick. The roof was supported by steel frames and built of three-inch planks. Most of the building was constructed in 1899 and 1900.

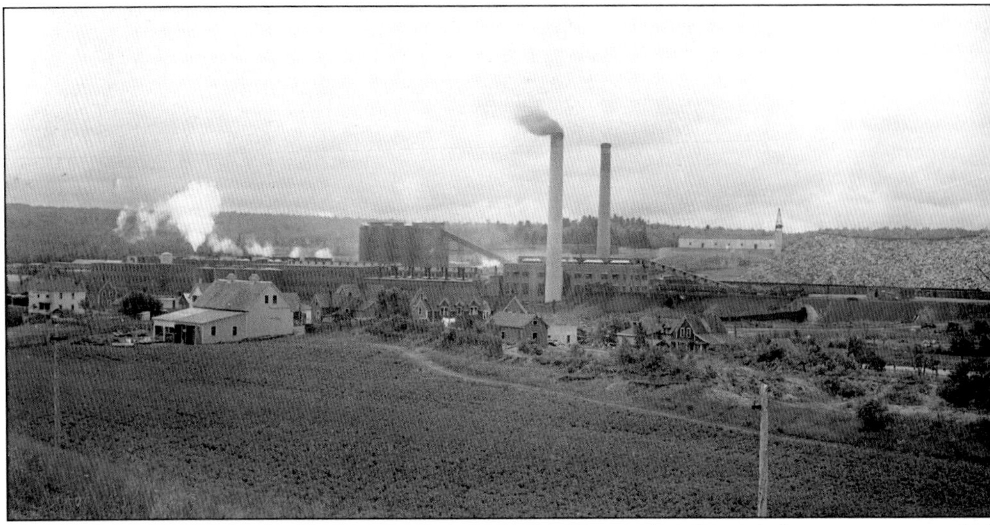

Little Italy was beginning to prosper as more money was earned and people became more settled. With the space available, the open land was used by the residents of Little Italy to grow vegetables in small gardens. Fred Peluso probably had the biggest of the gardens; he farmed potatoes for sale in his store. The site of his garden is now the location of the Granite Street School.

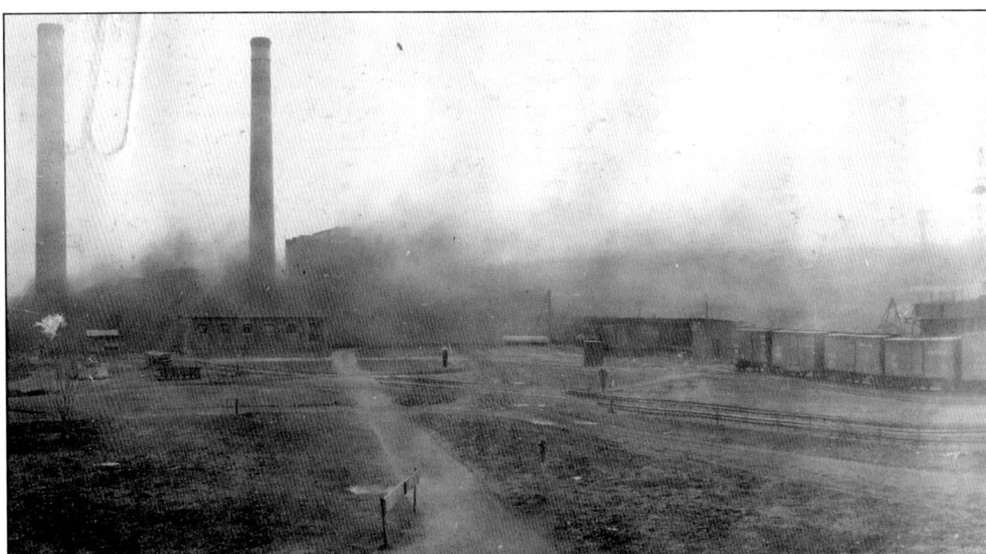

In order to feed the numerous boilers in the mill, coal was needed to fuel the fires. Unloading the coal was a dirty and messy affair, and coal dust filled the air with a dark cloud. The coal was delivered by rail car from the Bangor and Aroostook Railroad.

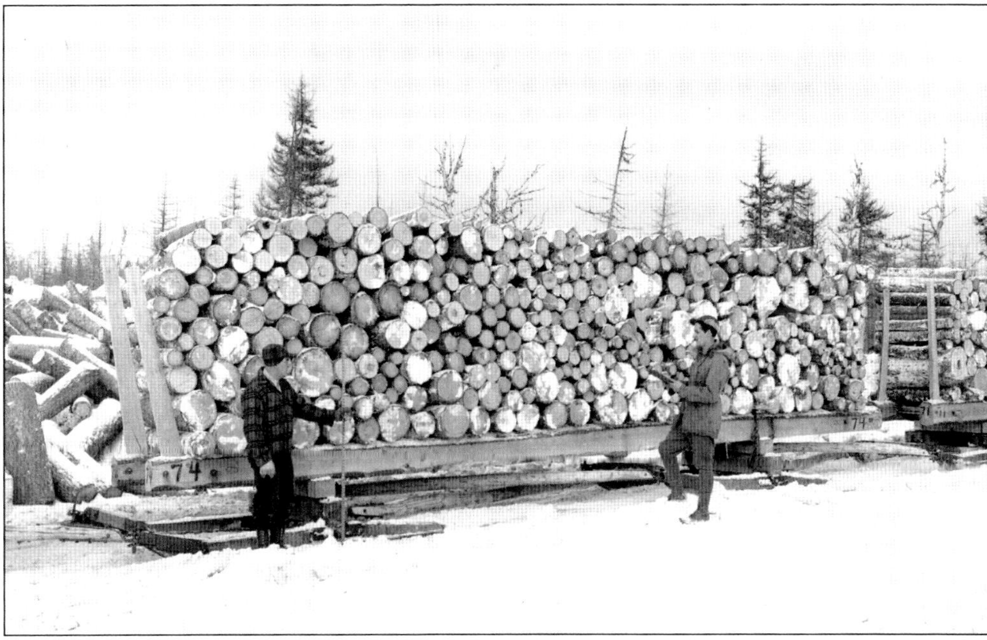

With the pulpwood loaded on a tractor-drawn sled, these men scale the wood for accountability. The man on the left measures the wood, and the man on the right records the results. The load seen here scaled in at a little over five cords. A cord of wood is traditionally considered to be four-foot logs stacked four-feet high in a pile that is eight-feet long.

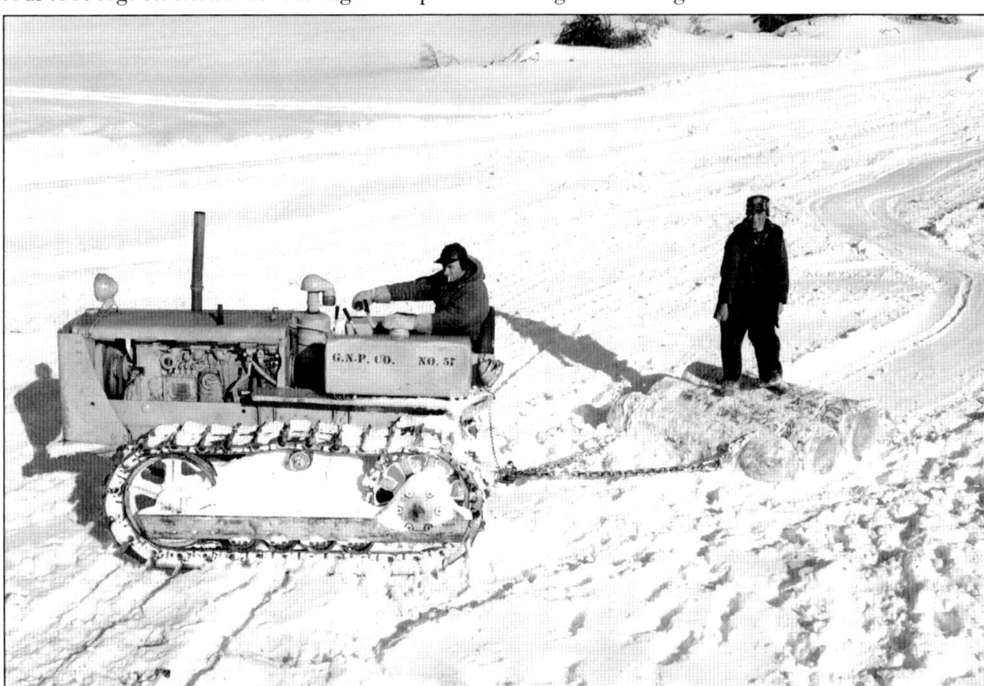

Trails could be broken deep into the woods with the tracks on the bulldozer. In order to help the teams of horses that were used, the bulldozer dragged logs behind it to pack down and smooth out the snow. Today the roads are plowed with heavy equipment.

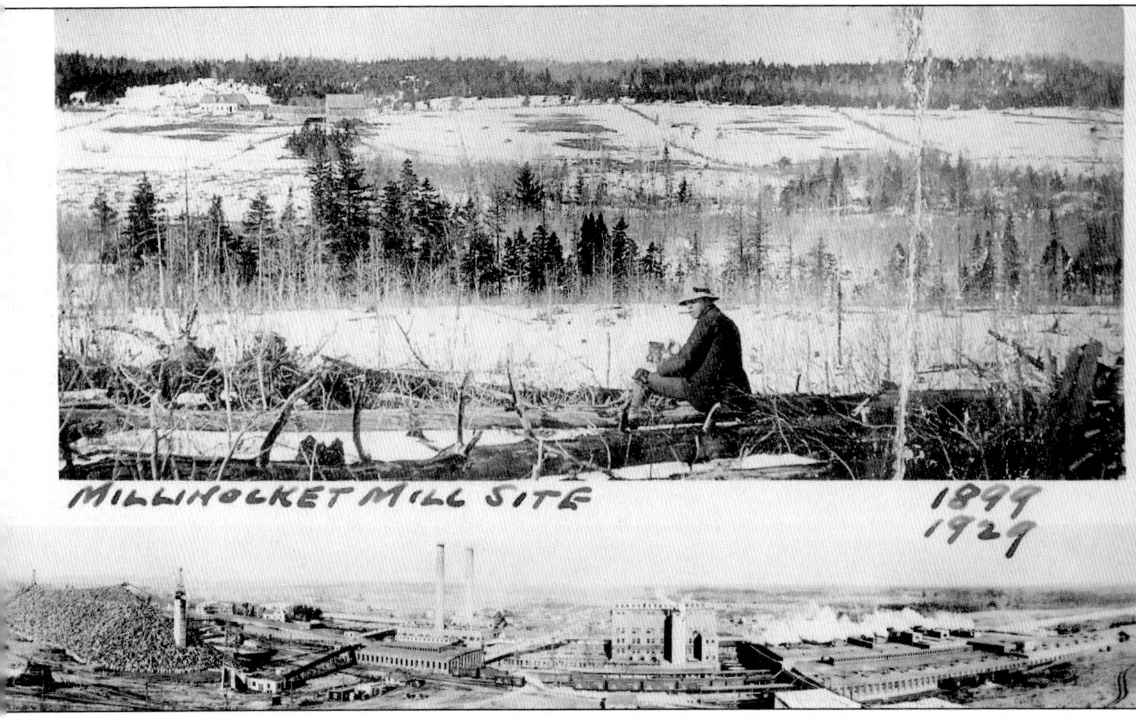

A unique, early postcard shows the Fowler farm before the mill was built. A few years later the mill occupied the site. Thomas Fowler Sr. sold his farm in 1882 to grandson Charles T. Powers and his wife, Eugenia. The site of the farm was to become known as Shack Hill, named after all the shacks that were hastily erected for the workers. The main residence of the farm was used for a time as a boardinghouse, and for a short time, it also served as the first post office in Millinocket. The Powers' sold the farm to the Great Northern Paper Company in 1899, and the construction of the mill began. It went from a peaceful and tranquil farm to the largest paper mill in the world, cranking out 240 tons of newsprint a day.

Two

The Magic City

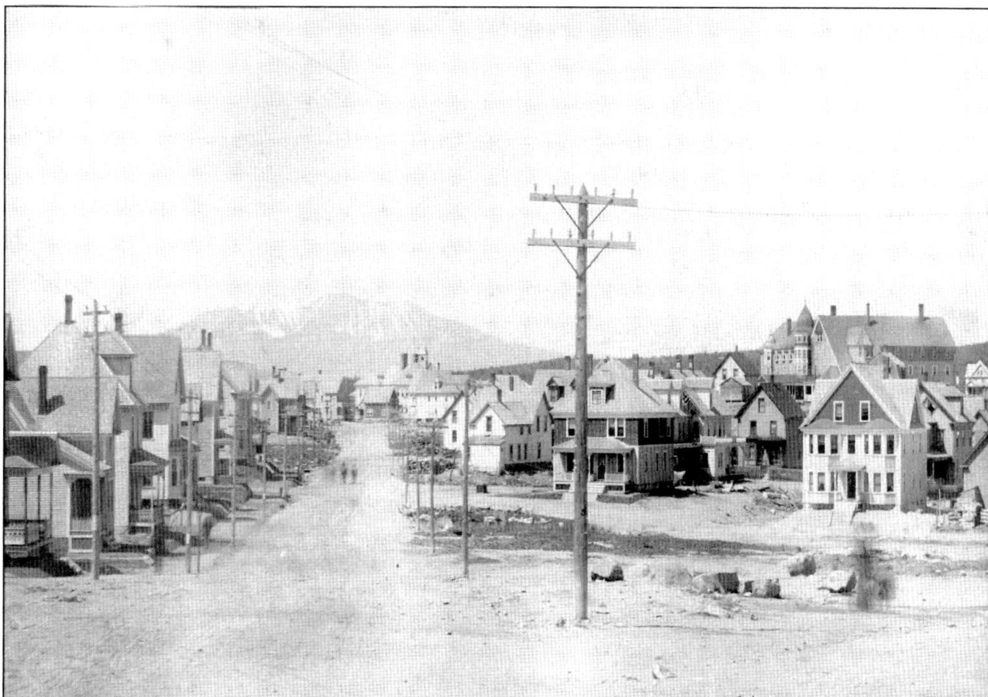

Looking down Katahdin Avenue, it is clear how the street was named, as Mount Katahdin appears off in the distance. The Great Northern Hotel sits on a small hill looking towards Mount Katahdin. Millinocket grew at such surprising speed that the newspapers of the day gave the name "magic city" to the town. It was created and existed for one reason—the Great Northern Paper Company. The town was carefully planned out and the first houses were built within walking distance of the mill. The Great Northern Paper Company was always there to lend a hand in building and supporting the town. The company sponsored various sports teams that provided recreation for the mill workers and townspeople. It goes without saying that the Great Northern Paper Company made Millinocket.

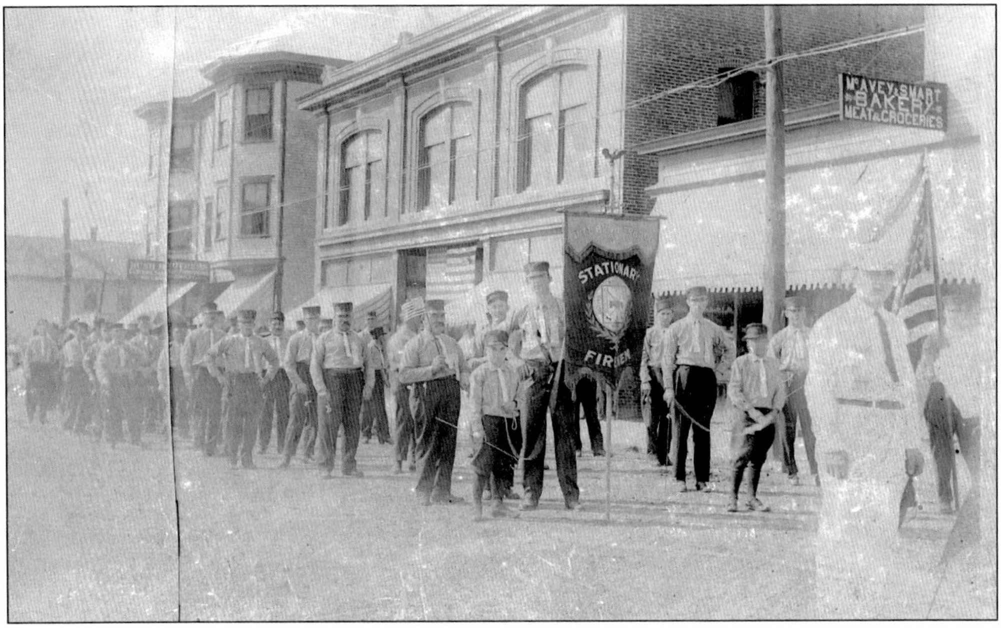

The stationary firemen are forming for a parade on Penobscot Avenue in Millinocket. In the background are the H. A. M. Rush building, the Eugene Rush building, and the McAvey and Smart building. Fires were a constant problem in the town because many of the early houses were not built from the best materials. If there was a fire in town, the fire whistle blew; if the mill whistle followed, then the volunteer firefighters rushed out to the fire.

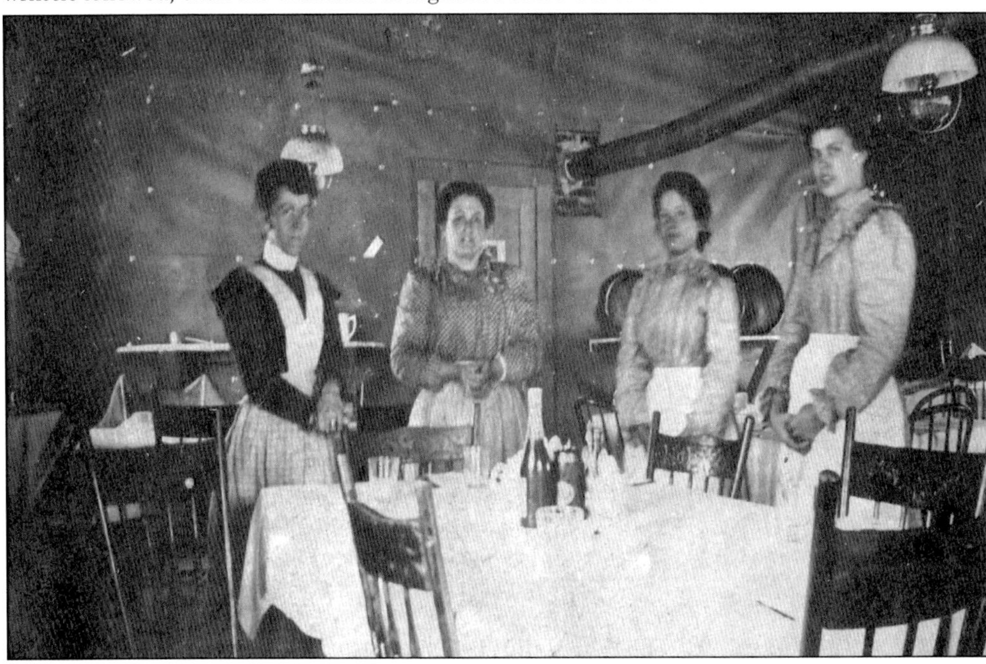

Shack Hill consisted of an odd assortment of shacks and other temporary shelters that seemed to spring up overnight. Boardinghouses were not much better than the shacks that were quickly built, but it was an improvement. Mrs. Flynn operated one of the boardinghouses on Shack Hill.

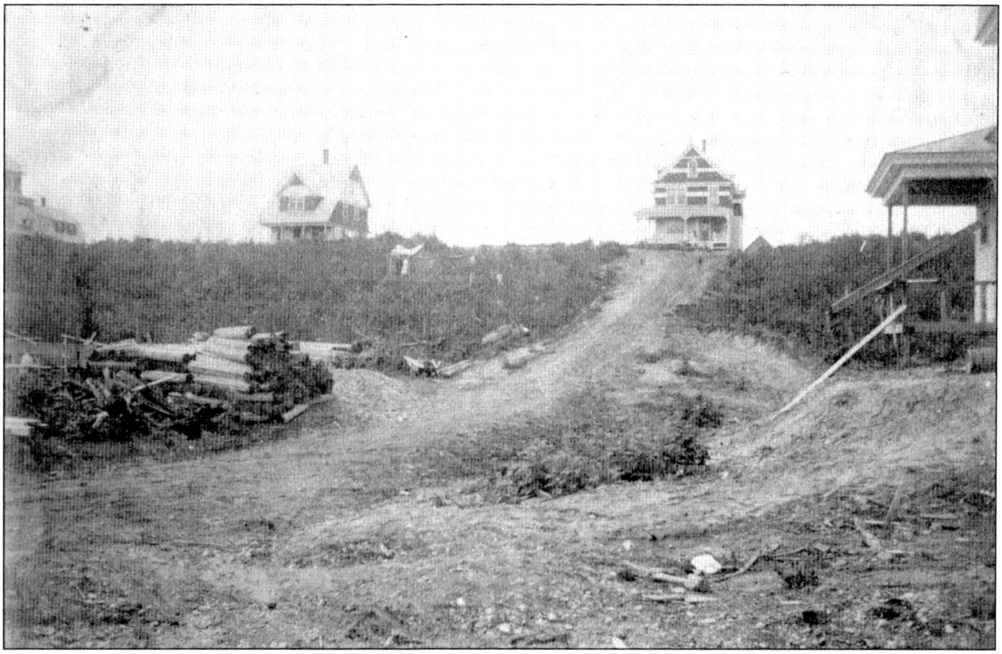

As the first houses were built, the land was open and barren. The conditions were harsh, and it took a hardy soul to carve out an existence in what was previously nothing but wilderness. There was no running water, electricity, or other modern conveniences of the day to help with everyday chores.

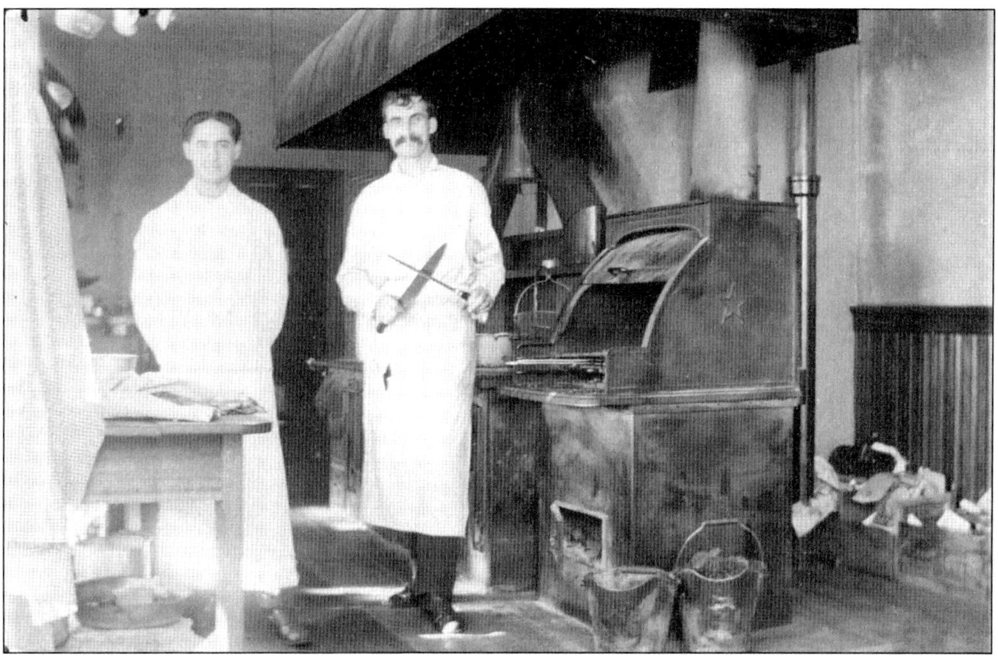

A good meal could be had at any one of the boardinghouses or eateries that thrived in town. Cooking with wood heat in large stoves probably made for a comfortable environment in the winter and perhaps an unbearable one in the summer. With the many nationalities represented in town, one could have a variety of food to choose from.

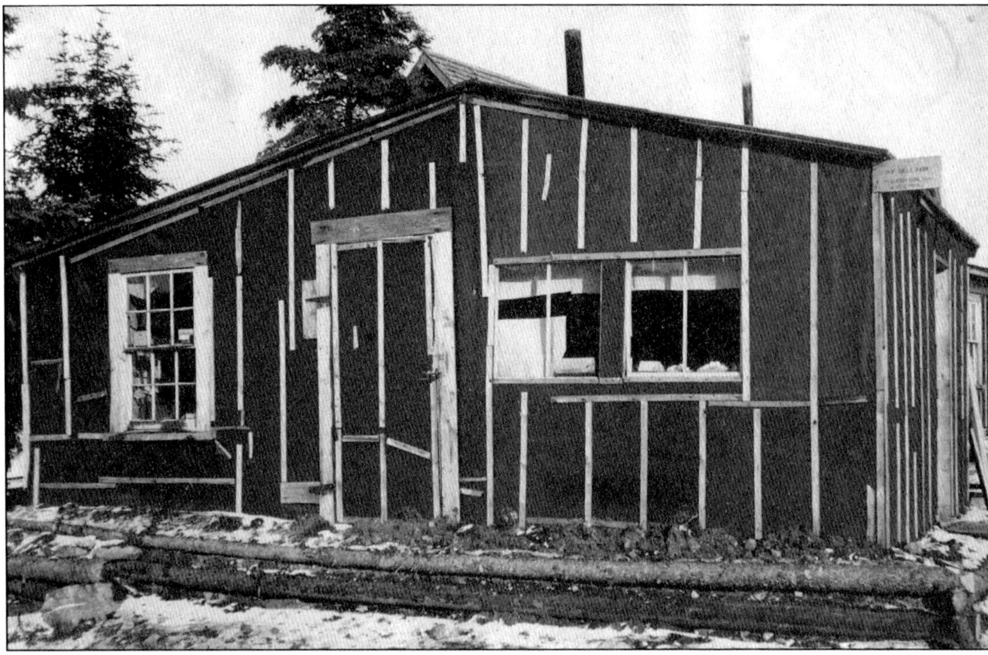

Tar paper shacks were a common sight that provided the shelter for the first inhabitants of Millinocket. In some cases the tar paper shack was an extravagance that some did not have, some of the first dwellings were also made of mud and straw or dug into the ground. A local land mark was called Shack Hill due to the numerous shacks that populated the hillside.

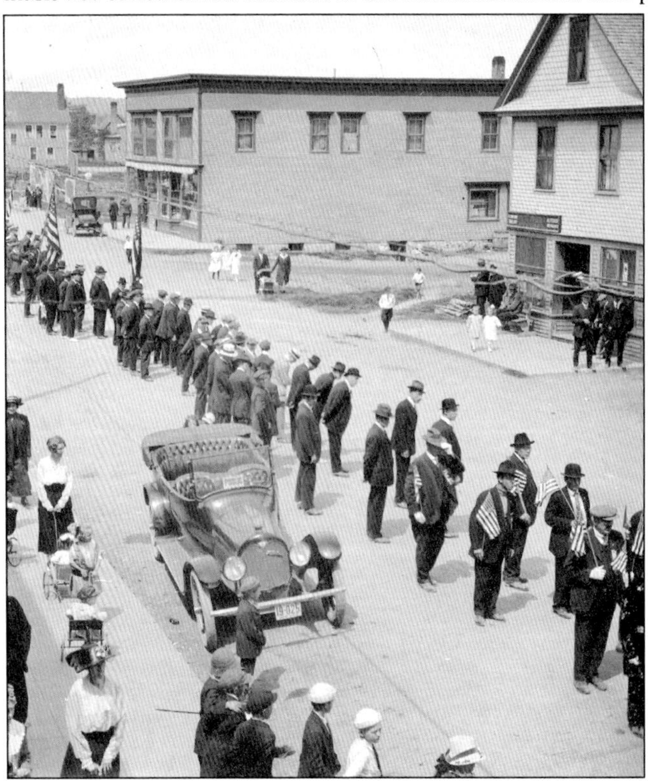

A group of men are gathering to either march in a parade or to view a parade, as seen here on Penobscot Avenue in the early 1900s. A. Simpson had one of the early tailor shops in town and can be seen on the other side of the street on the right.

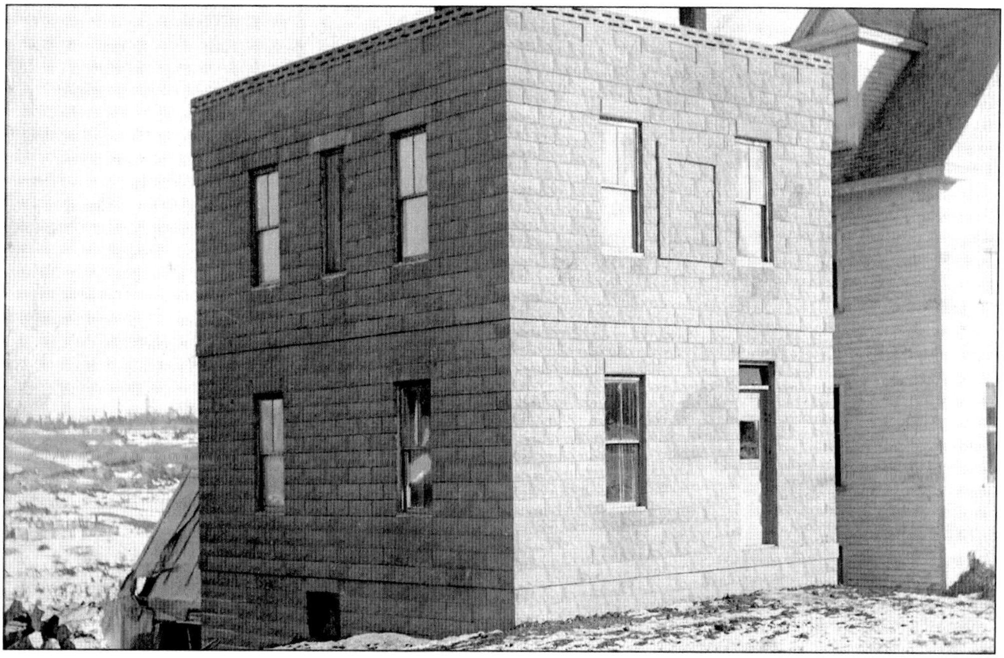

Tom Clowes built the first concrete block house in Millinocket on Aroostook Avenue. Concrete block houses were not common at all; with wood in abundance, and it was the preferred building material of most people. Given the lack of insulation in most homes during that era, one can only imagine how hard it must have been to heat this house in the winter.

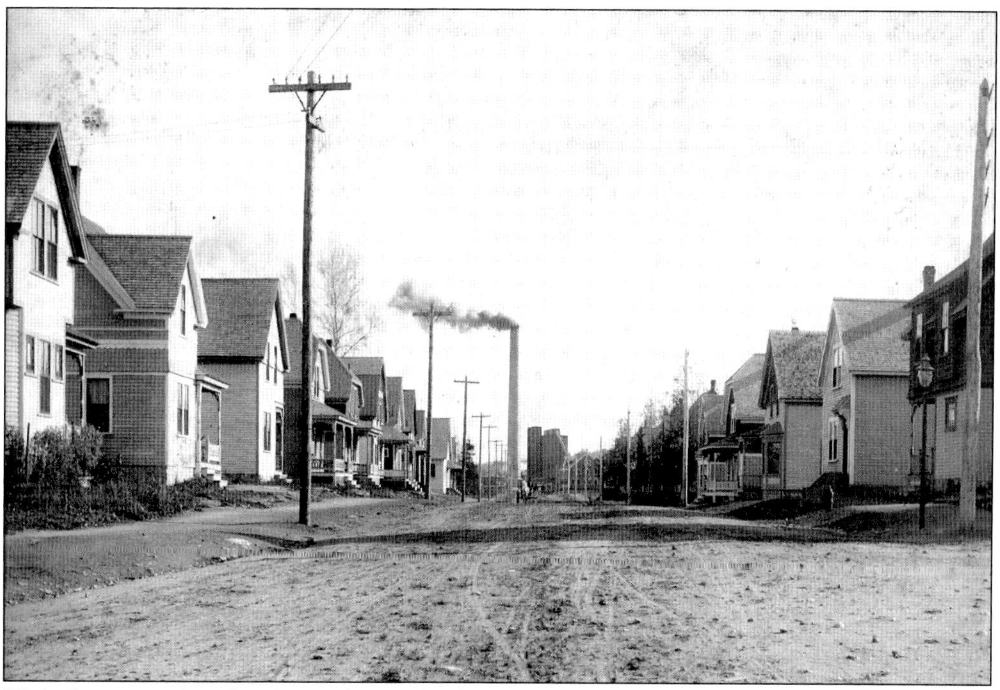

Wide dirt streets lined with new homes lead directly to the mill. Most of the town was initially built so that the workers were within walking distance to the mill. It was awhile before Millinocket saw paved streets.

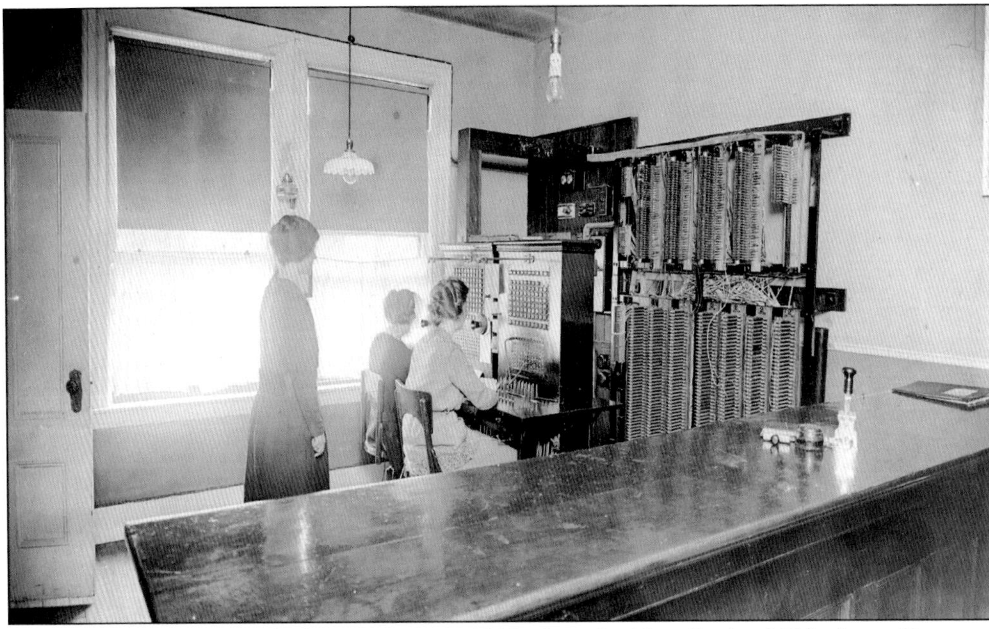

Millinocket got its first telephone service in 1902 when the New England Telephone Company installed telephones for the mill and the town. Mabel (Rowe) McLish can be seen standing as the supervisor watching over the operation of the switchboard in 1921. Theresa (Pinette) Arnold is on the left, and Helen (Lewis) Farquhar is on the right. The switchboard office was located on what was called the Gonya Block on the corner of Penobscot Avenue and Central Street.

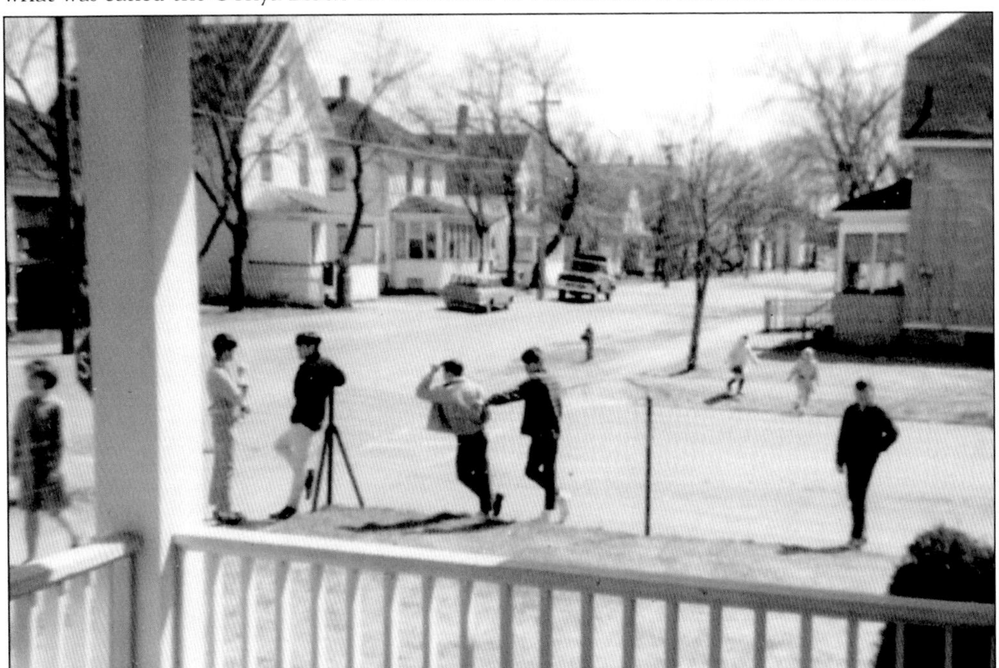

A group of children gather on the street corner in town. In the early days, it was not uncommon to find children picking berries and selling them door to door. With the mill operating in three shifts, play time often revolved around the working or sleeping habits of the mill workers.

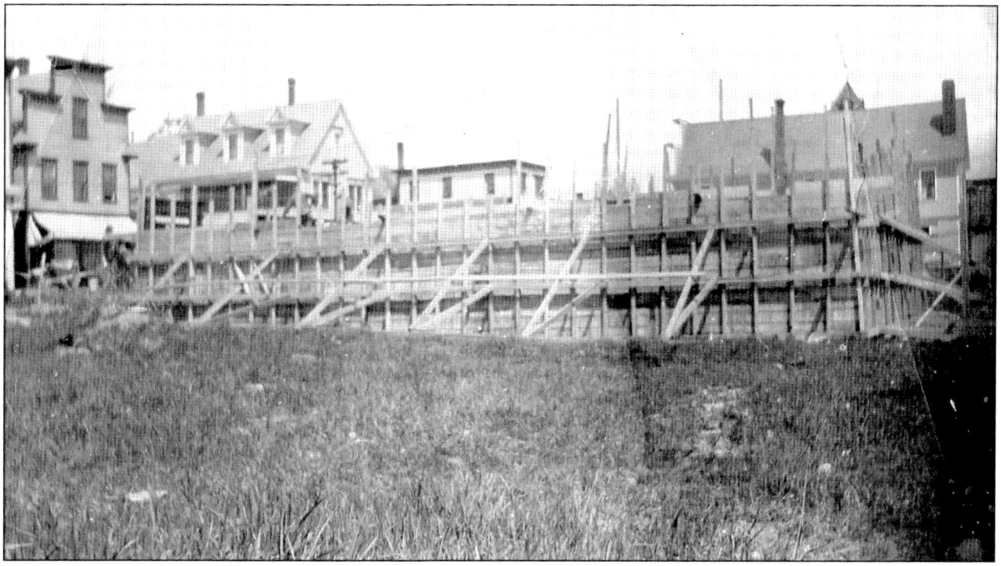

The Odd Fellows building was constructed in 1924 on the main street. It was a popular gathering spot, and the building still stands today. The building was used for fraternal purposes and had a lodge room, kitchen, and dining area. The building helped improve the appearance of the business district of the town. It is an impressive two-story brick building and was a welcome asset to the downtown area. The main street in Millinocket is actually Penobscot Avenue, and it was developed as the principal business area in town. Penobscot Avenue, Central Street, and Katahdin Avenue formed a triangle that was the center of town.

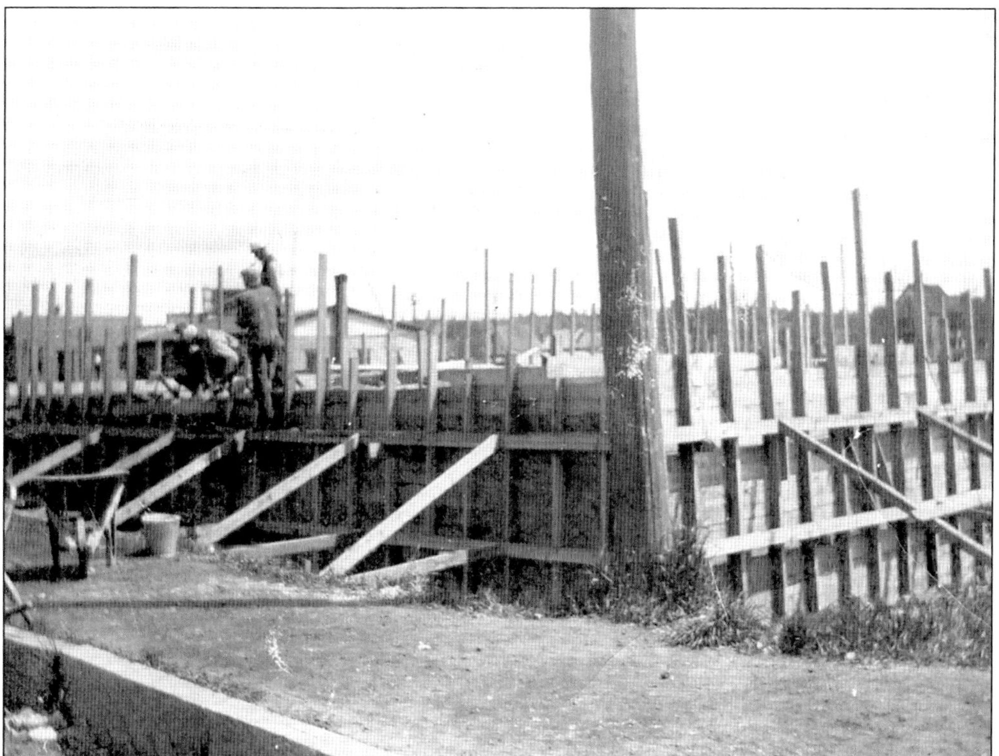

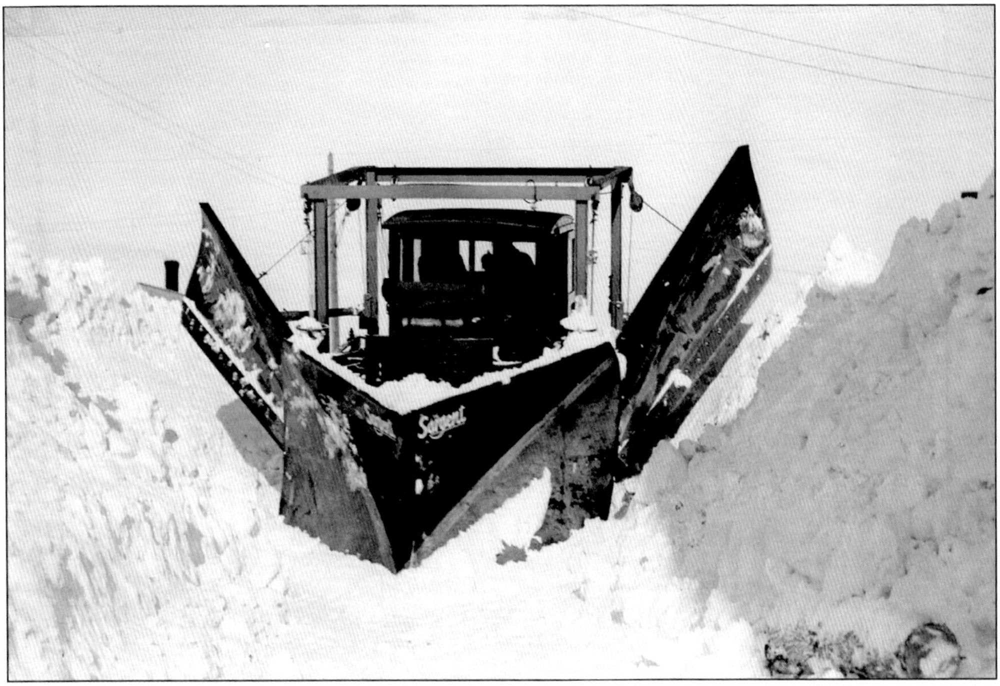

Enduring the harsh winters is a way of life in Millinocket. This picture, dated February 7, 1934, shows a snowplow with its V-shaped plow pushing through the snow. Dealing with the large amounts of snow was a constant problem that took a lot of ingenuity on the part of the town road crew.

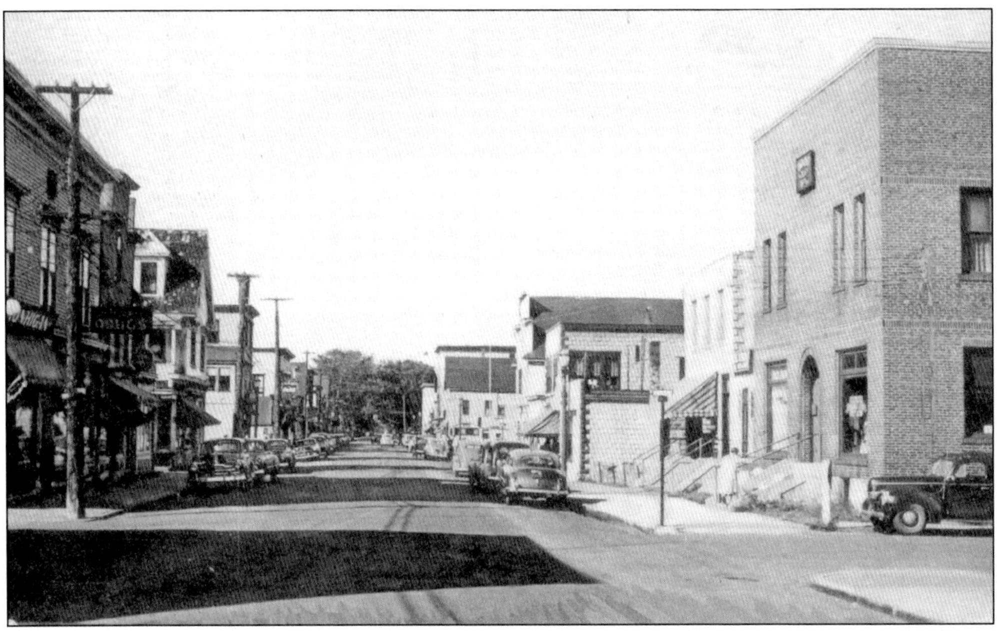

The Odd Fellows building stands as a dominant building on Penobscot Avenue. Penobscot Avenue has developed nicely, with all of the stores offering many varieties of products for the consumer. The days of dirt roads and horse-drawn carriages are gone, as it has all been replaced by pavement and automobiles.

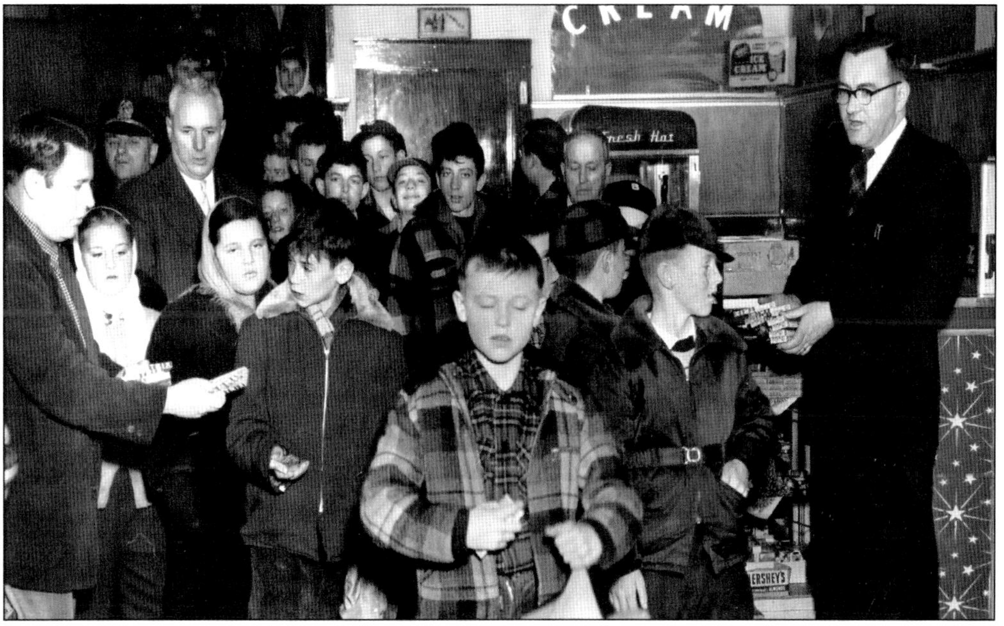

Movie theaters were popular in Millinocket. Movies were shown in the Millinocket Opera House at different times as well as in the Millinocket Theater and later in the K-Cinema on Central Street. The Millinocket Theater was owned by Frank LePage and operated on Penobscot Avenue until the 1950s. While undergoing repairs, the theater caught fire and burned. It was replaced by the Millinocket Bowling Alley.

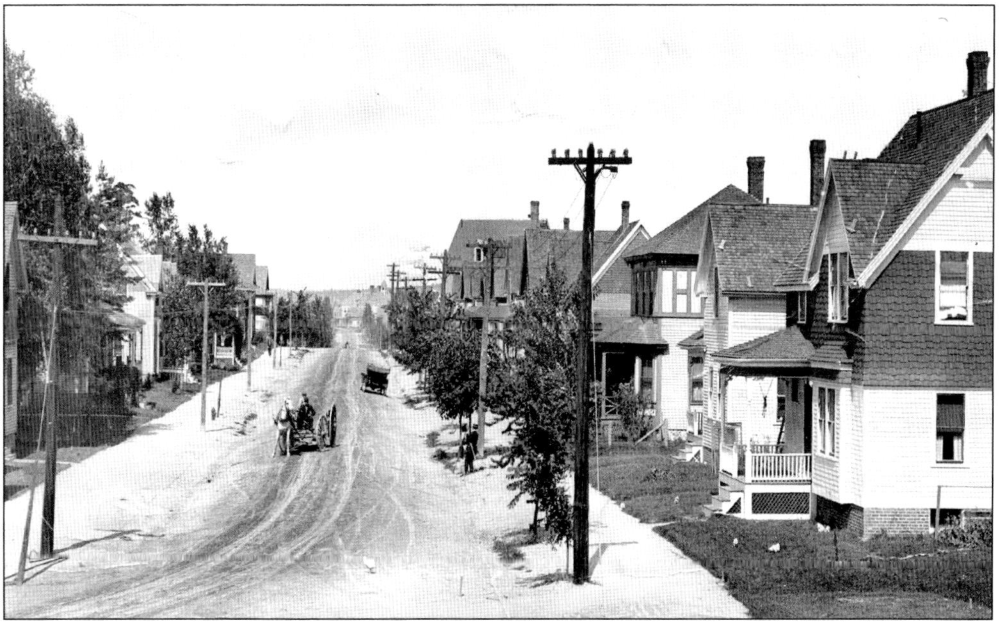

This image looks up Mill Street towards Mount Katahdin from the administration building. The steeply graded dirt street still sported both horse-drawn wagons and automobiles. The transition from horses to automobiles was not an uneventful one; many a startled horse reacted in surprise at the noisy contraption. Mill Street ran from the Great Northern Paper Company administration building down to Cherry Street where it became Katahdin Avenue.

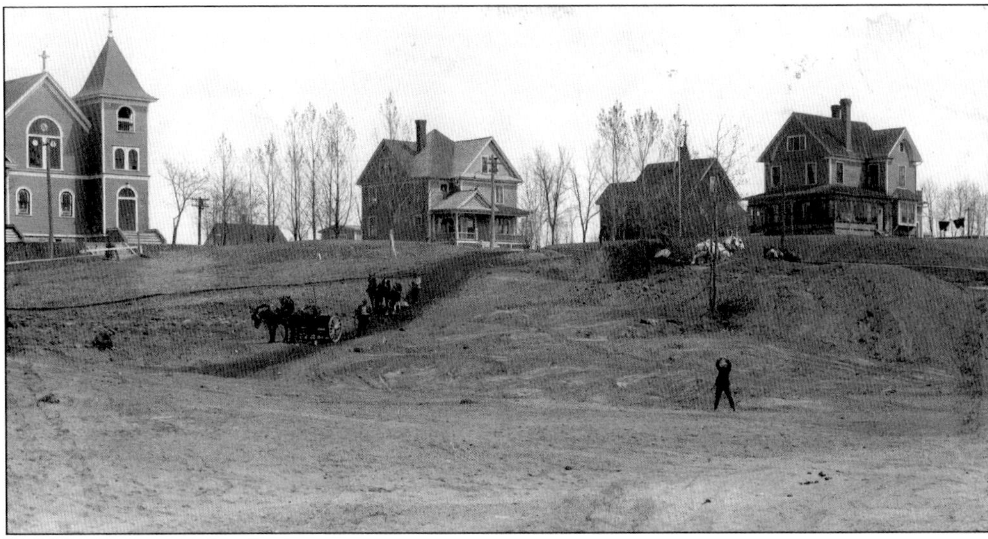

The Millinocket High School burned to the ground on November 13, 1921. The town was in need of a new school and work soon began on its construction. Shown here is the future site of the George W. Stearns High School. The building still stands today and is known as Stearns Assisted Living. From left to right beyond the building site stand the St. Martin of Tours Catholic Church, the church rectory, St. Andrews Episcopal Church, and the John Corrigan house.

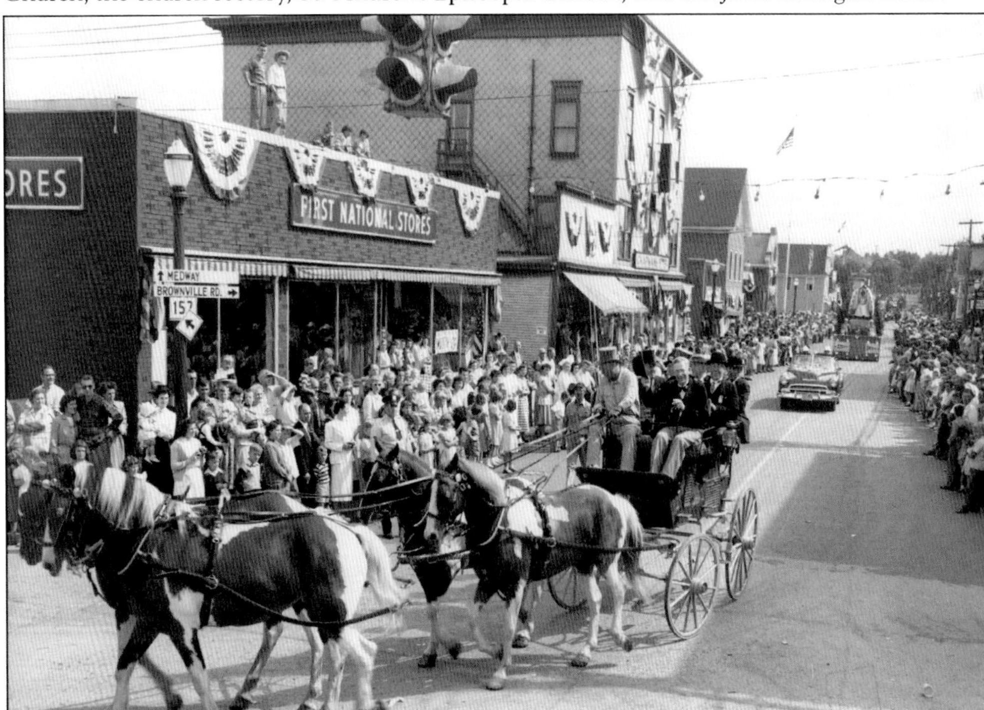

During the town's 50th anniversary parade, A. J. Cole guides his horses around a corner. Cole is a prominent businessman from the Bangor area who started Coles Transportation. The First National Stores building on the corner of Penobscot Avenue and Central Street is now the site of Magic City Golf.

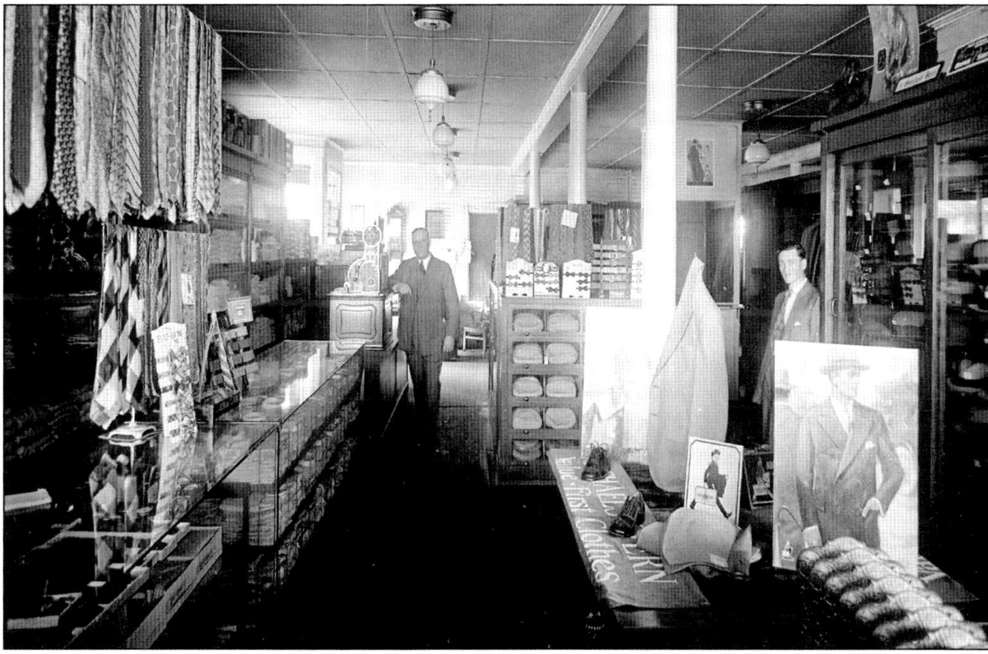

H. A. M. Rush is standing near his cash register ready to do business. Harry A. M. "Bud" Rush is standing over to the right. The clock on the wall beyond the cash register is now on display in the Millinocket Historical Society Museum. The store operated for many years and outfitted many gentlemen in fine male clothing.

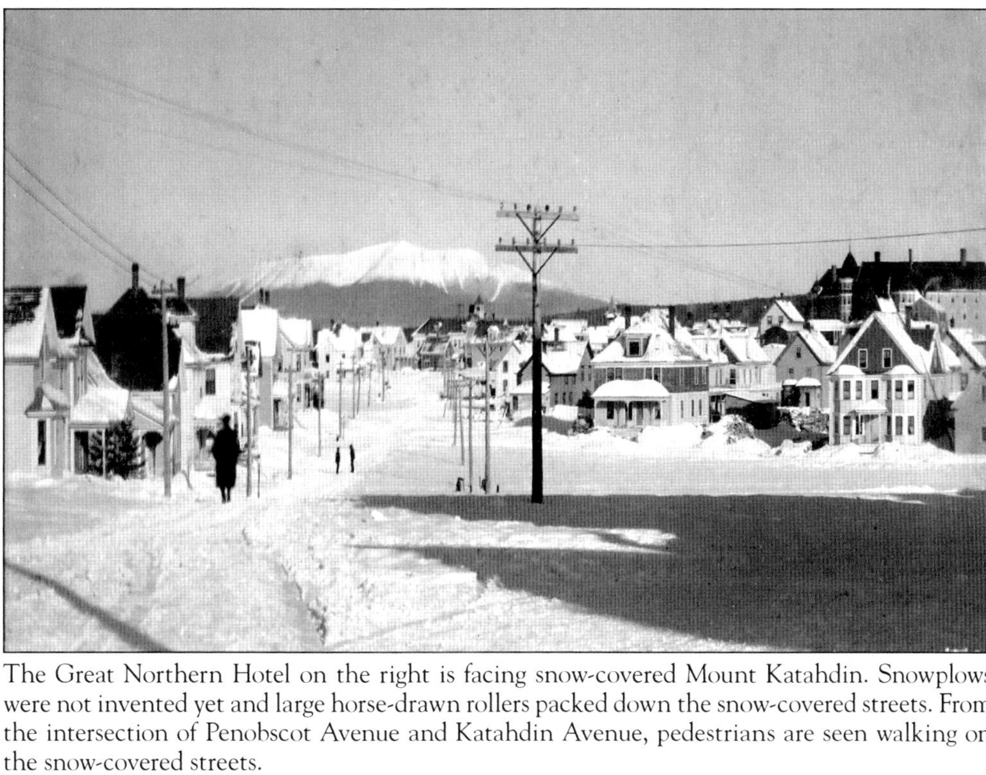

The Great Northern Hotel on the right is facing snow-covered Mount Katahdin. Snowplows were not invented yet and large horse-drawn rollers packed down the snow-covered streets. From the intersection of Penobscot Avenue and Katahdin Avenue, pedestrians are seen walking on the snow-covered streets.

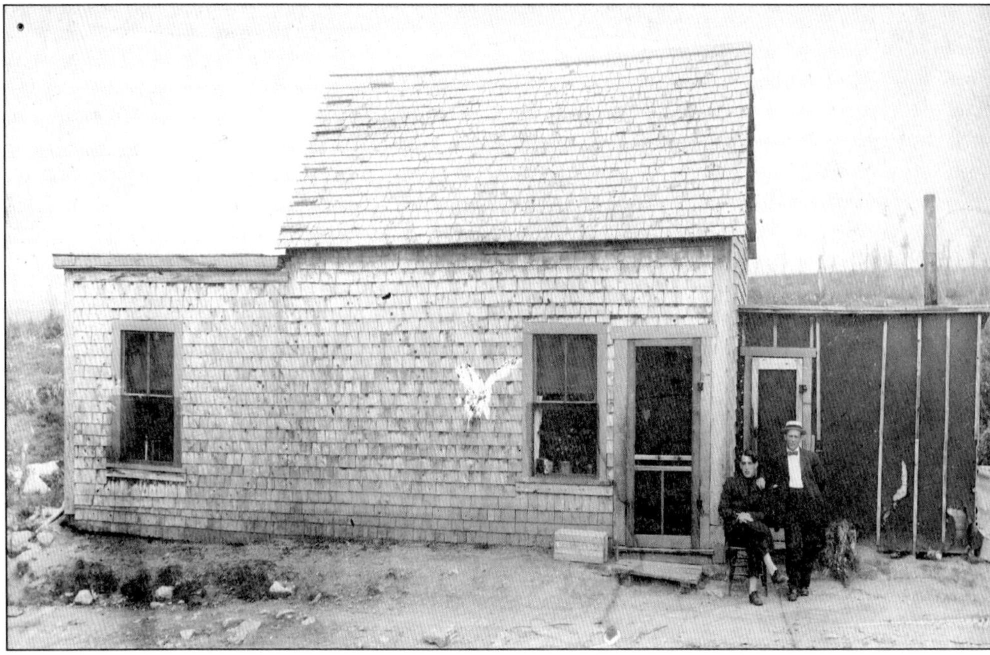

Dick Herbert and a friend pose in front of his house on Shack Hill. Hastily built shacks were thrown up almost overnight on the hillside overlooking the mill, which is how it came to be known as Shack Hill. There are no more houses on the hill, as it is now part of the land owned by the Great Northern Paper Company.

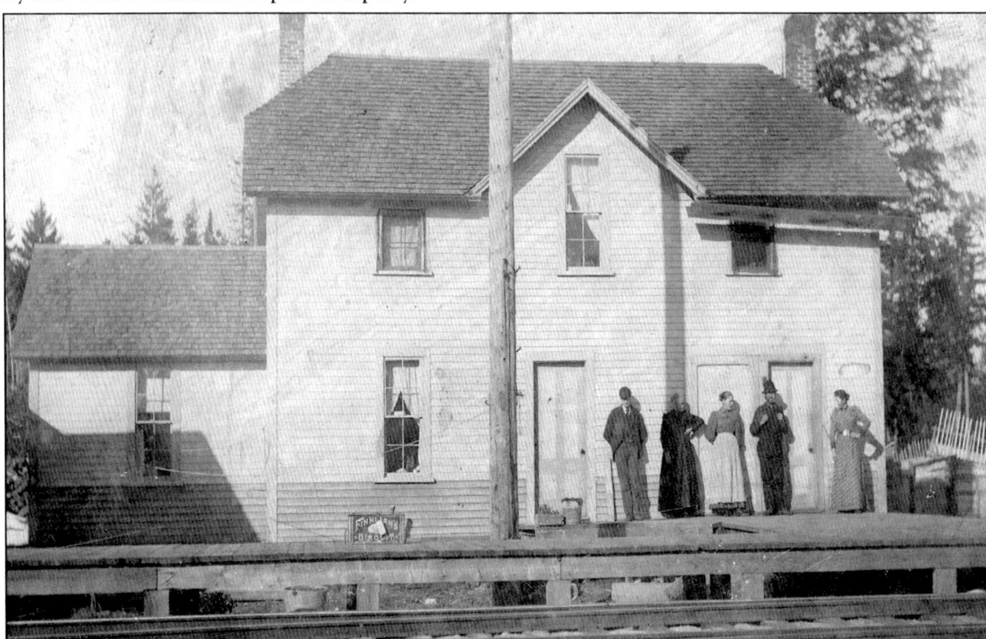

The Bangor and Aroostook Railroad saw the potential in the new mill and realized a need for more tracks. The railroad knew that the largest mill in the world was being built and was willing to invest heavily in a new station in Millinocket. The tracks were expanded to handle up to 500 cars. Pictured here is the first railroad station that was built in the iron bridge area.

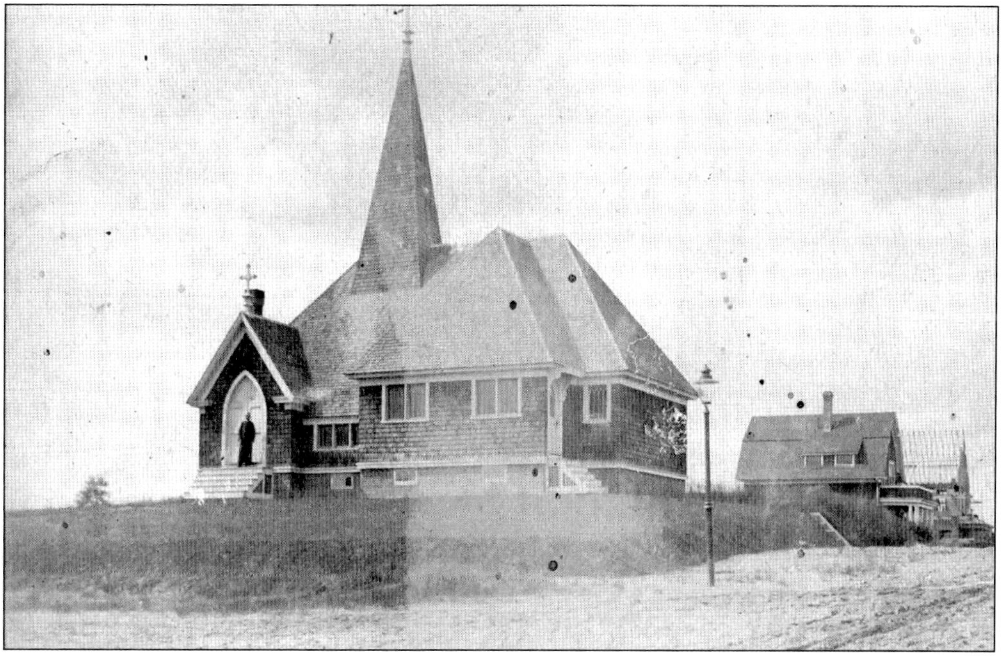

Fr. George Robinson of Winn was the first Episcopal priest of this Tudor-style church in 1901 when it was on the corner of Colby Street and Highland Avenue. In 1964, it was moved to its present location behind the library on the corner of Highland Avenue and Hill Street. This spot was where the old Great Northern Hotel had stood previously.

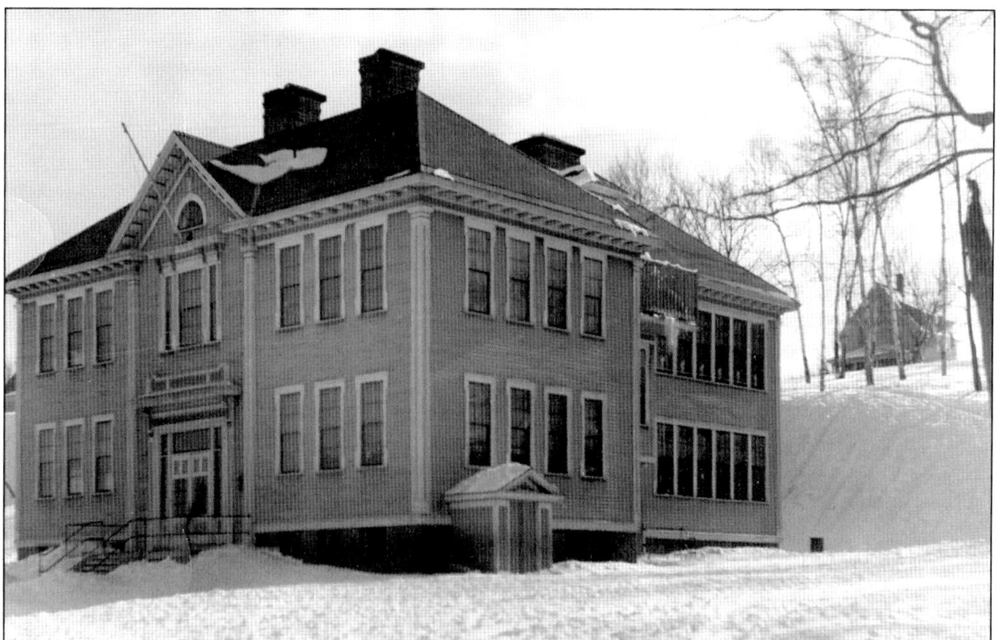

The Oxford Street School opened in 1907 as a small four-room schoolhouse. In later years, it was expanded into an eight-room school. It was deeded to the Veterans of Foreign Wars (VFW) in 1943, and it is still occupied by the organization. It has been heavily remodeled, but it still stands as impressive as it ever did.

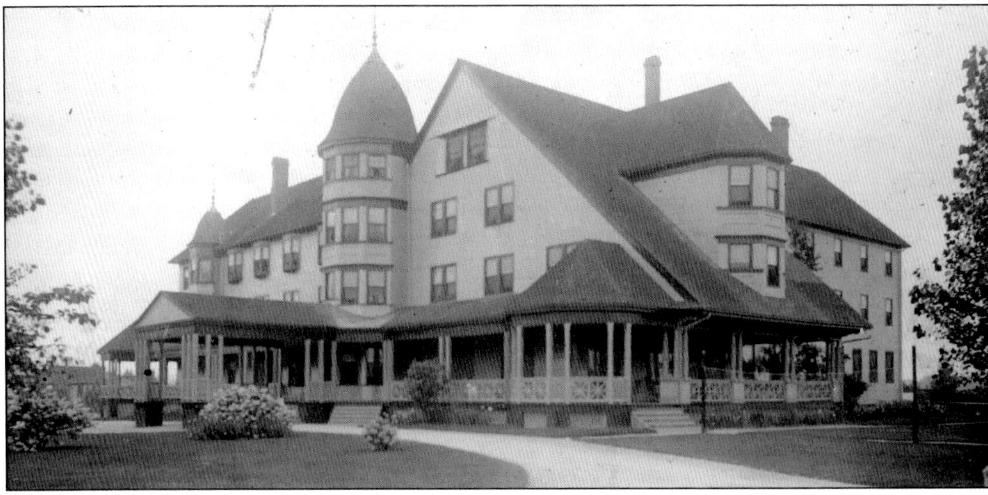

Known as the "palace in the woods," the Great Northern Hotel was a sight to be seen in the new town. Construction was started on the hotel in 1899, and it was a hub of social activity for many years. It was a grand hotel that rivaled many of the finer resorts dotting the coast of Maine. Its grounds were well manicured and planted with many native plants and trees. There were gravel walkways around the grounds, and it sported a tennis court for the pleasure of the guests. The hotel was torn down in the early 1960s, and the town library and the Episcopal church now stand on the site.

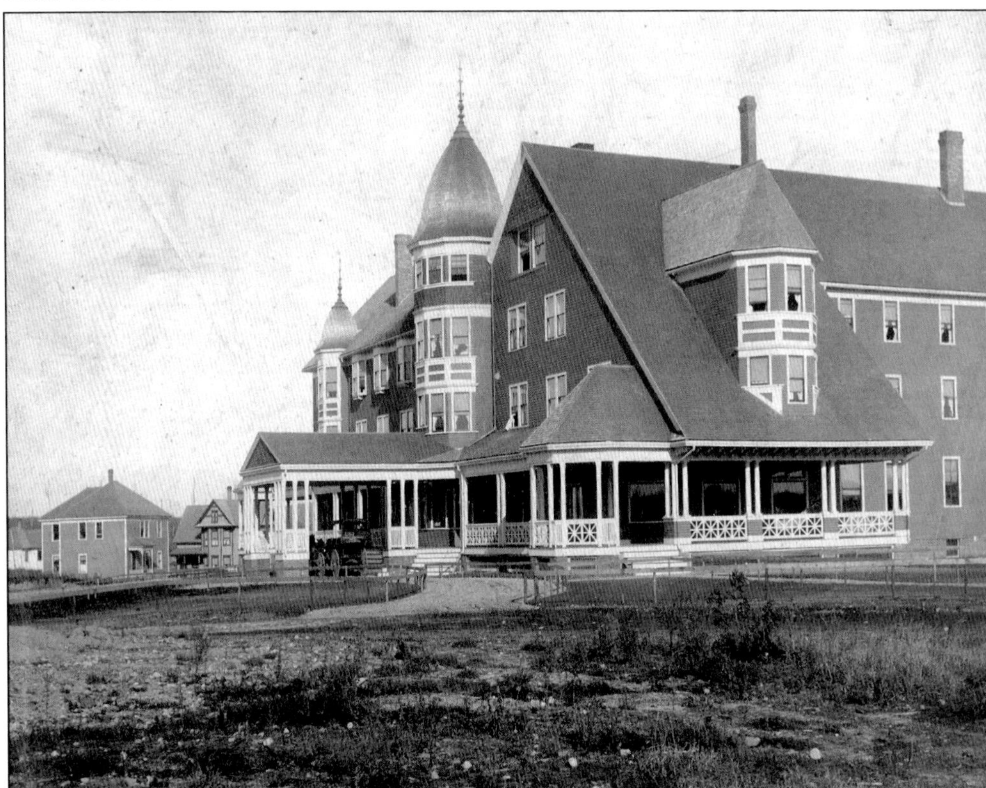

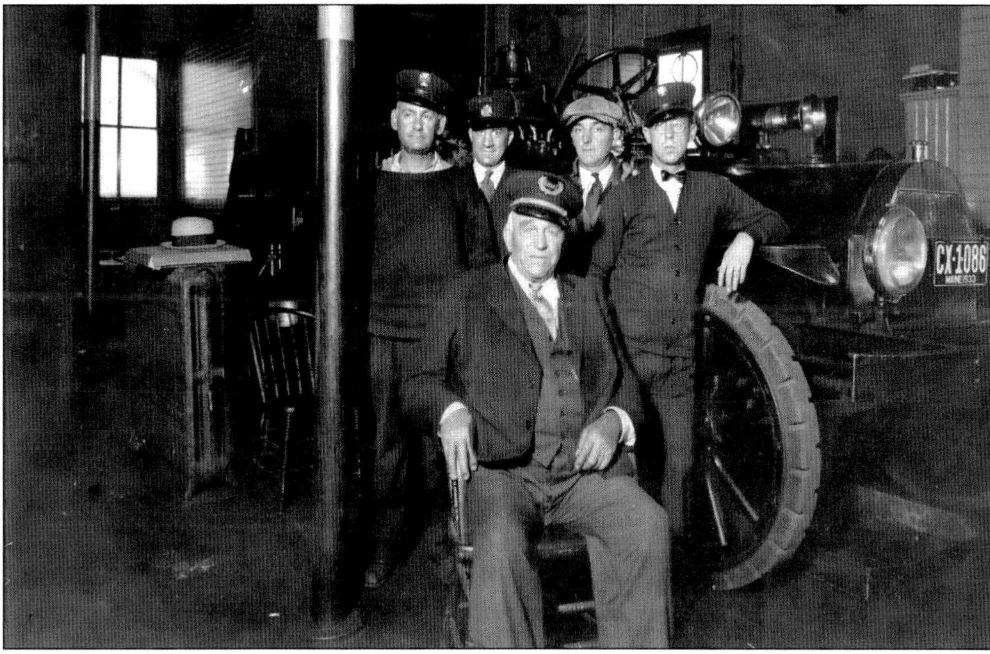

Chief Fred M. Gates is seated here in front of the Knox fire truck. Standing from left to right are James Murch, George Grant, unidentified, and Fred Gates Jr. Fred M. Gates was the first fire chief, having held the position from 1902 to 1936. The Pioneer Hose Company No. 1 was formed in May 1901. By 1905, the fire department had its own fire station on Penobscot Avenue.

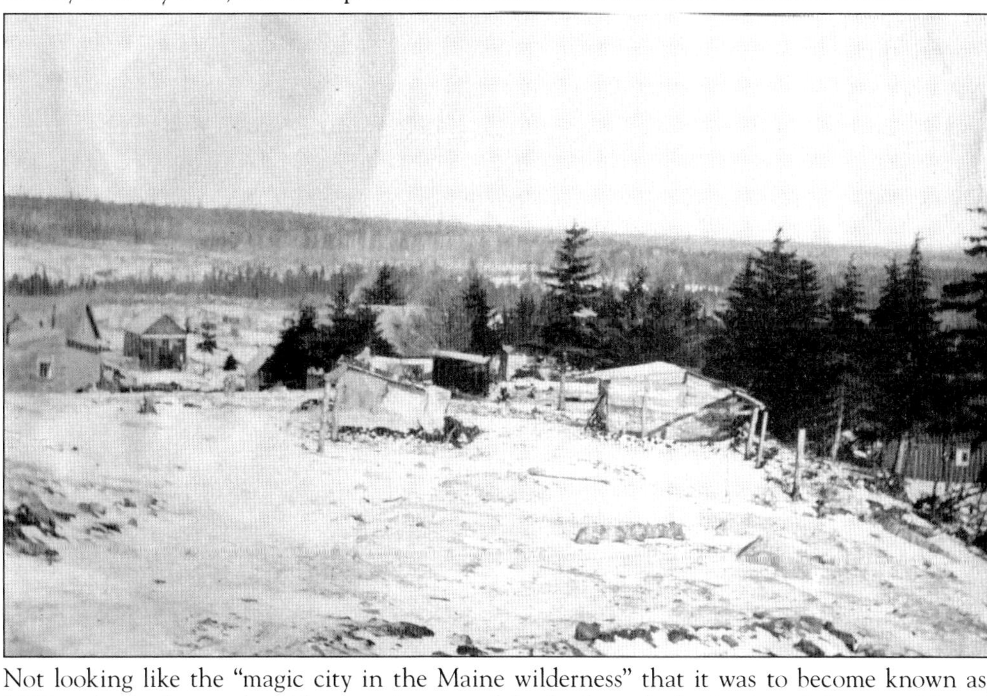

Not looking like the "magic city in the Maine wilderness" that it was to become known as, Millinocket had a very humble start. A group of shacks show the beginning of the town. Houses seemed to be almost an afterthought, since the construction of the mill was the most important business at hand.

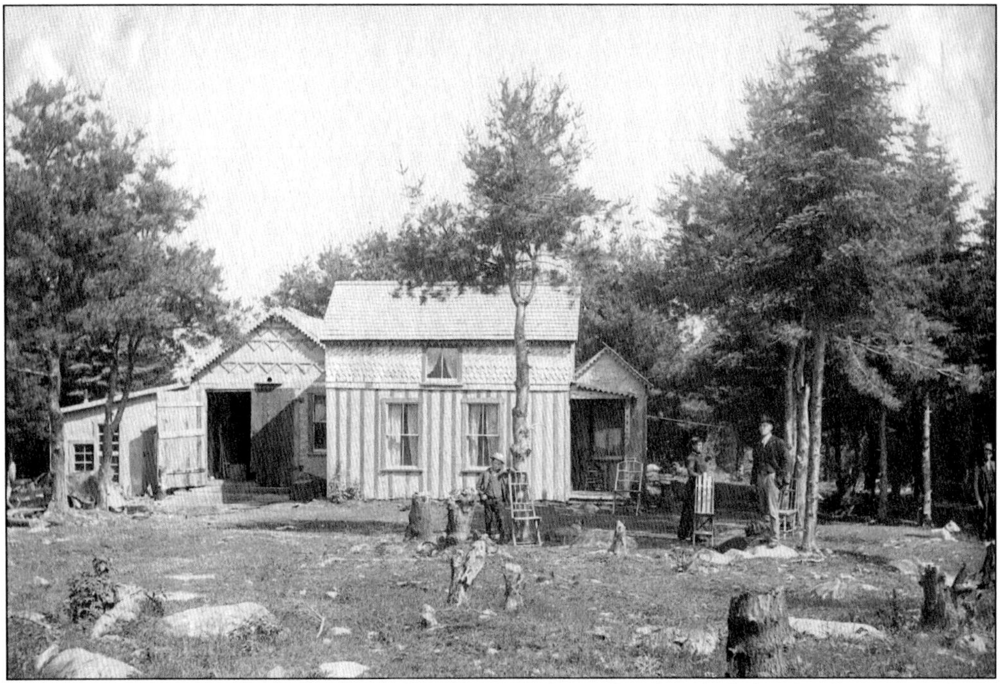

Shack Hill was a bustle of activity until 1906, when the mill ordered all the dwellings torn down to make more room for the mill. The Butterfield family own one of the more elaborate homes that was built on Shack Hill. Note the fancy trim and wood work on the house and shed.

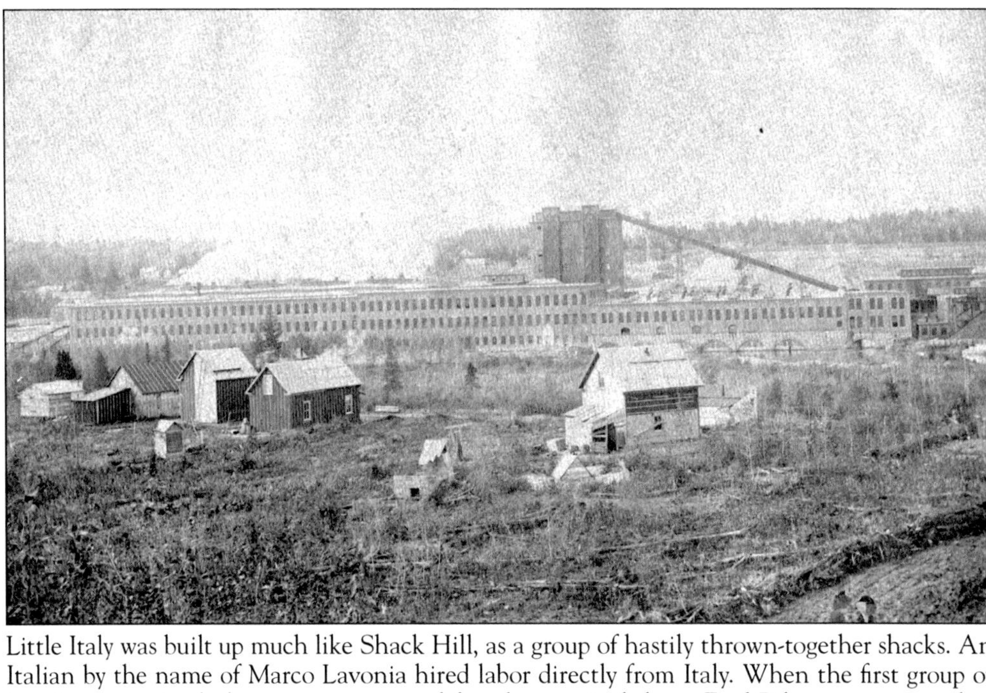

Little Italy was built up much like Shack Hill, as a group of hastily thrown-together shacks. An Italian by the name of Marco Lavonia hired labor directly from Italy. When the first group of immigrants arrived, they were unprepared for what awaited them. Fred Peluso was assigned to watch over the men, and he saw to their every need. He earned the title of *padrone*, or king of Little Italy.

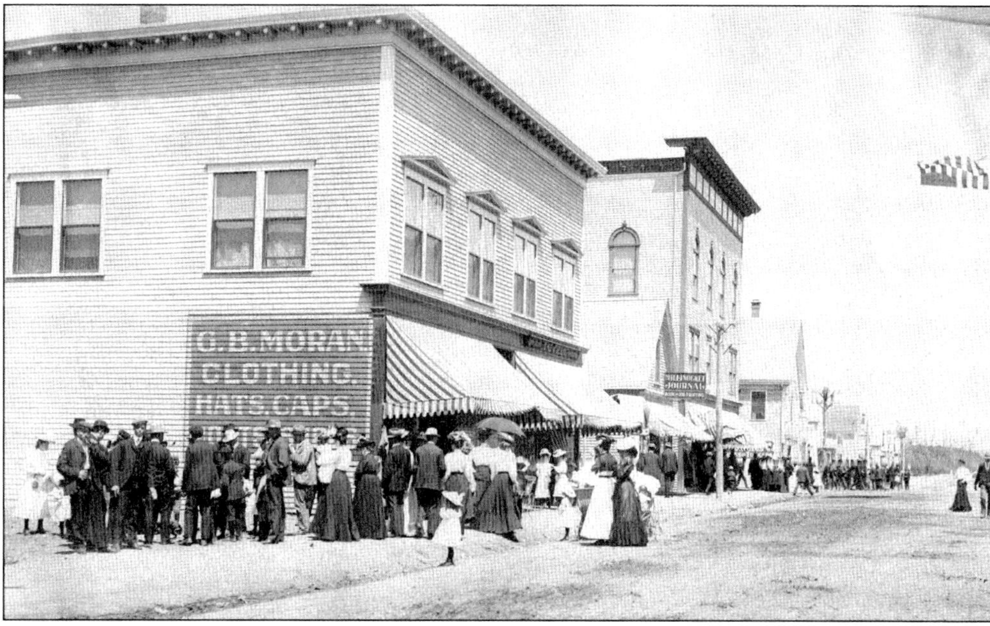

People are gathering on Penobscot Avenue on the dirt sidewalks. The G. B. Moran Clothing Store occupies the building next to the small office of the *Millinocket Journal*. As a small weekly newspaper, the *Millinocket Journal* started printing as soon as the town got its charter. Gil Moran kept the clothing business going until his death in 1951. His son Burton Moran carried on with the business until 1968.

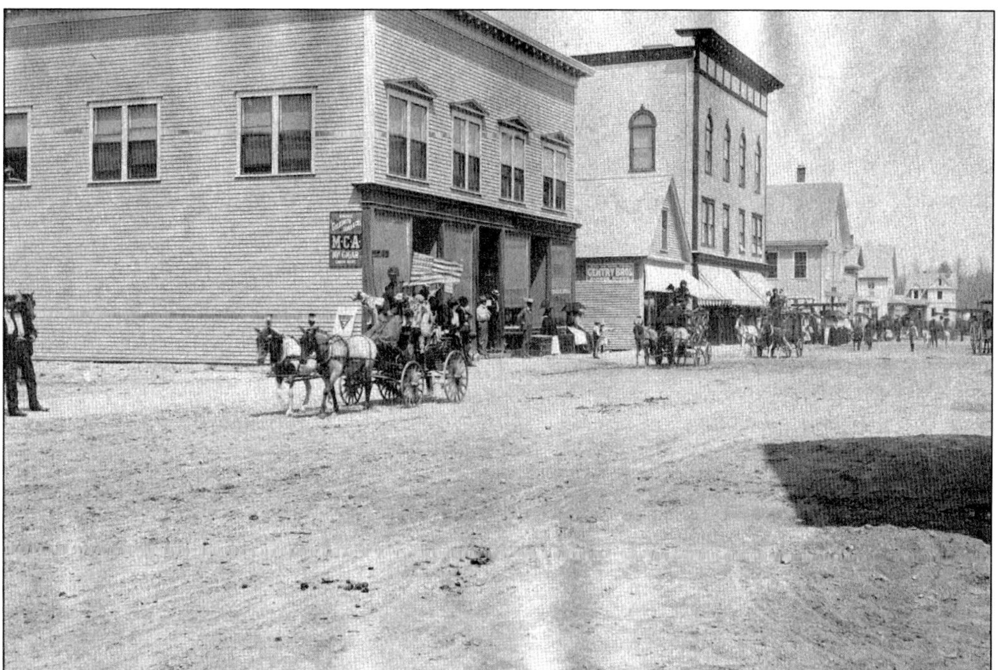

An odd and curious assortment of pony-drawn carriages move down Penobscot Avenue. The small wagons might have been part of an early traveling show that came through Millinocket to entertain the public. The Gentry Brothers store is tucked in between the two taller buildings.

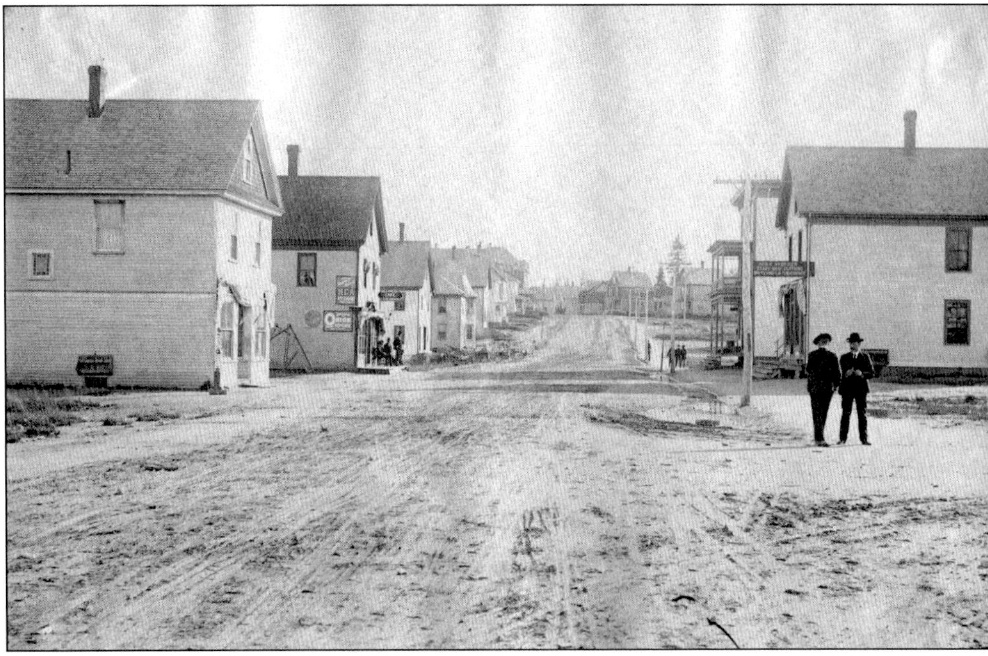

John Simon set up his clothing store across the street from the 10¢ Millinocket Cigar Café on the lower end of Penobscot Avenue. He also advertised the availability of home furnishings in the store. The tract of land at the end of Penobscot Avenue on the upper right was to become the location of the town park.

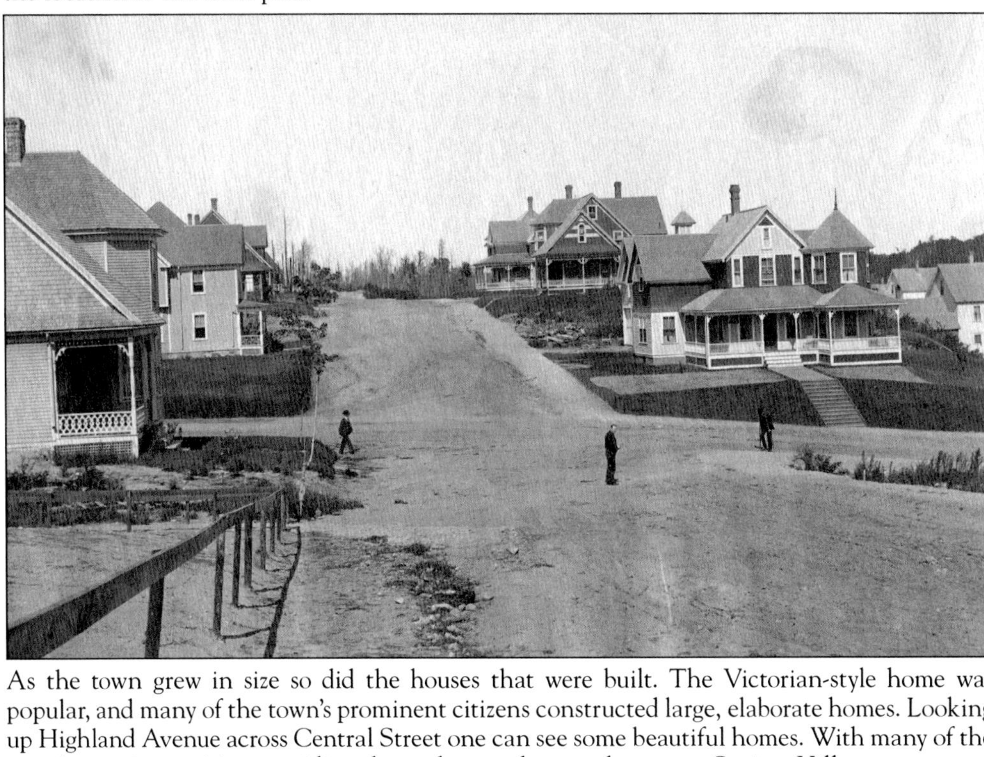

As the town grew in size so did the houses that were built. The Victorian-style home was popular, and many of the town's prominent citizens constructed large, elaborate homes. Looking up Highland Avenue across Central Street one can see some beautiful homes. With many of the town's prominent citizens residing there, the area became known as Society Hill.

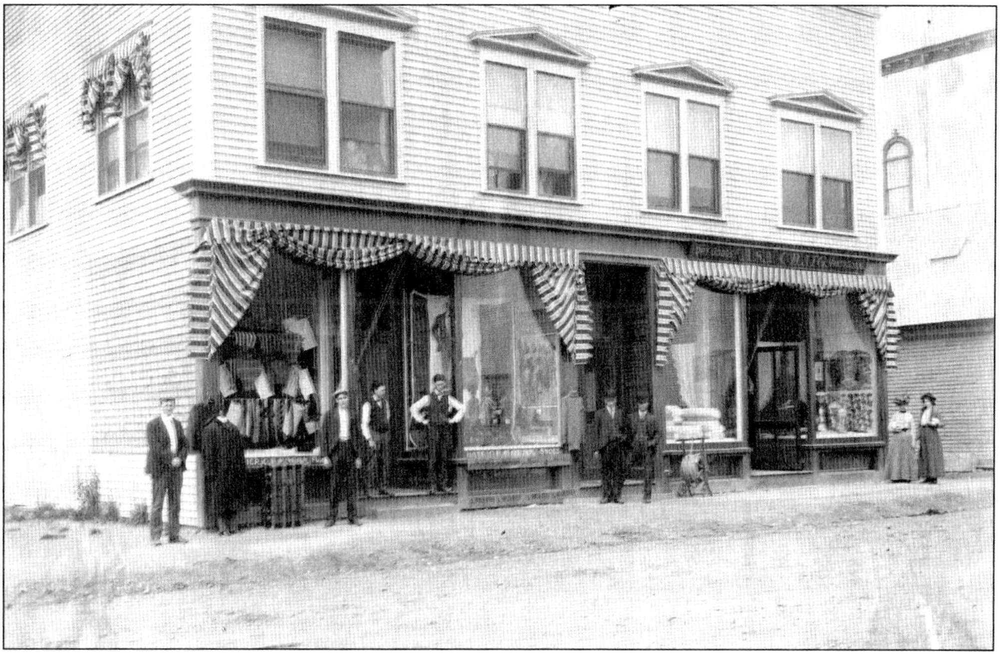

G. B. Moran Clothing Store sold clothes to the lumberjacks and was considered to be one of the finest clothing stores in town. On payday, many loggers hurried to purchase the heavy wool clothes that were needed in the woods during the winter months. His store was beside the dry goods store of Asa Craig on Penobscot Avenue.

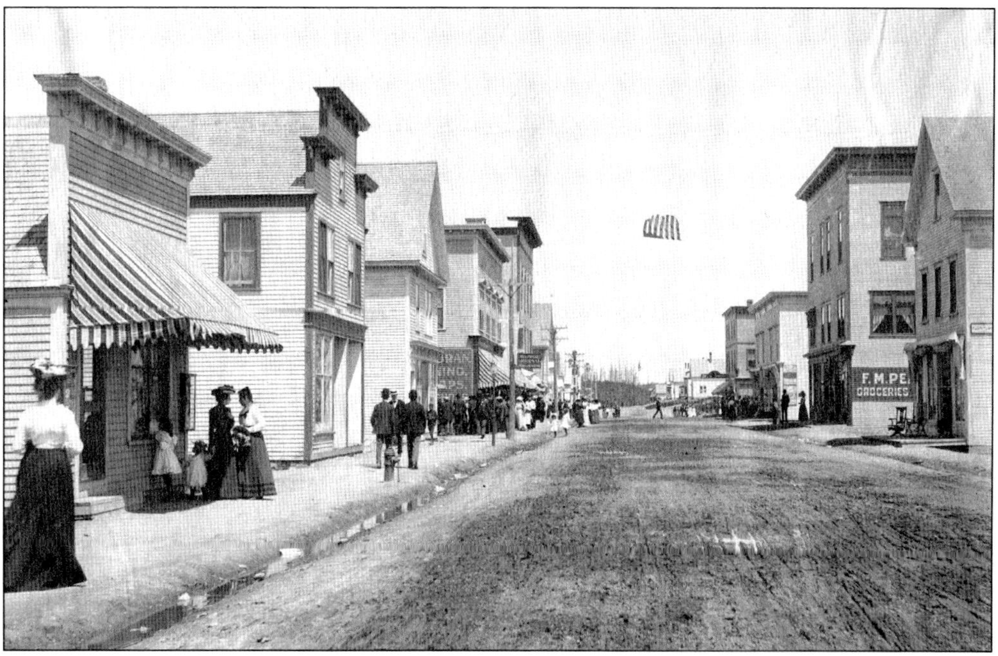

Penobscot Avenue was the main street of Millinocket with numerous stores opened for business. The business district stretched from Poplar Street to Central Street. Some of the names that were familiar along Penobscot Avenue included Moore Block, Bishop Block, Hayden Block, Rush Block, Decker-Gonya Block, McCaffrey Block, and Kimball Block.

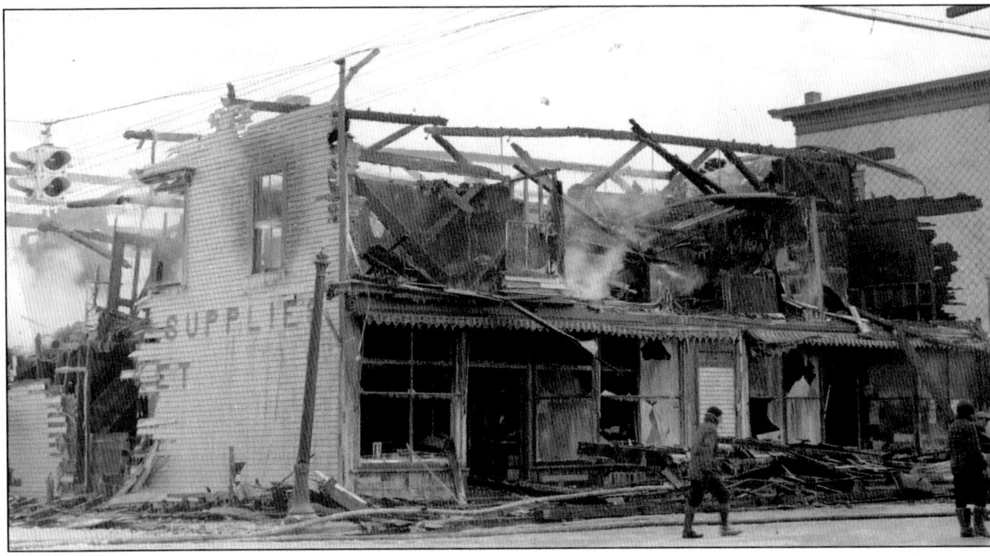

The Kimball Trading Company sat on the corner of Penobscot Avenue and Central Street. Customers could purchase dry goods, meats, and other groceries in the store. The cashier had a unique way to deal with the money. When payment was made, she placed the cash in a small container, and with the pull of a handle, the money was sent on a wire to another cashier who made the proper change and returned the container.

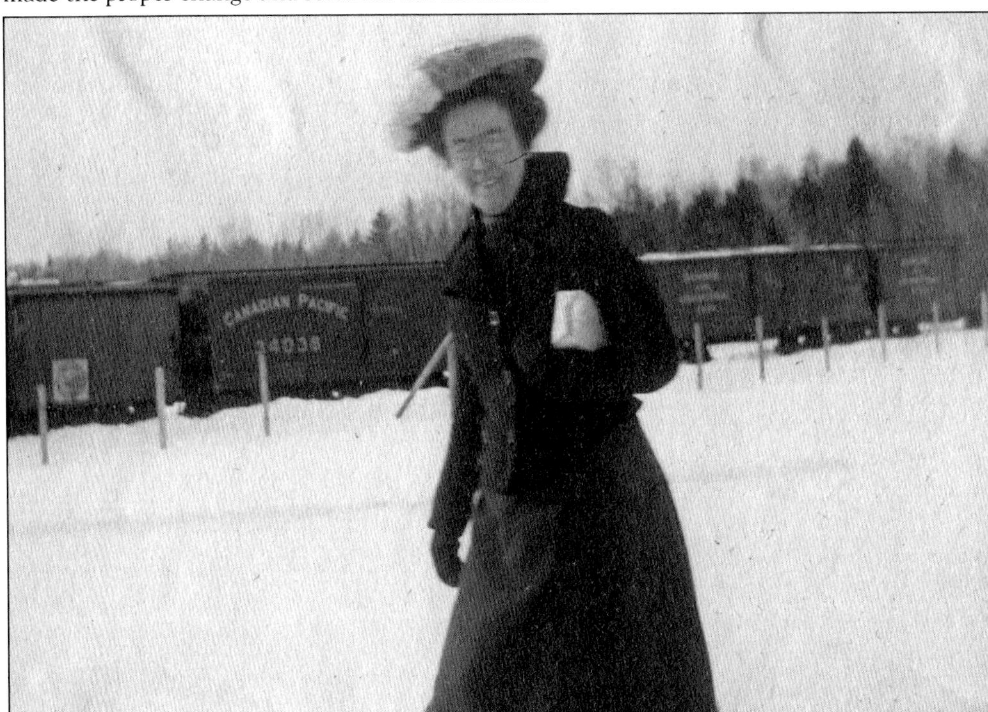

Shopping and running errands was no easy affair in the winter. Dressed in long, wool dresses and fancy hats, it was hard walking through the snow on the unplowed streets. When it was possible, extra supplies were purchased ahead of time to cut back on the number of trips to the store in bad weather.

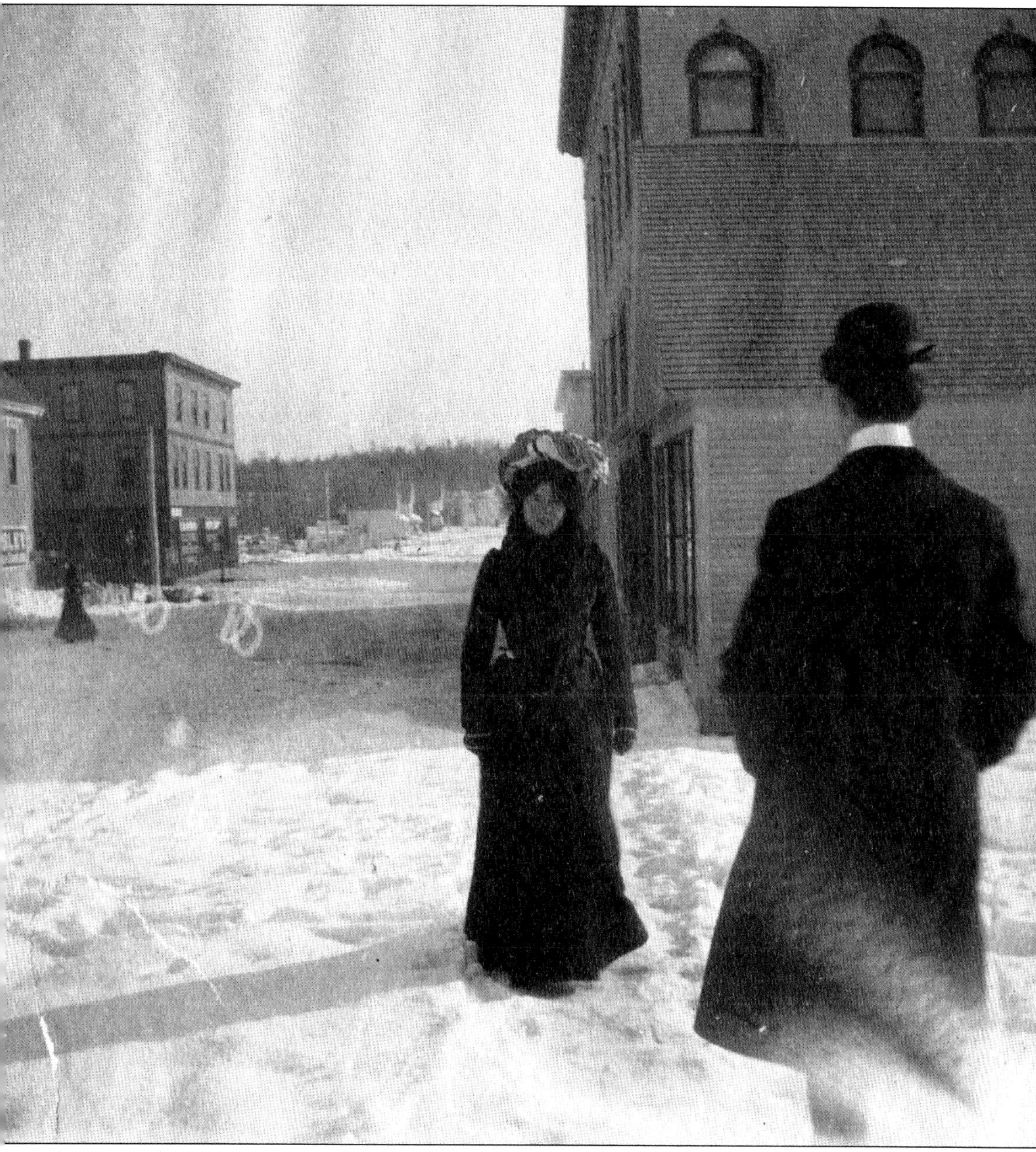

A man and a woman are out for a stroll on Central Street on a nice winter day. Fred Peasley opened a hardware store on the corner of Central Street and Penobscot Avenue. The store was later known as Fogg and Clifford's hardware store. The three-story building across from the hardware store was known as the Bishop Block; it is no longer there and was replaced by an automobile dealership. On the back side of the Bishop building, Mr. Butterfield had a livery stable until it caught fire and burned to the ground. Directly behind the lady walking was the location of the town library when it was on Central Street. In the tall building beside the library, Dr. George W. MacKay had his office. Without the now-familiar snow banks, the streets look somewhat odd with all the snow covering them. Snow removal was not considered during that time, and it was acceptable just to leave it unplowed.

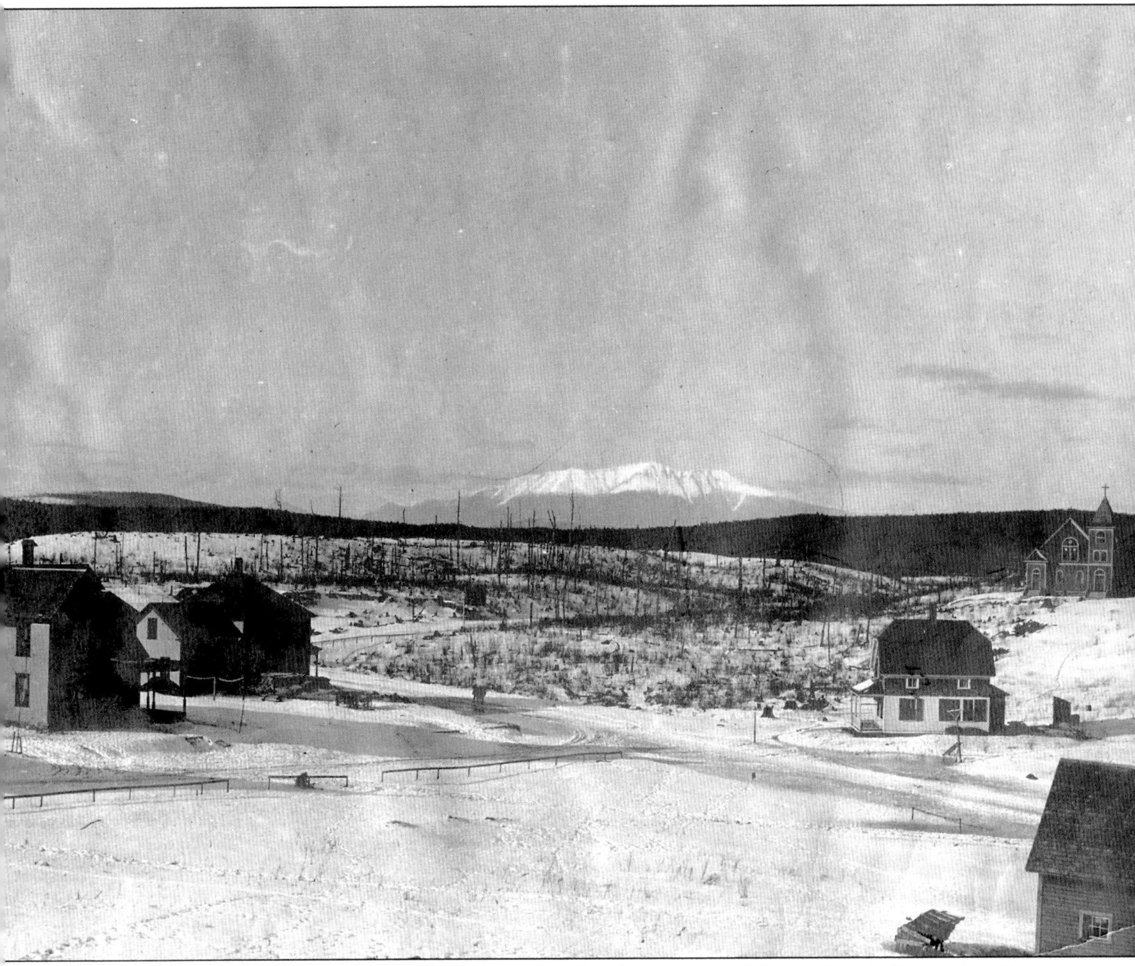

Guests in the Great Northern Hotel had a breathtaking view of Mount Katahdin in the distance. At the intersection of Central Street and Maine Avenue, the town was still bare of trees and open to the cold north winds blowing down from the mountain. Much of the land close to town was clear-cut in order to supply the need for mill production and the building of houses. In later years, a more responsible practice was instituted for the cutting of trees. Now the town has many beautiful trees that have grown back over the years. The early St. Martin of Tours Church sits off to the right on a small hill looking over the town. The open space in front of the hotel is now the site of the Great Northern Guest House.

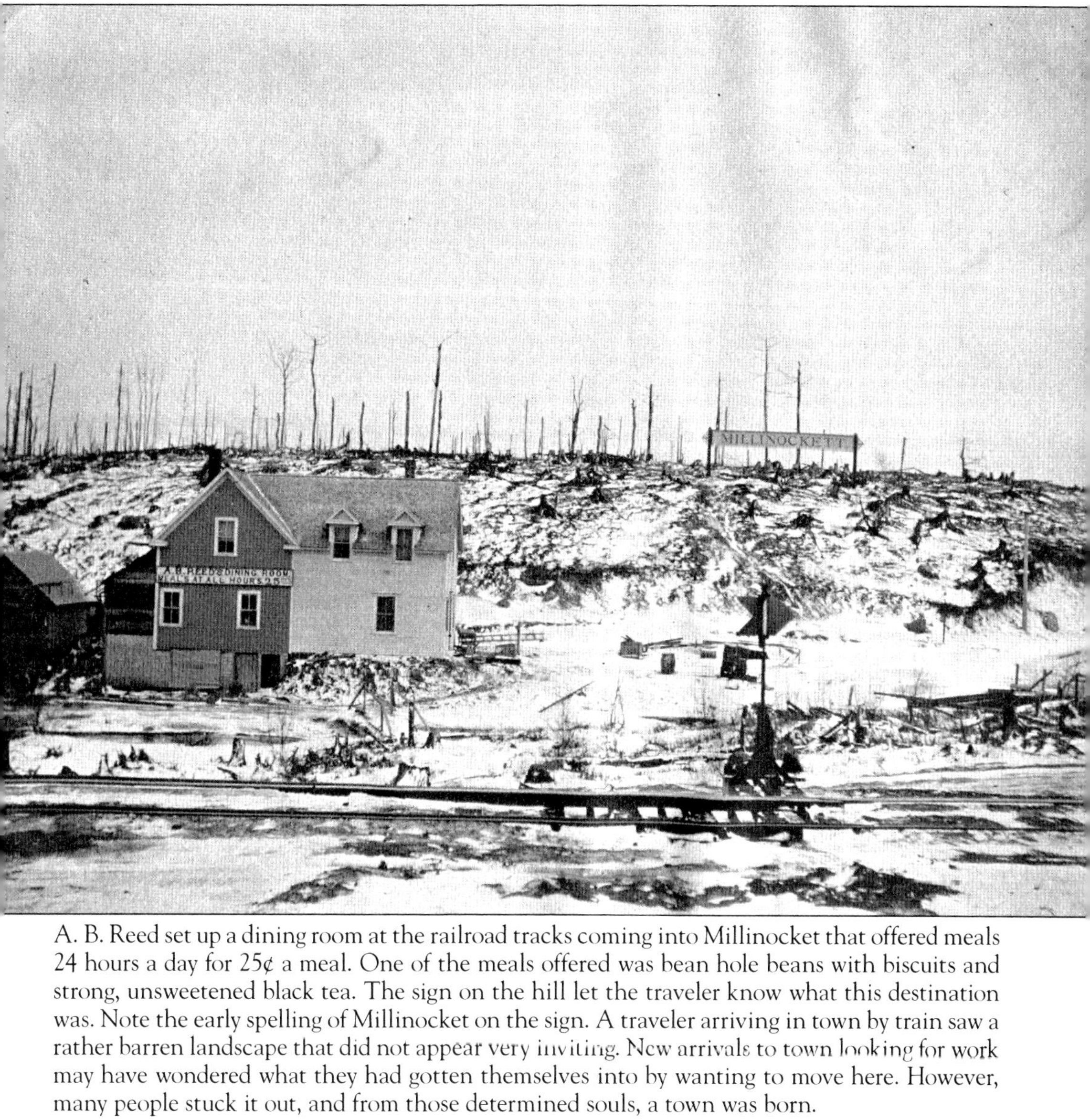

A. B. Reed set up a dining room at the railroad tracks coming into Millinocket that offered meals 24 hours a day for 25¢ a meal. One of the meals offered was bean hole beans with biscuits and strong, unsweetened black tea. The sign on the hill let the traveler know what this destination was. Note the early spelling of Millinocket on the sign. A traveler arriving in town by train saw a rather barren landscape that did not appear very inviting. New arrivals to town looking for work may have wondered what they had gotten themselves into by wanting to move here. However, many people stuck it out, and from those determined souls, a town was born.

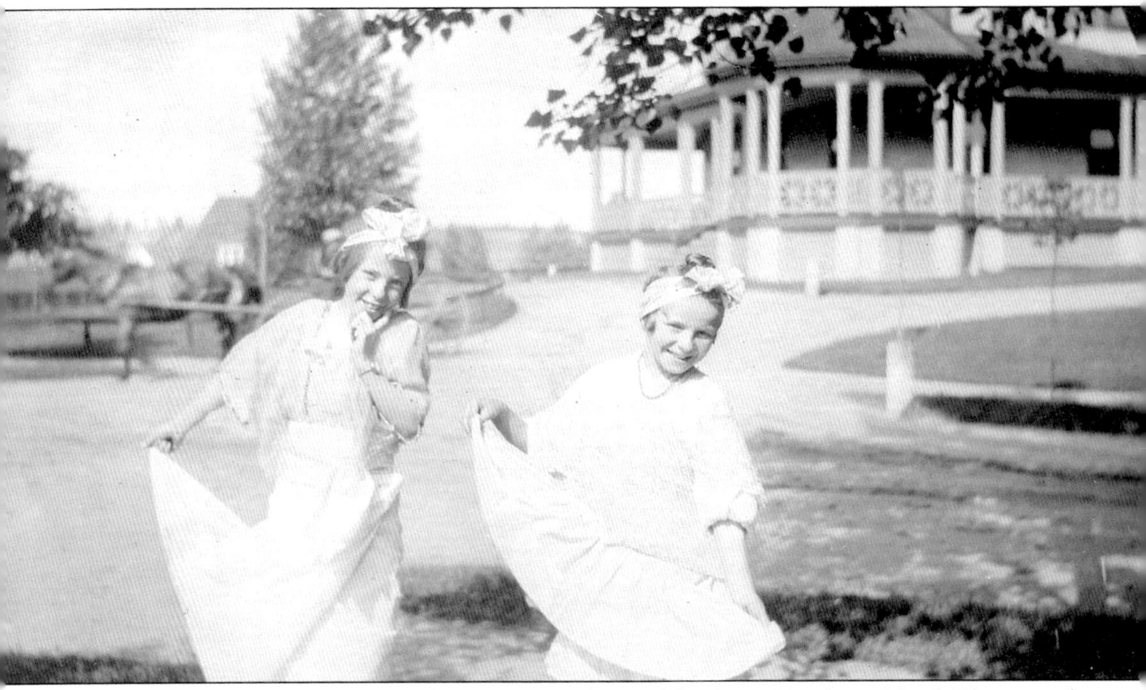

Two angelic-looking girls are striking a pose in front of the Great Northern Hotel. The veranda on the hotel was a favored spot for guests to relax and socialize. The veranda wrapped around the hotel and allowed for a view of the town from all sides of the building. Travelers arriving by train were picked up at the train station by the local hackney and brought to the hotel. There they were greeted with warmth and luxury like no other place in the north woods. The lobby was large and open and was filled with potted plants and chairs to sit in and rest tired feet. The hotel dining room was a formal dining area, and many local businessmen met with clients there. The Great Northern Hotel was a prized establishment in its time. It was torn down in 1961.

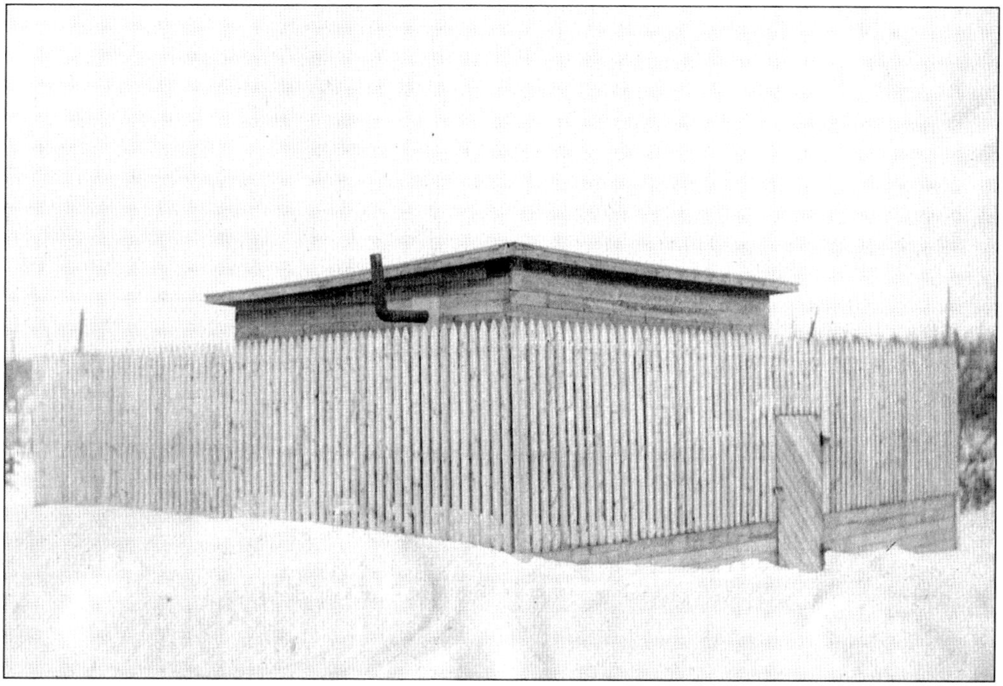

The first jail in Millinocket was on Shack Hill and consisted of a one-room building with a barred window that was enclosed by a high picket fence. Benjamin Bragdon served as the first deputy sheriff of Millinocket until Fred M. Gates arrived from Old Town and was appointed as the first police chief. Gates was known as a firm but fair officer of the law. Millinocket was a rowdy town in its early days, and Gates was a busy man. The jail was upgraded to a more modern facility, and the old shack was torn down.

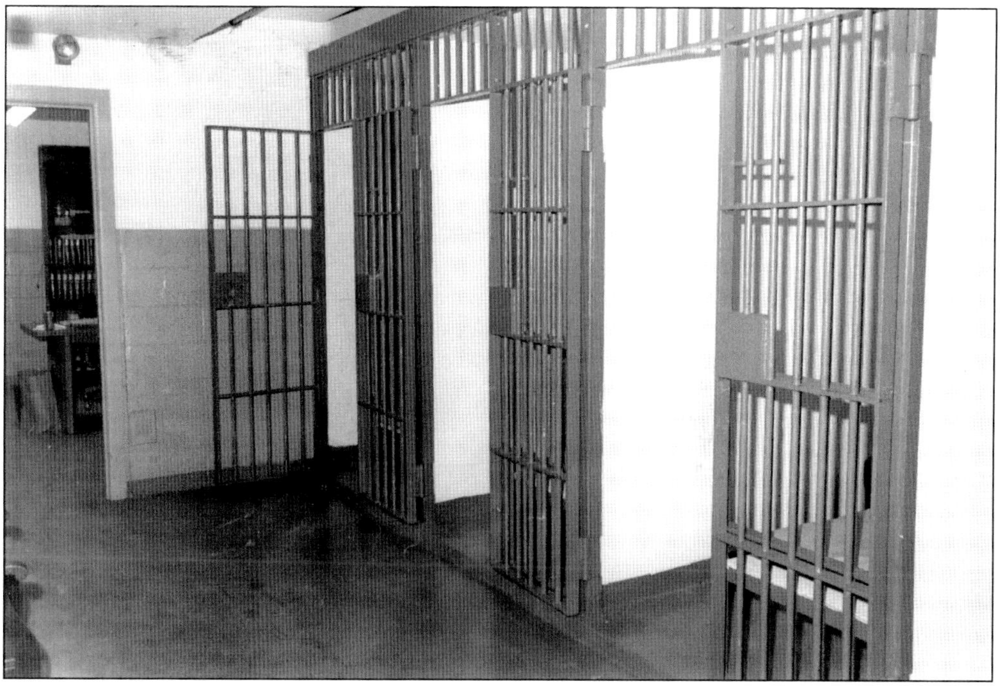

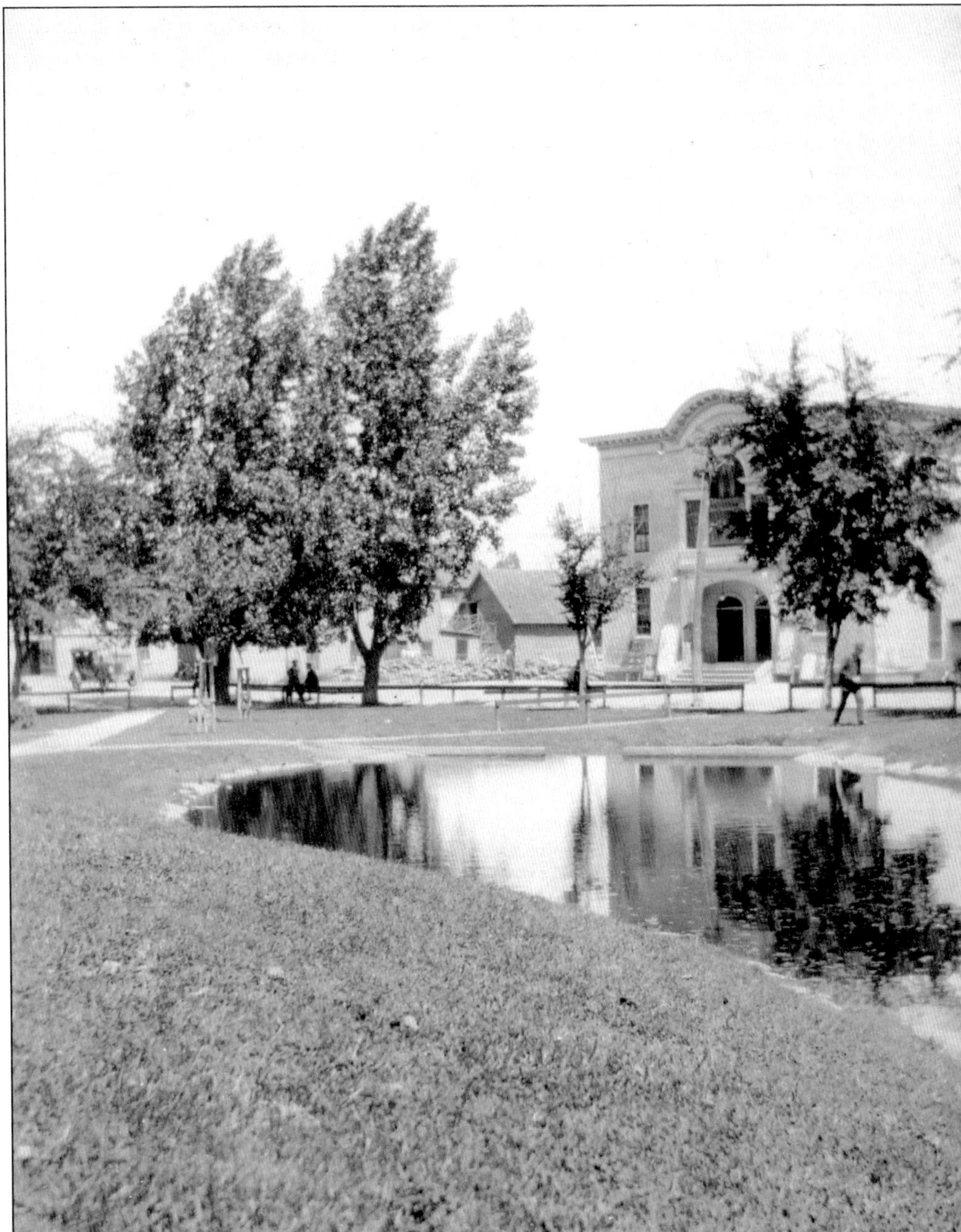

The Millinocket Opera House was built in 1912 to replace the Woodmen Hall that burned that year. The Millinocket Opera House was on Poplar Street and overlooked the town park. For a short time, the park was used as a cemetery and held the graves of two children and a man. A marker on the grave of the man identified him as Ossinger. A small pond in the park was supplied with water by Ferguson Lake and formed a small wading pool. Eventually the town located a bandstand at the park, the cemetery was moved to another location, and the pond was filled in for a parking lot. The Millinocket Opera House was the center of community activity and served as the civic center for the town. Movies and plays were shown, and dances were held there. The Millinocket Opera House is no longer standing.

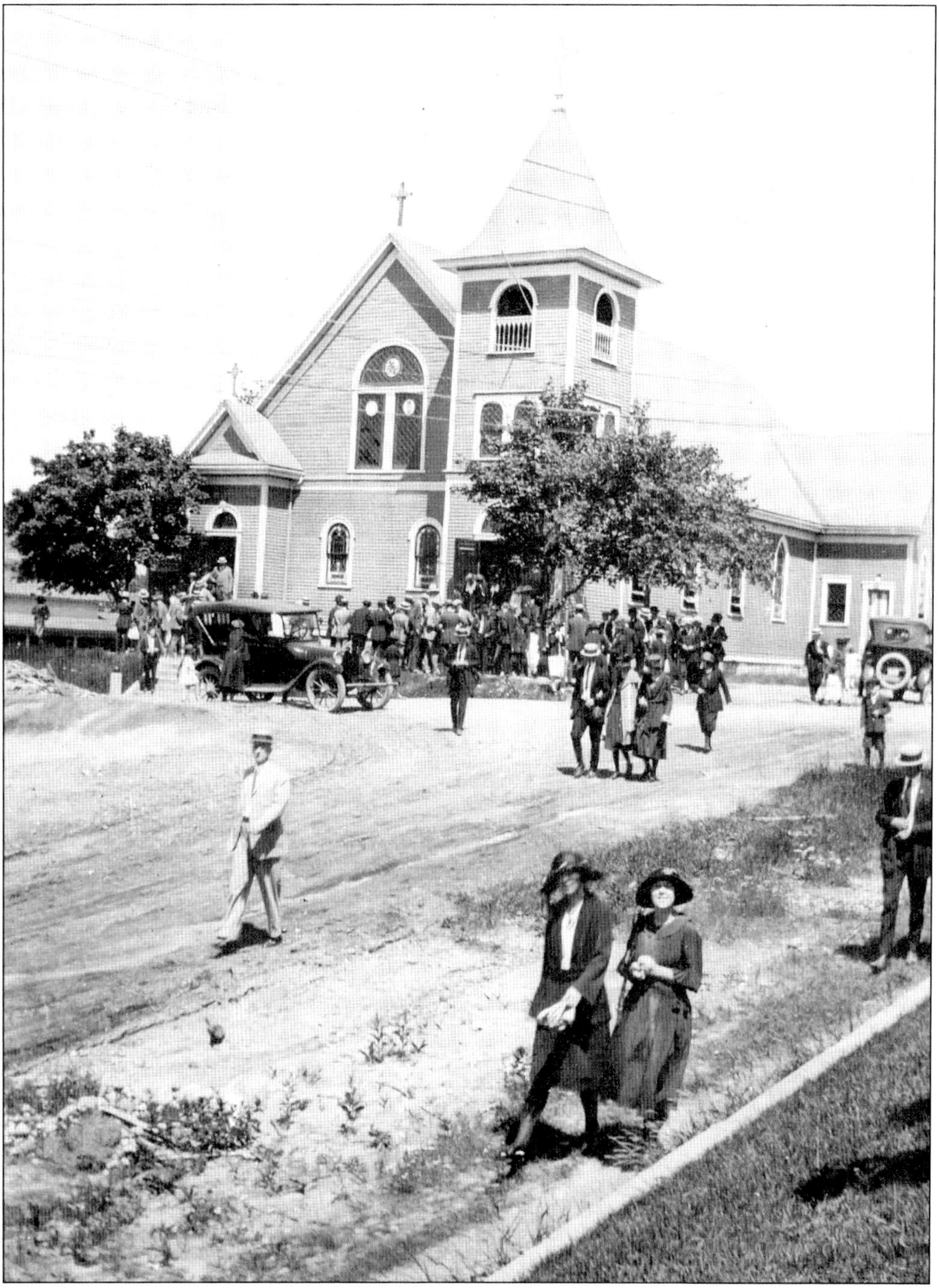

In 1899, St. Martin of Tours was the first church built in Millinocket. Fr. Martin Clary was the first rector of the church when it was located at the corner of Colby Street and Maine Avenue. The building had a tall belfry and stained-glass windows. It was the oldest church in town until it was torn down in 1970 and replaced with another building nearby. Church life is important to the people of Millinocket, and many of churches served the population. Church is letting out for these people on a nice, sunny day.

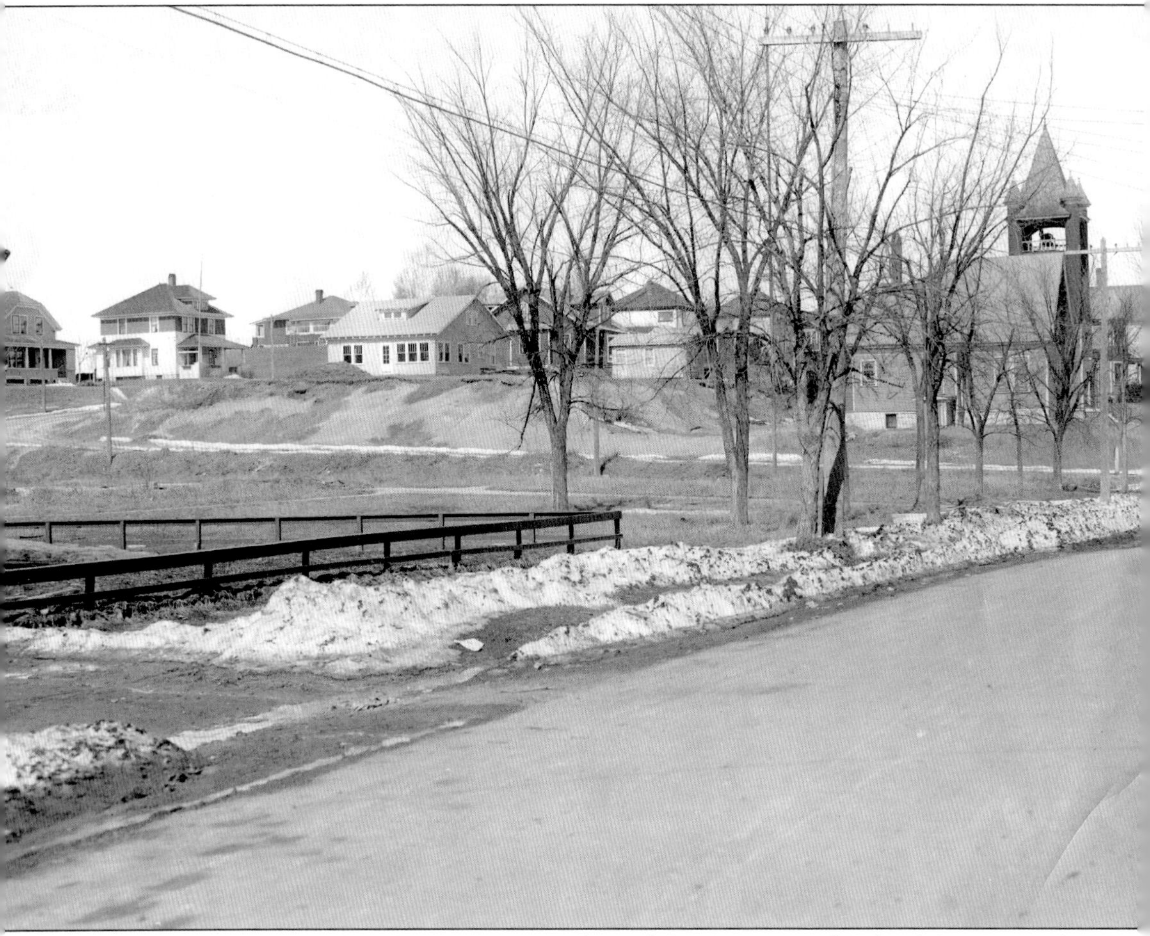

The open tract of land at the intersection of Katahdin Avenue and School Street was the location for the Katahdin Avenue School. At an earlier time, the Millinocket High School occupied this spot but was left vacant when it burnt. The steeple of the First Congregational Church can be seen off to the right. The church was built in 1904 and Rev. W. J. McNeil was its first minister. The church has changed over the years, but it is still located in the same place. The open steeple seen here has been nicely rebuilt to enclose it slightly, but it has not affected its beauty. Except for a few storage units, the location of the Katahdin Avenue School is once again open and vacant.

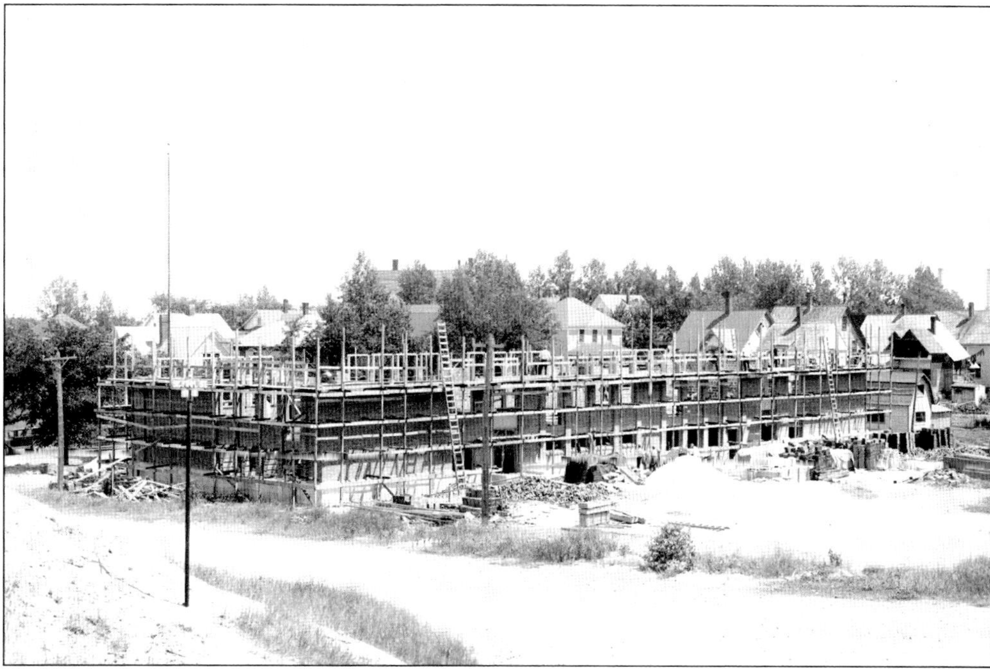

At the former site of the Millinocket High School on Katahdin Avenue and School Street, the new Katahdin Avenue School was built in 1931. Originally designed as a single-story schoolhouse with eight classrooms, it was expanded in the 1960s when additional classrooms and office space were added. The single-story brick structure was built for less than $62,000. The ornate front of the school was an impressive sight when it was completed, with its high, columned main doors and stone decorations on the roof. The school no longer stands and has been replaced by storage units.

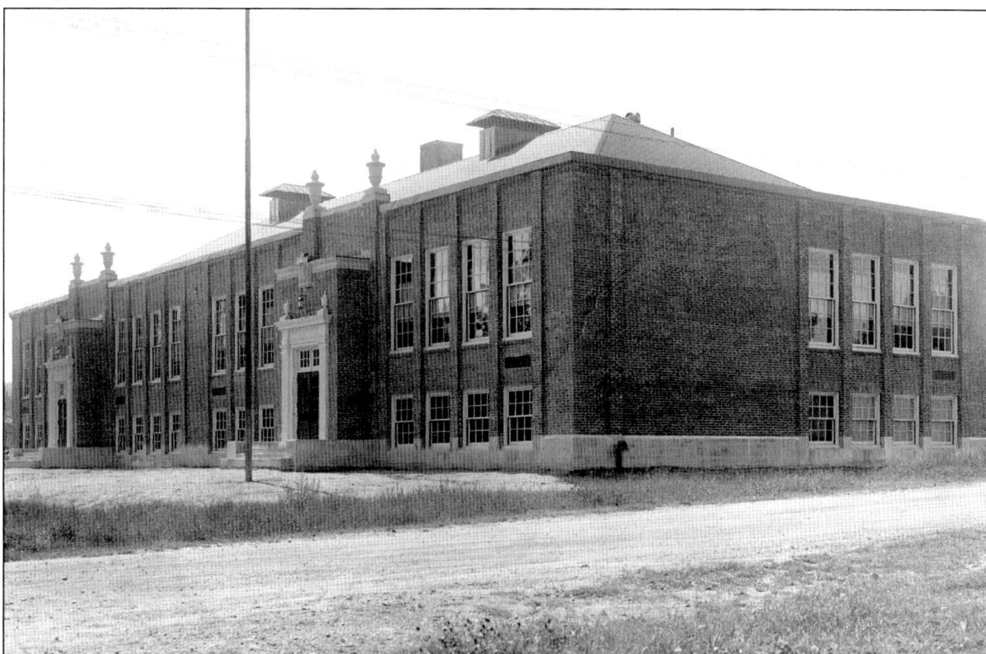

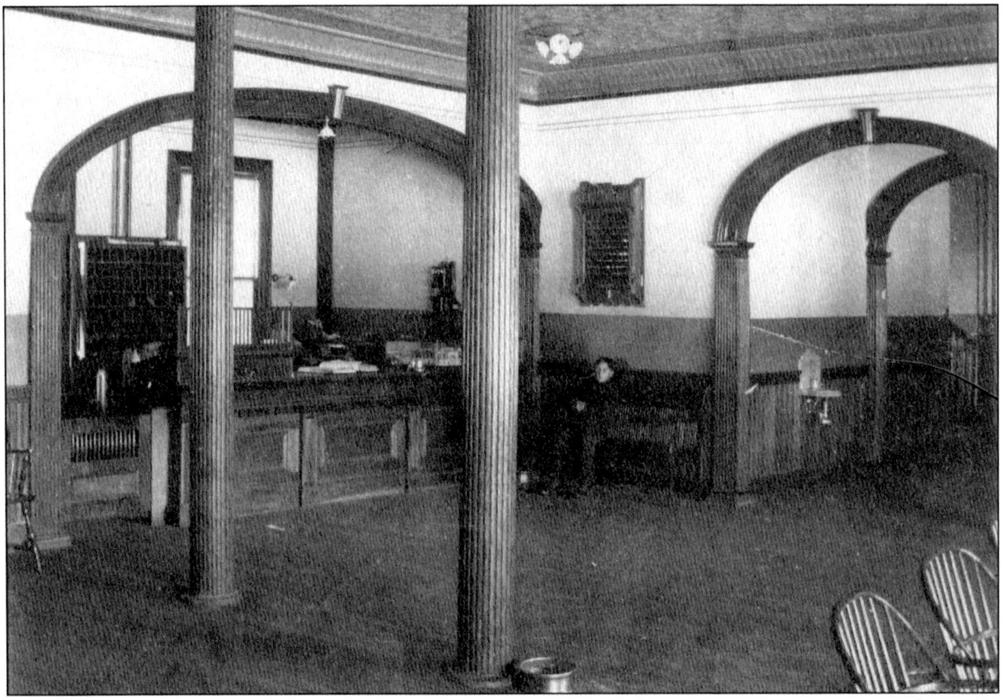

With high columns and tin ceilings, this lobby area is a far better improvement over the early shacks that first appeared in Millinocket. The attention to detail in the woodwork adds to the beauty of the room. A small child is sitting on one of the benches patiently awaiting someone's arrival.

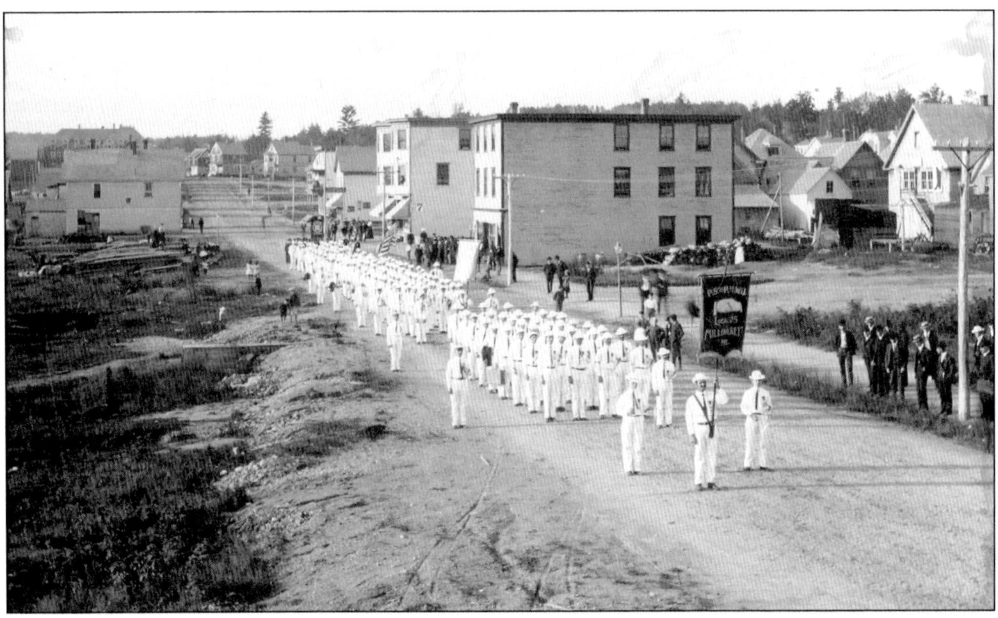

Organized labor unions were developed early in the forming of the mill. For a time, employees worked 12-hour days seven days a week for an average of $1.50 a day. The union eventually changed that to three shifts of eight hours in an attempt to improve working conditions. To show its solidarity, a labor union parades down Penobscot Avenue sporting its flag.

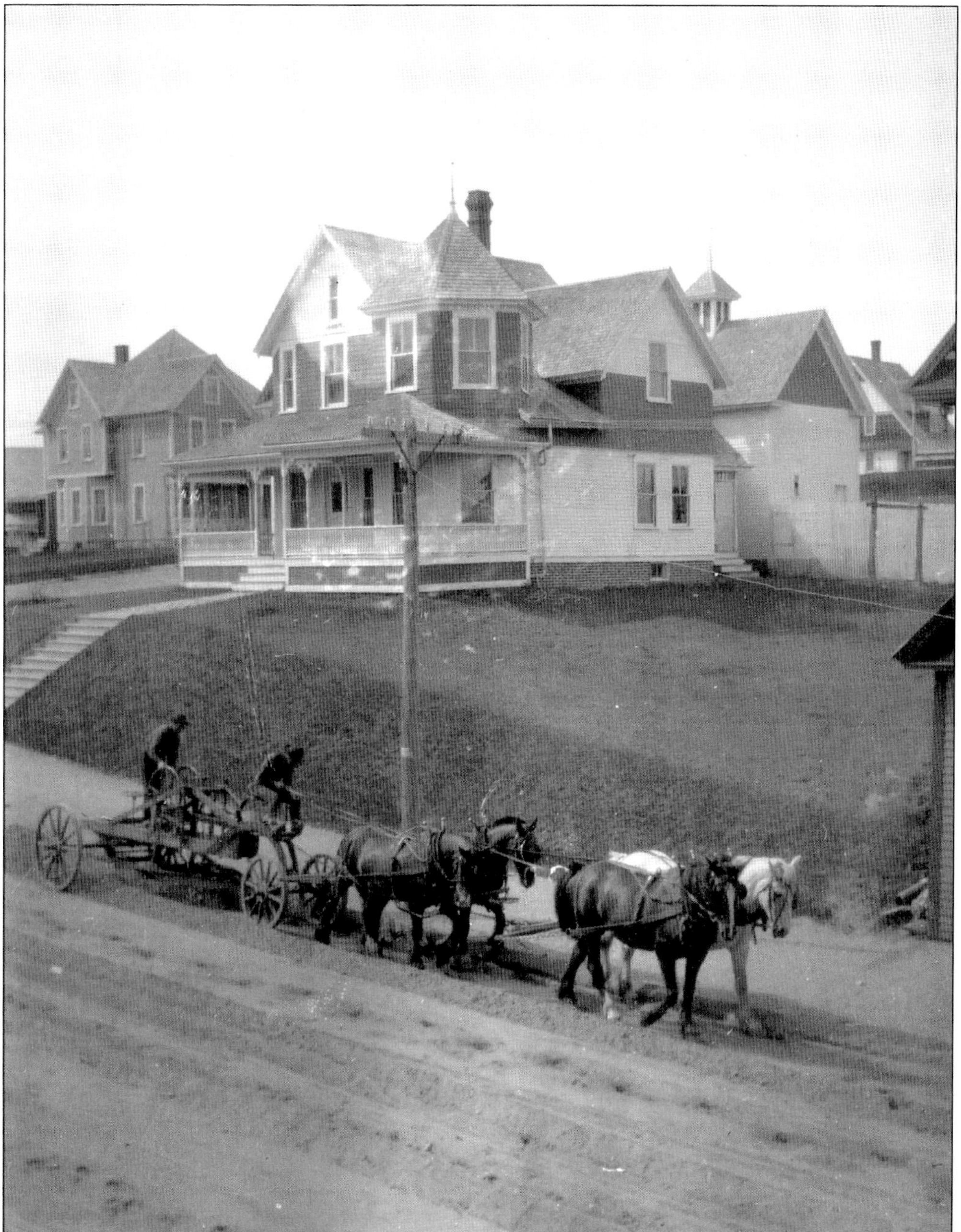

The streets of Millinocket were not only built at a steady pace, but they were also maintained. A road crew is plowing Central Street with a double team of horses and a plow to keep the dirt street smooth and passable. The man in the front drove the team of horses, while the man in back operated the plow. Hardy Ferguson's office had the job of designing the mill and the layout of the town. Millinocket was first planned out to cover 500 acres of land, but the terrain was not very well suited for a town due to all of its large boulders and trees. However, the location was ideal for a mill. Once the streets were laid out, they were given names of local trees, counties, or colleges. (Courtesy of Fred Fowler.)

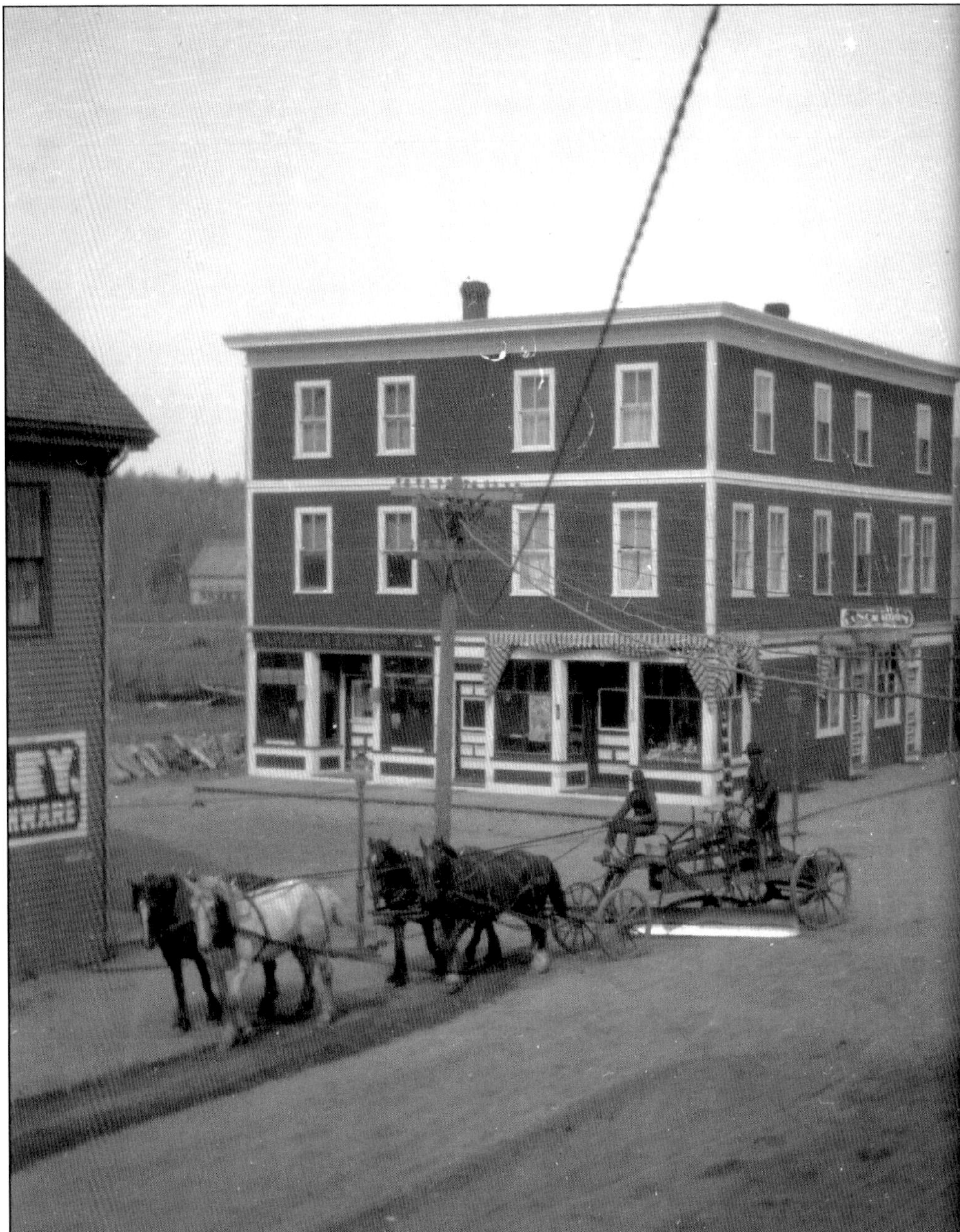

Seeing the Bishop building across the intersection of Central Street and Penobscot Avenue, Dr. G. W. MacKay could watch the road crew working its team of horses from his office. MacKay started his dental practice in the Windsor Hotel in 1900 before he moved to the Gonya building on Penobscot Avenue. He served the town of Millinocket for 62 years as a dentist and relieved many a toothache during that time. In later years, he moved the dental practice to his house, which was just beyond the church on Highland Avenue. On the Central Street side of the Bishop building is a small lunchroom, and on the Penobscot Avenue side there is an American Express office. Today the Central Street and Penobscot Avenue intersection is busy, with one of the two streetlights in town safely directing traffic. (Courtesy of Fred Fowler.)

Looking down the deeply rutted Katahdin Avenue, Mount Katahdin is just a faint outline in the distance. During the spring thaw, the roads were almost impassable for the wagons and the early automobiles. More often than not, it was easier just to walk to one's destination. Paved roads made for easier travel around town. (Courtesy of Fred Fowler.)

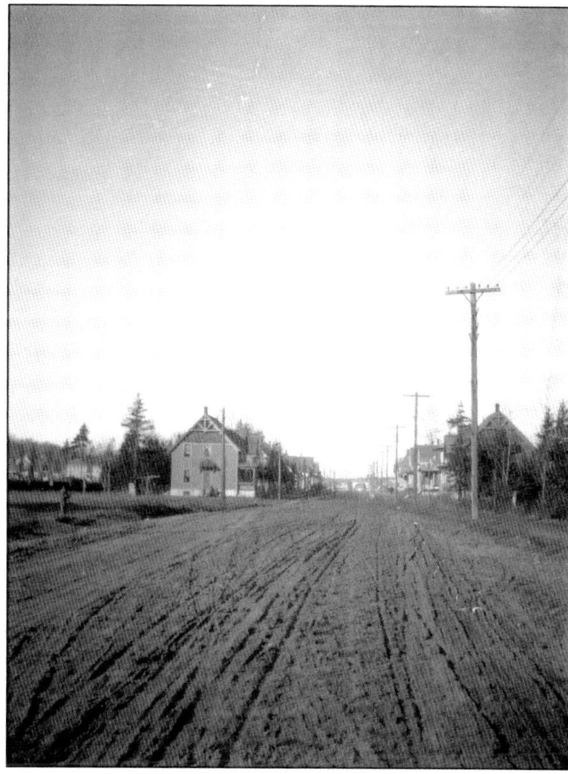

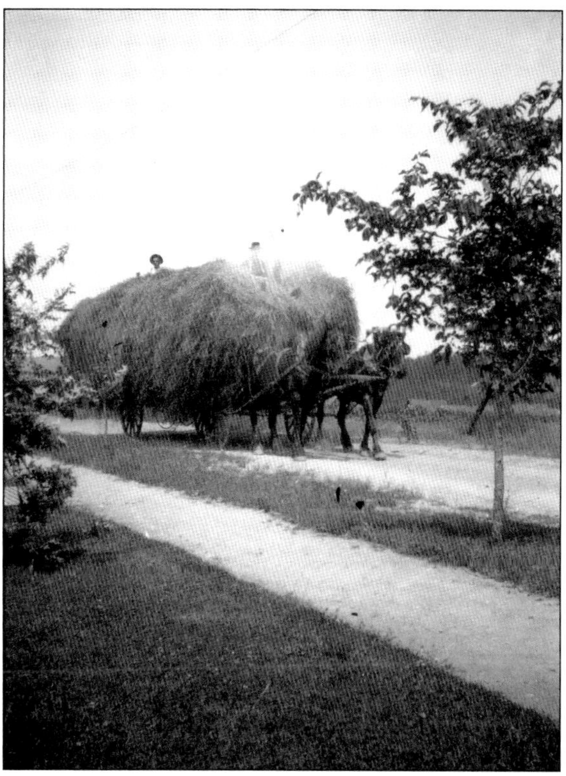

With probably more horses and oxen than people in the Millinocket area, it was a constant challenge to have enough feed on hand for the animals. The Great Northern Paper Company had large barns spread around the region to house and feed the livestock used in the woods operations and the construction of the mill. (Courtesy of Fred Fowler.)

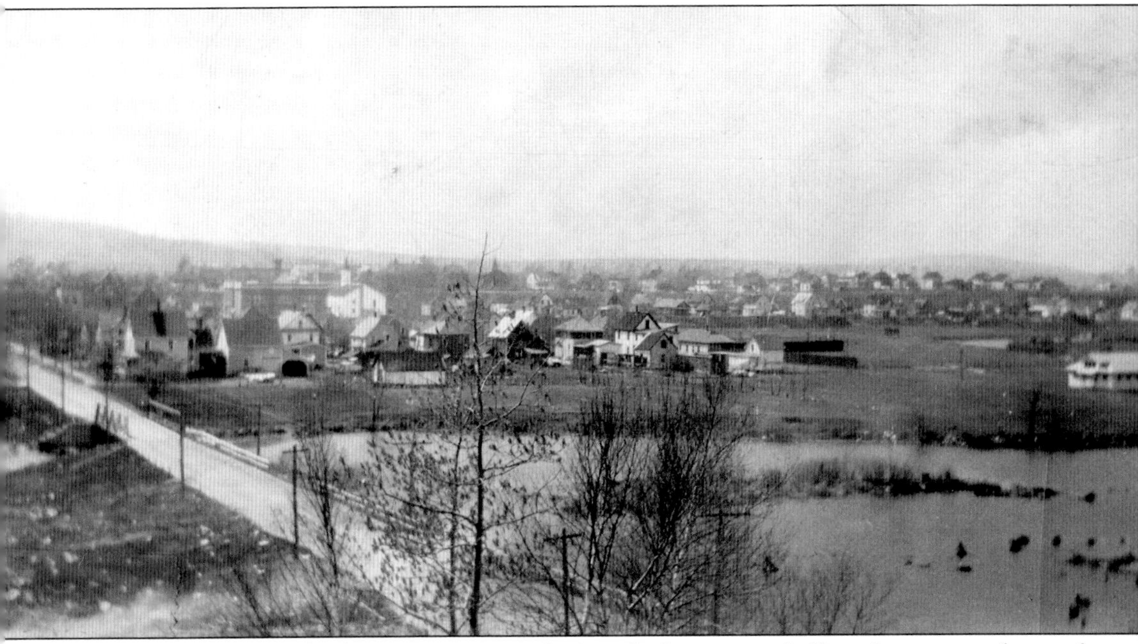

The Central Street bridge was constructed of stacked stones and allowed access to the sand banks of the stream on the other side. A short distance over the bridge, the road curved to the right, and in later years, it became Medway Road. Central Street was built over the hill, and it was later extended all the way to East Millinocket. To the left of Central Street on the hill was an area called Skunk Hollow. The Millinocket Pest House, which was a bungalow-type hospital used to quarantine patients with smallpox and the flu, was located on a stretch of land known as the flats. During epidemics, the hospital had armed guards to keep the patients in and to prevent the spread of disease.

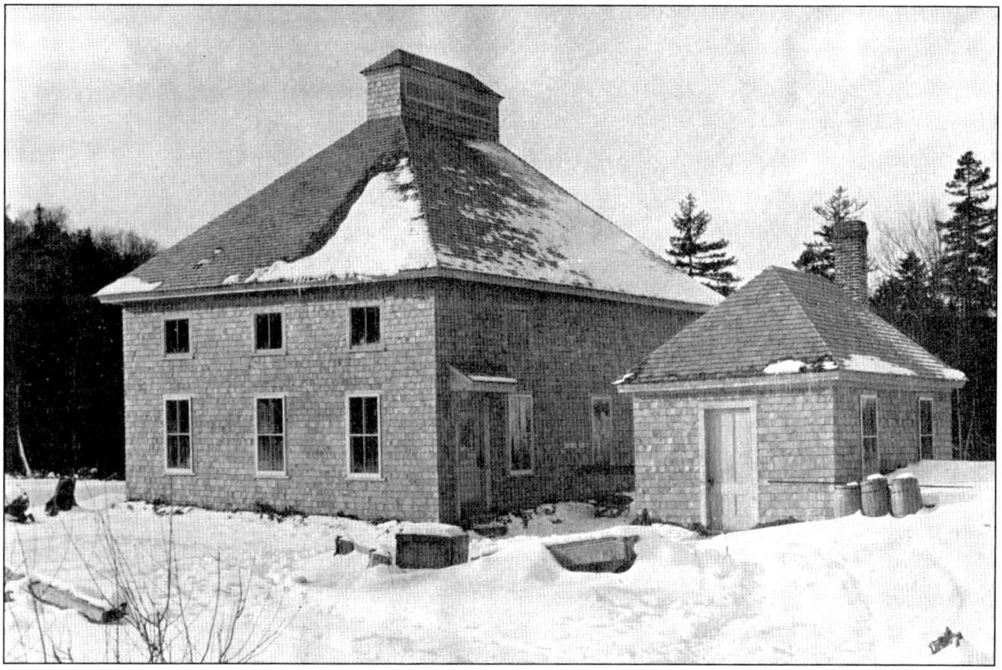

The Millinocket Light Company installed two generators in 1920 and started providing electricity to the town, which replaced the acetylene-powered streetlights. The light company constructed its gashouse behind Millinocket High School on Katahdin Avenue. By that time, the mill had already been generating electricity for its own use.

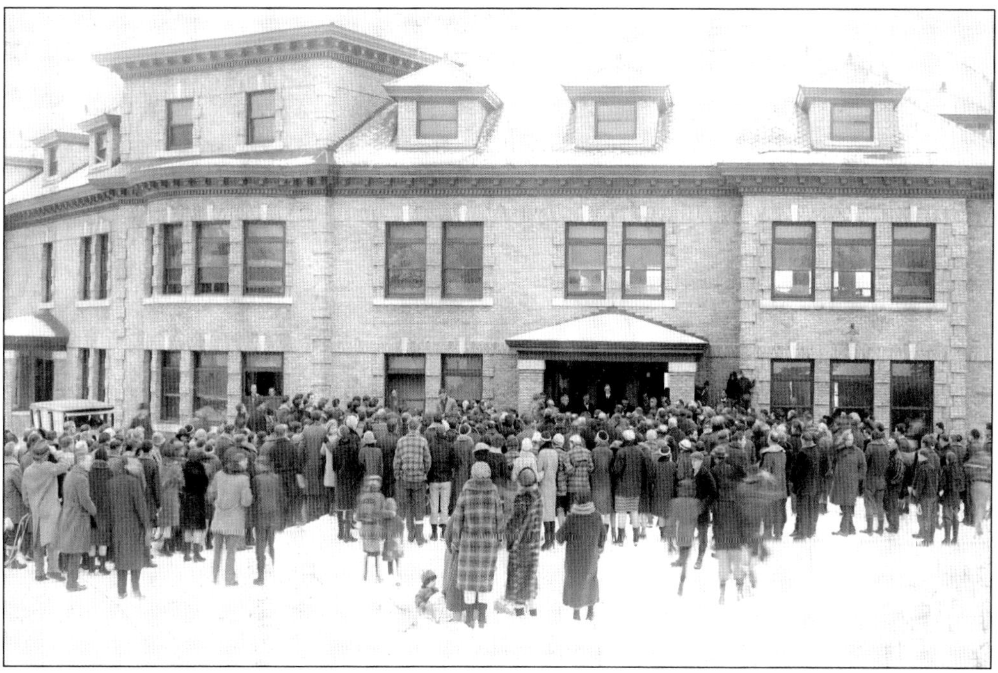

The Great Northern Paper Company administration building, a large, imposing brick structure, is the focal point at the Katahdin Avenue entrance. The company cornered a large part of the newsprint market and was well known for the manufacture of high-quality paper.

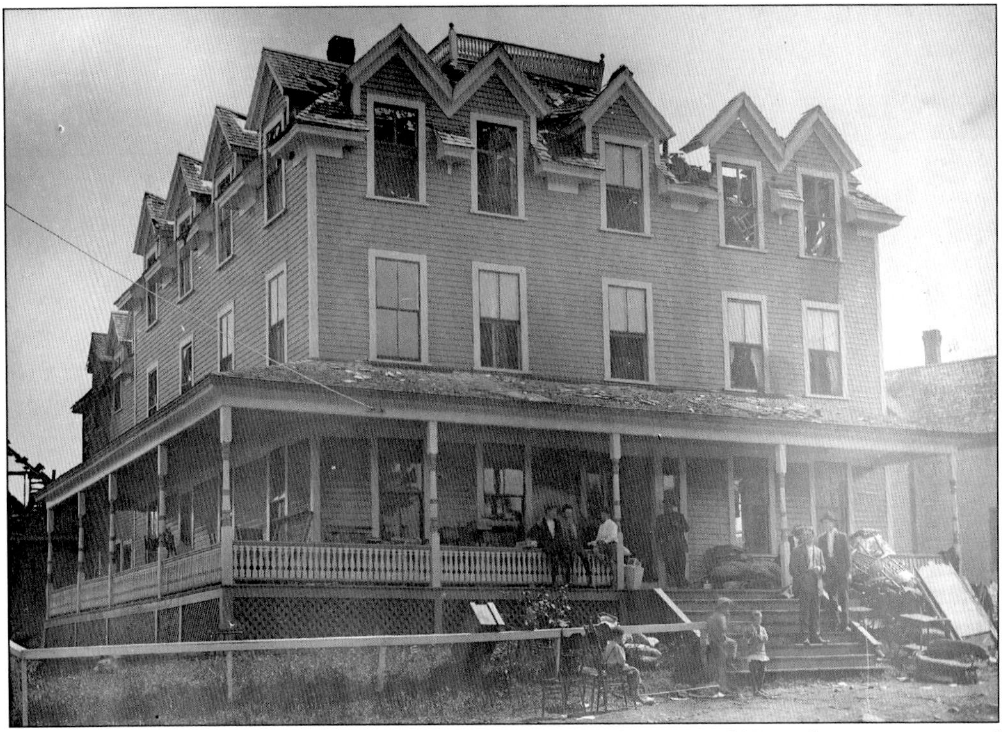

Shine and Curren of Bangor built the Mountain View House in 1899 at the intersection of Penobscot Avenue and Katahdin Avenue. The building had a balustrade topping off the roof. In 1903 during a typhoid outbreak, a part of the hotel was used as a hospital. It was torn down in the 1940s, and by 1954, the New England Telephone Company erected a small brick building in its place.

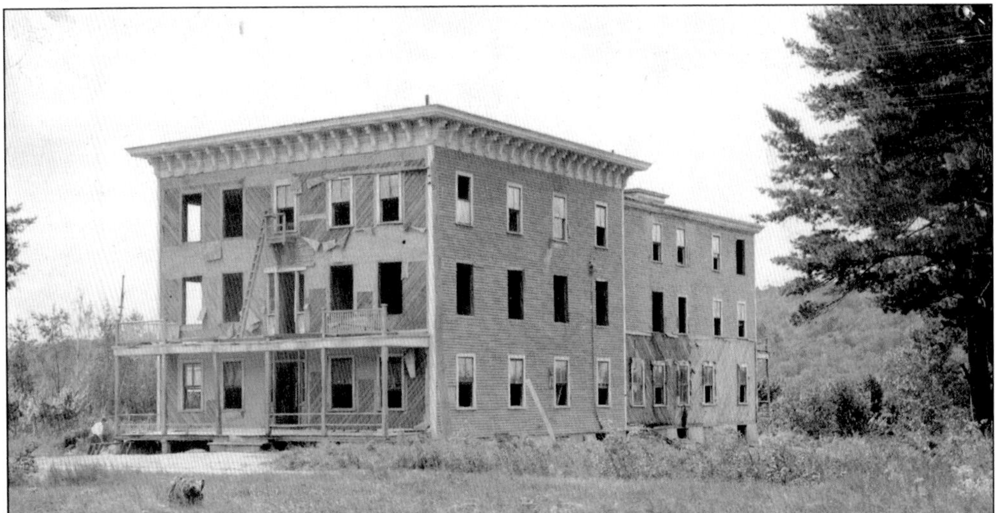

The tiny settlement of Dolby was destroyed when the dam was built and the Dolby Flowage was created. As water took over the land, the buildings were torn down, including the Dolby Boardinghouse seen here. The Dolby Flowage also flooded out the McCauslin farm and the Thomas Fowler Jr. farm.

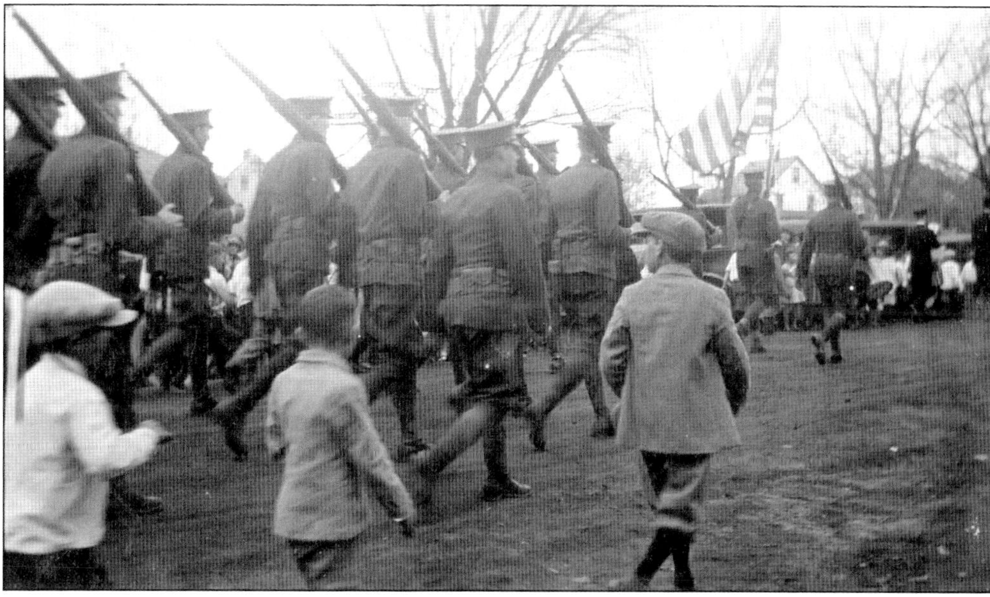

A veteran of the Spanish-American War, Capt. William Glenn was in command of Company I of the 3rd Maine Regiment in the initial days of World War I. During the war, Company I was attached to the 26th Division and served bravely in Europe. More than 100 men and women from Millinocket served in the military during the conflict. Marching down the streets of Millinocket, Company I was an impressive unit and made the town proud. Children ran alongside the uniformed young men, staring in awe at them. The American Legion Post No. 80 was named after the first casualty of the war from Millinocket, Donald V. Henry.

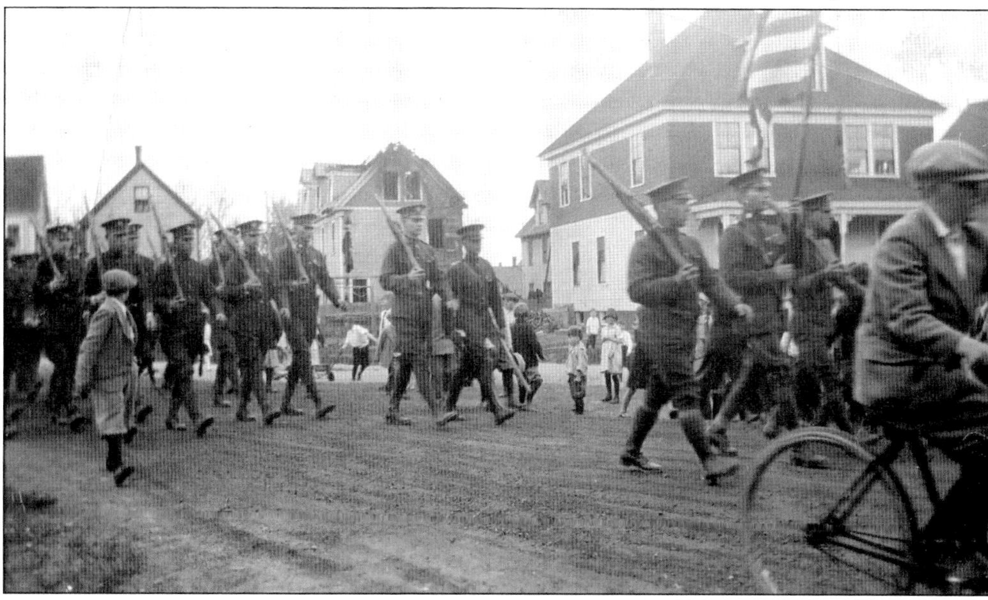

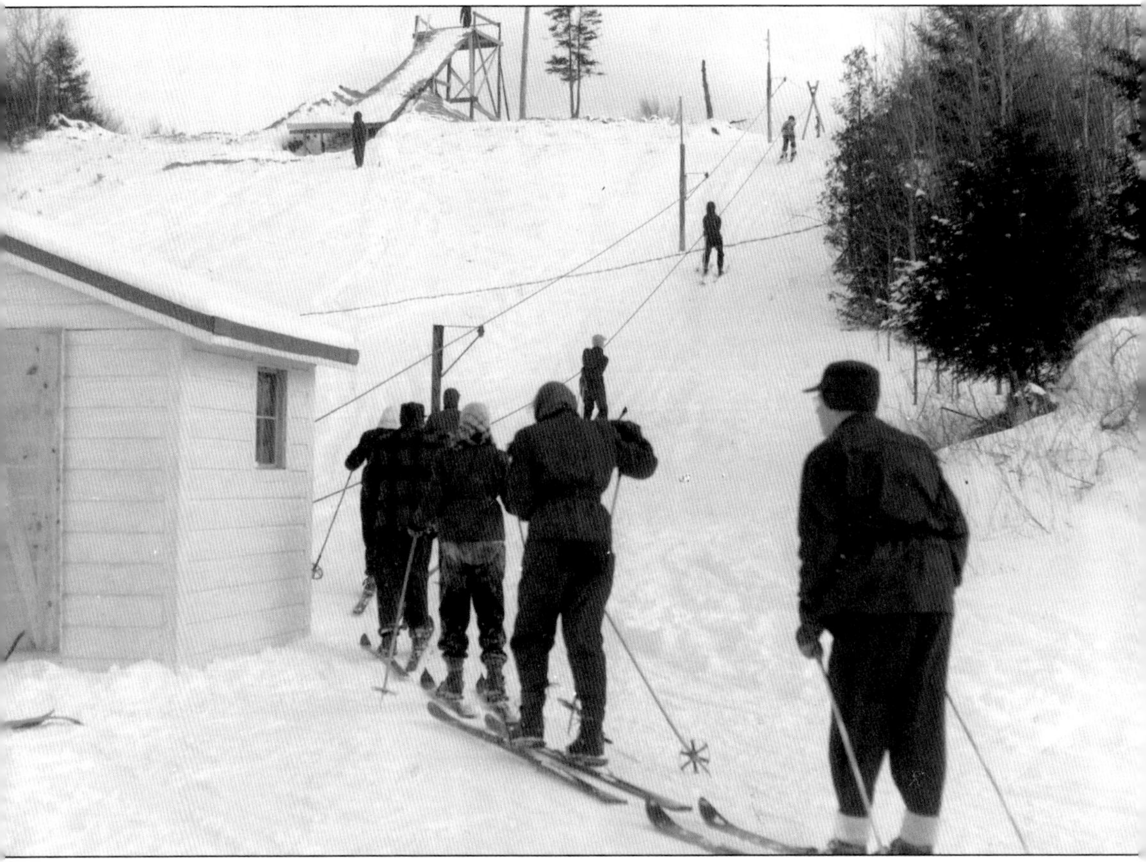

On a hill in town, a ski tow was built to help skiers get back up. For the more adventurous, there was a ski jump off to the side, standing ready for the brave soul who dared to try it. The Katahdin Outing Club was formed by a group of skiers, and a ski lodge was built at Black Cat Mountain. The club did not last long, and the ski lodge is now gone. For a time, the hill on the upper end of the recreational complex that was part of the Hillcrest Golf Course was available for skiing. Today Millinocket is a hub for many miles of cross-country ski trails that snake through the woods around town. The trails are well groomed and offer an opportunity for outdoor enthusiasts to get out and explore the Maine woods in the winter.

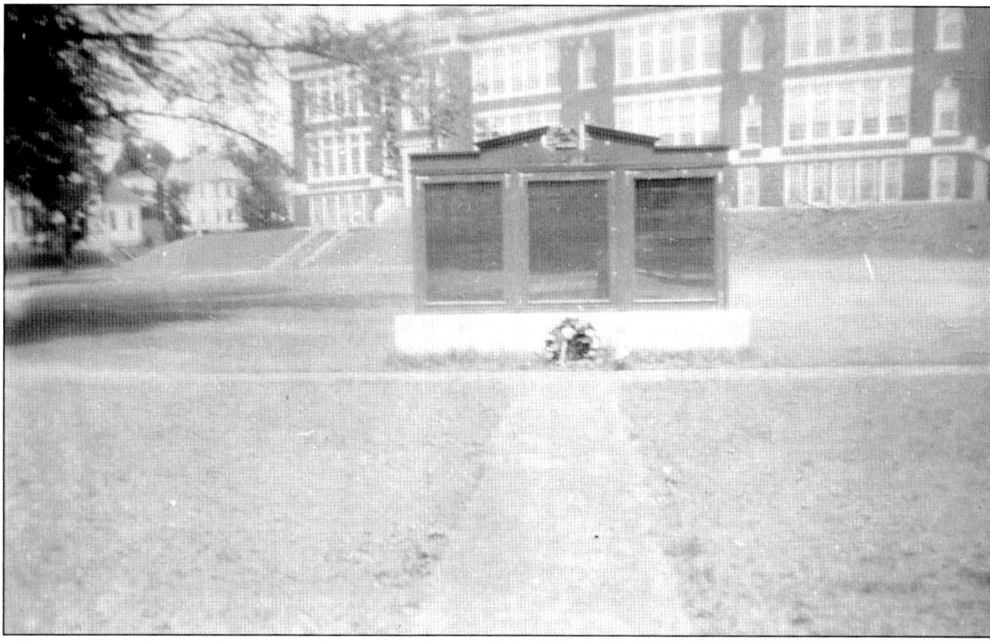

Memories of those who gave their lives for their country were preserved on the honor roll that was placed at the intersection of Central Street and Maine Avenue. There is now a larger honor roll at the town park. This photograph was taken in 1949.

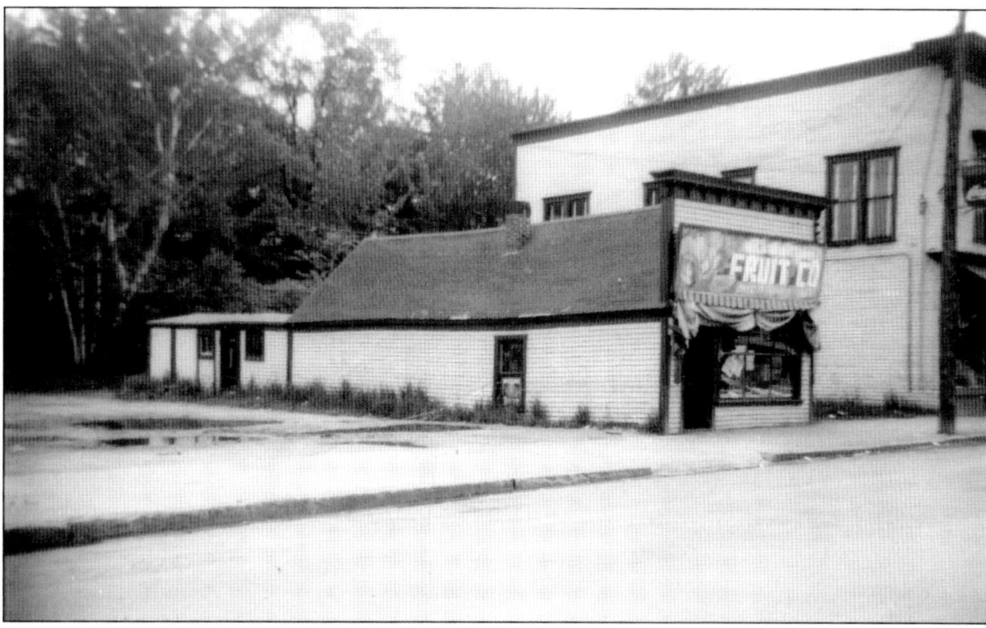

The Millinocket Fruit Company was one of the many stores to buy food at in Millinocket. The Matangelo brothers operated it for many years. In order to make the tiny stores look bigger than they really were, a large, flat front was built onto the building to give the appearance of a large store. This building burned in 1958.

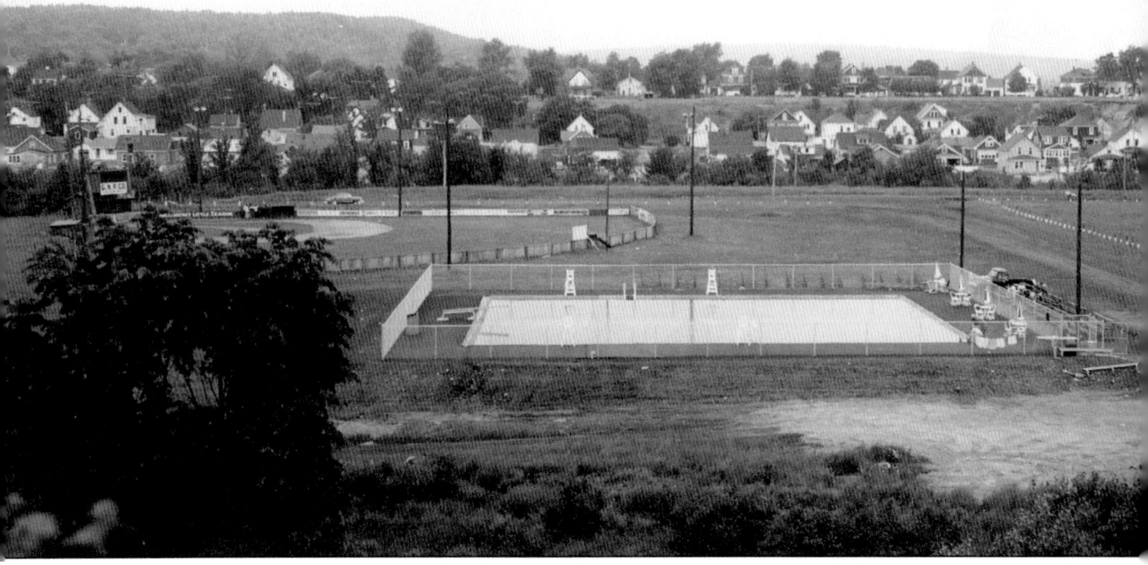

Little Smith Brook emptied into Millinocket Stream at an area called "the pines." In the early 1900s, Frank Rush operated a sawmill there and built small houses for his workers. In 1926, a committee was formed and directed by Kenneth E. Reed and Charles Madden with the intent of constructing a swim area on Millinocket Stream. Two bathhouses were built and a beach area was made on the stream's edge. The swimming area at the pines was a popular spot for many years and served the community well until a large pool was built in July 1954. The site of the new pool was at the new recreational complex in the flat, open area to the side of Millinocket Stream. The pool was often filled with laughing and playing children cooling themselves on a hot summer's day.

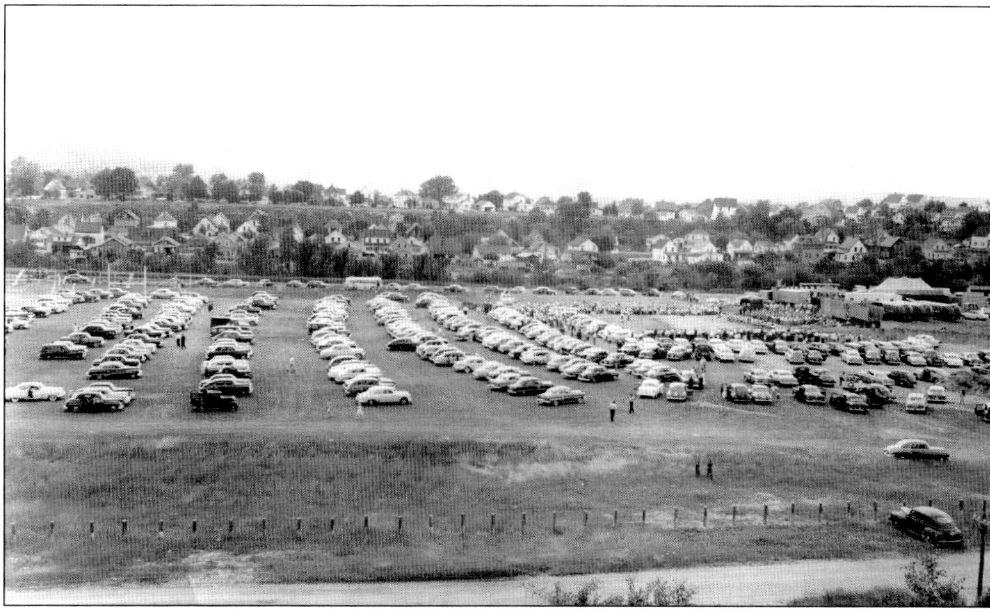

The recreational complex was a flat, open place that afforded the opportunity for various activities, including the fair, when it came to town. Arthur Russell owned a farm in this area until the town started developing it as a recreational complex. Today this area is home to the Millinocket Middle School and George W. Stearns High School. There are baseball diamonds, a hockey rink, tennis courts, a track, a football field, and a soccer field. Just recently, a large, modern swimming pool facility was opened to replace the aging pool. As it always has in years past, when the fair comes to town, it still sets up in this same spot at the recreational area.

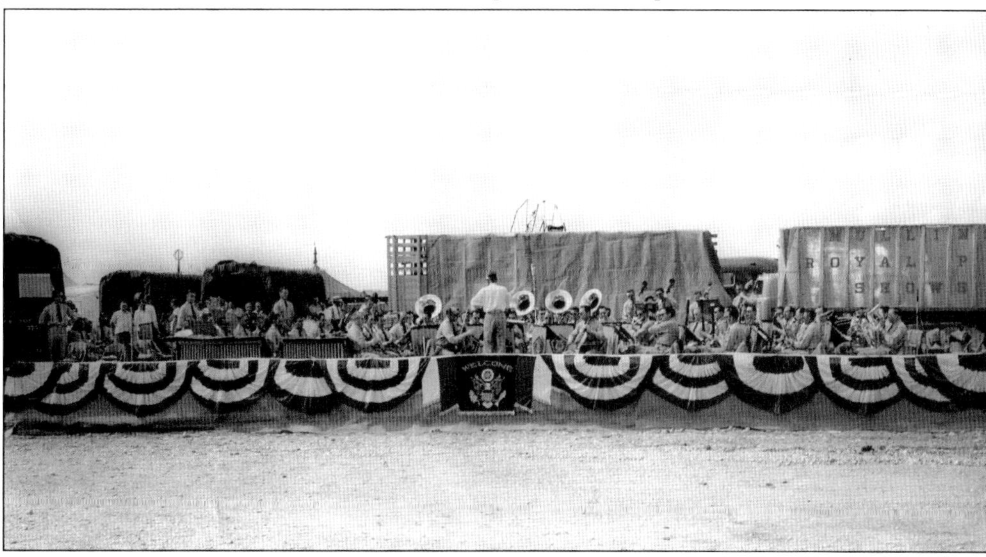

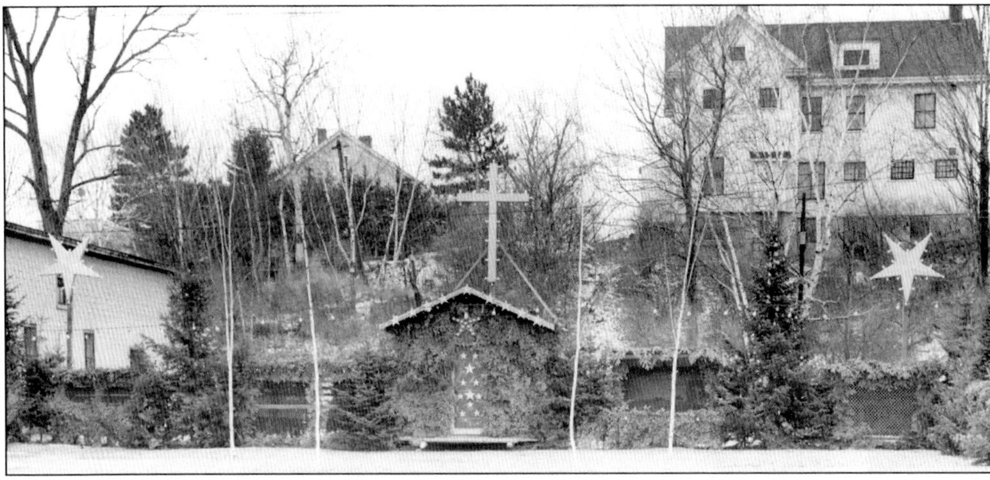

The municipal parking lot was created by the town to help with the parking problem in the downtown area. Santa came to the magic city at Christmastime and set up the Santa's Zoo in the lot. Children went through the brightly adorned display and pet the animals that Santa brought for them to see. Christmas was always a magical time of year in Katahdin country, and when Santa brought his pets to Millinocket for the children, it added to the magic.

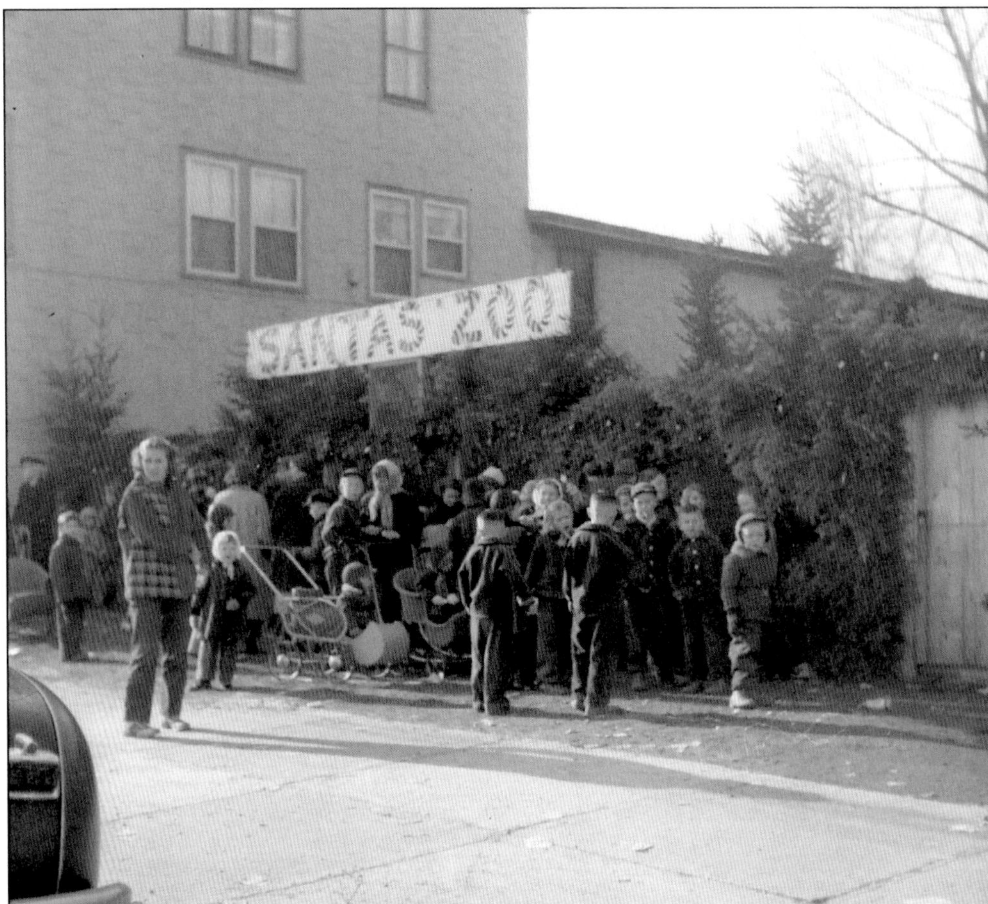

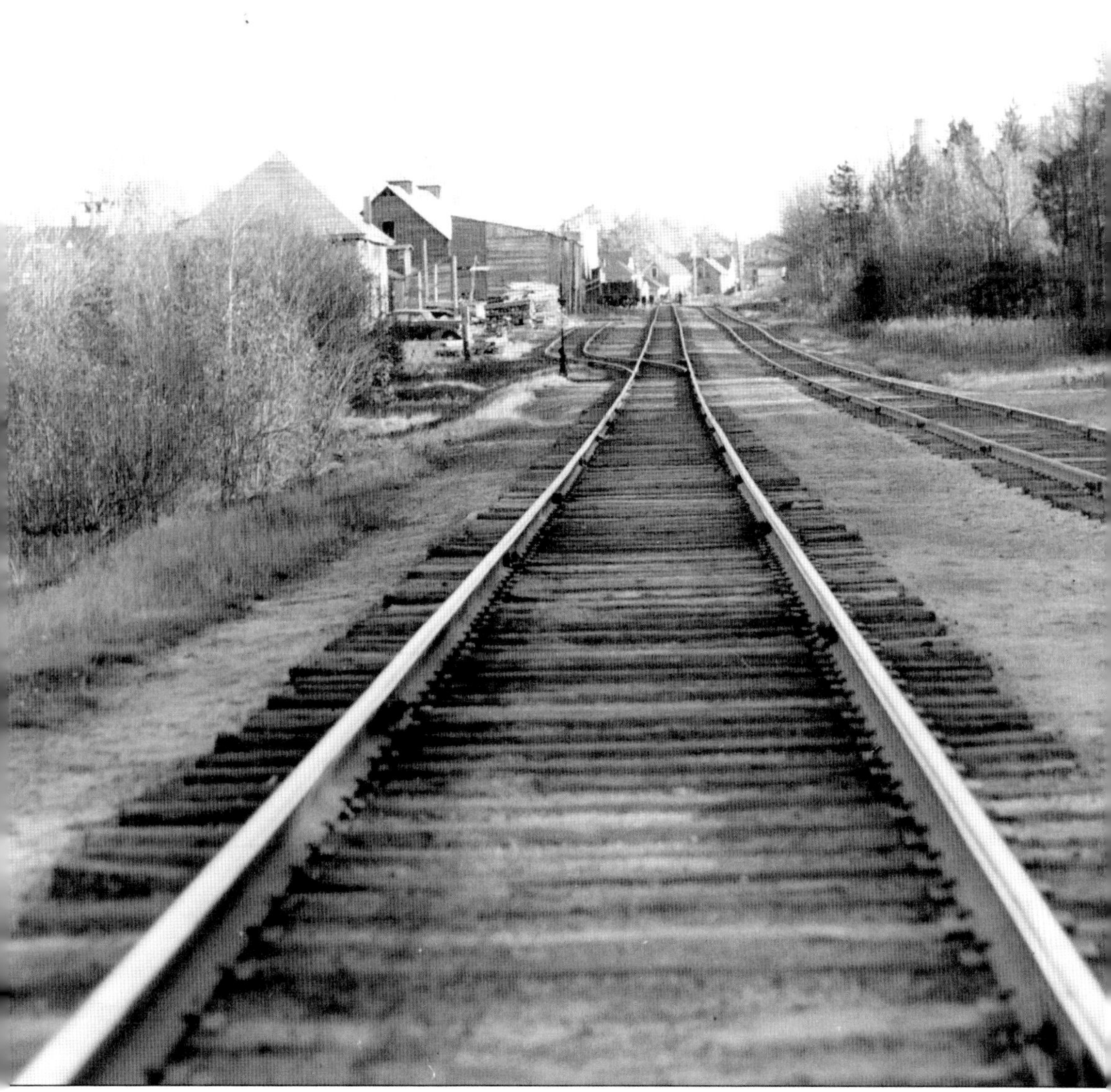

The Bangor and Aroostook Railroad played an important role in the development of Millinocket and the Great Northern Paper Company. There were no roads leading to Millinocket, so the primary route of travel for the early settlers and the transportation of goods was the railroad that passed through the area on its way to Houlton. The railroad also allowed people the means to travel to places as far away as Boston. With more passenger travel on the tracks, a parlor car was added to the regularly scheduled run between Bangor and Boston. Doctors also took advantage of the train service, as they could make house calls to their patients between Norcross and Grindstone. A spur off the main track passed along Katahdin Avenue and went into the mill complex to deliver supplies and pick up the completed paper product.

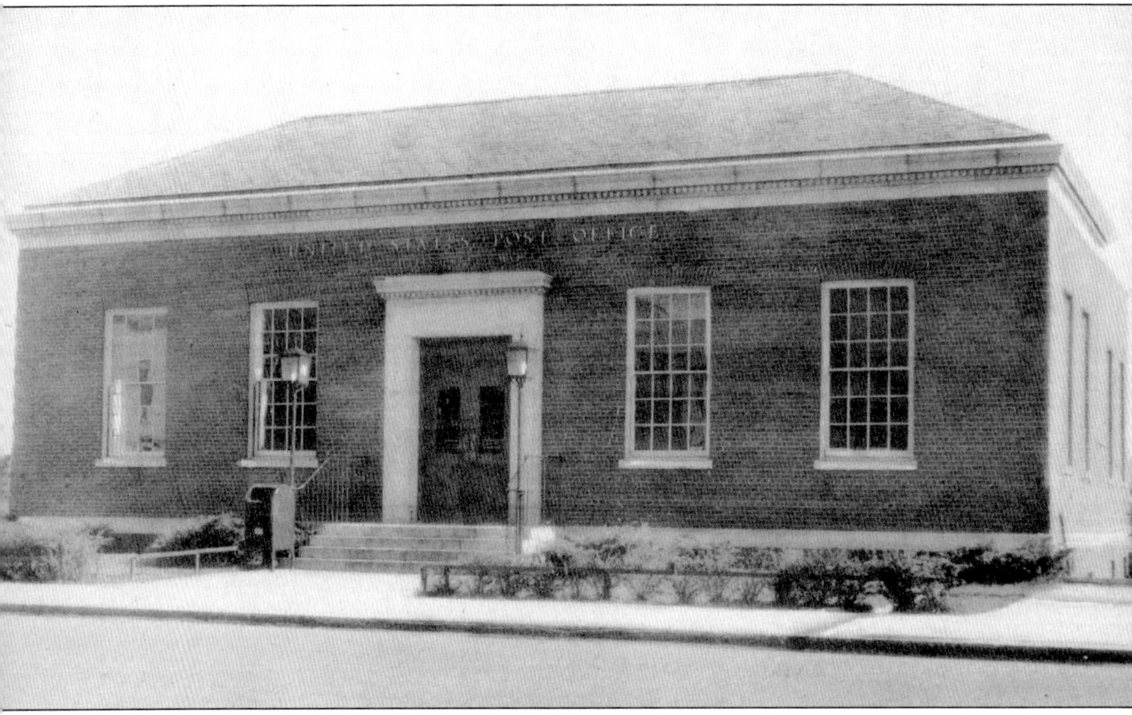

The cornerstone for the Millinocket Post Office was laid in 1937 on the corner of Penobscot Avenue and Spruce Street. Prior to the one central post office, people got their mail from various places all over town. The Powers farm on Shack Hill served as the town's first post office until the building was torn down. In the days of the Great Northern Hotel, mail could be picked up there. Often times the railroad station was the place to wait for mail, since it arrived by train anyway. Displayed inside this new post office, the federal government commissioned a painting under the Public Works Administration. The painting is a fitting one for Millinocket; it depicts a lumbering scene in the north woods.

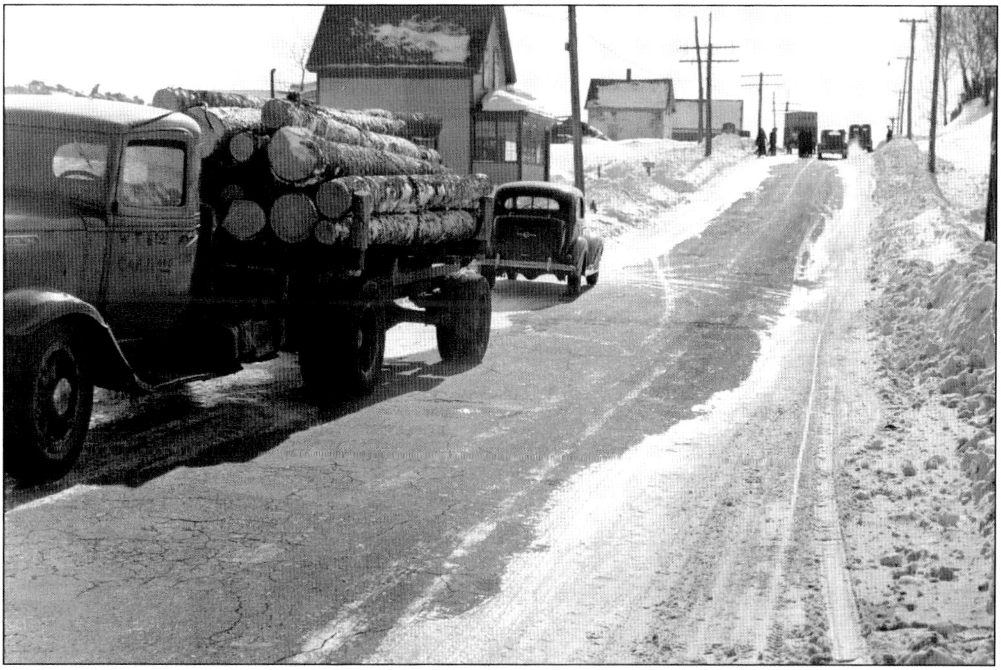

The Medway Road was built along a preexisting trail that led from Medway into Millinocket. Central Street was eventually extended and became the primary route of travel to East Millinocket. When the town constructed the airport, it was placed out on Medway Road. Driving on these early roads was a treacherous task, as snow tires had yet to be developed, and sanders on plow trucks had not been invented. Prior to automatic sanders, men had to shovel sand off the back of the truck as it traveled down the road. Early log trucks seem tiny compared to the large trucks that travel the roads today.

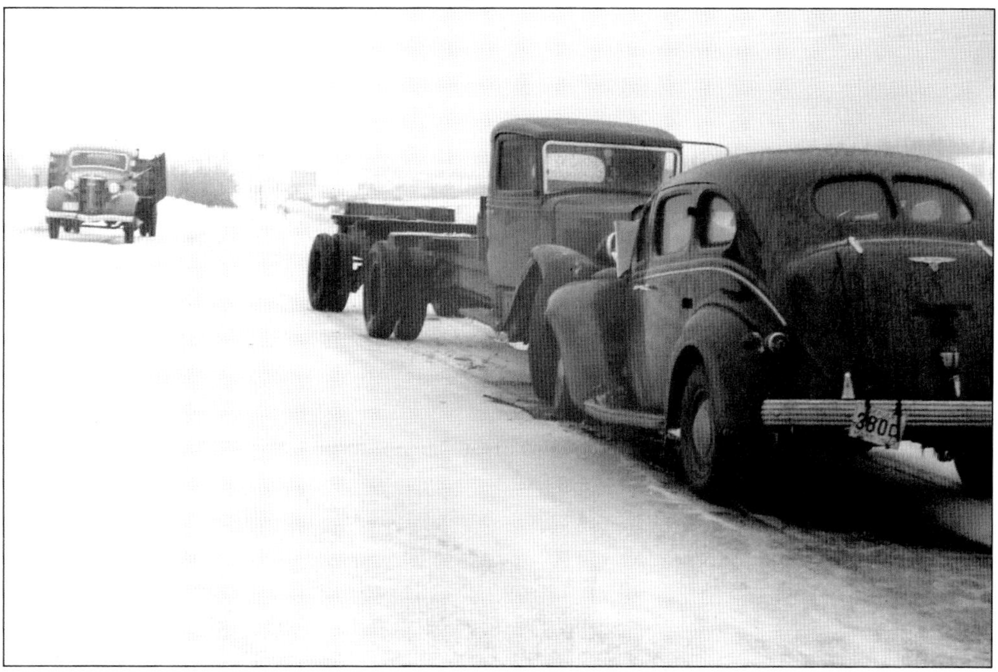

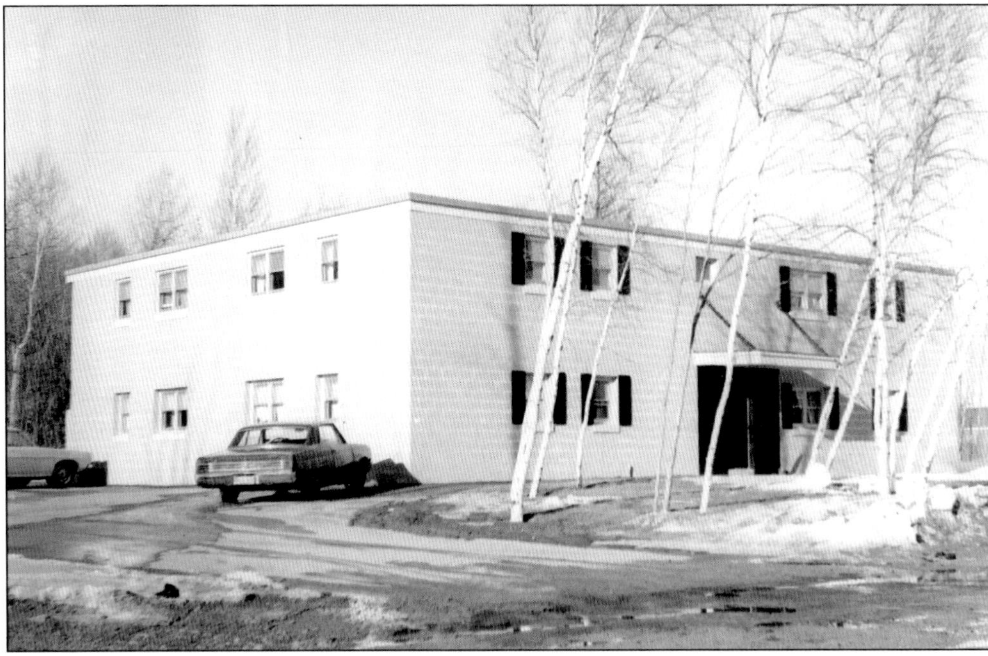

Jim Pratt built an apartment building on the corner of Walnut Street and Wassau Street where a number of other apartment buildings were built. From the beginning, apartment buildings were an important part of the development of the town. The boardinghouses of years past were gone, but the apartments helped fill the gap in housing.

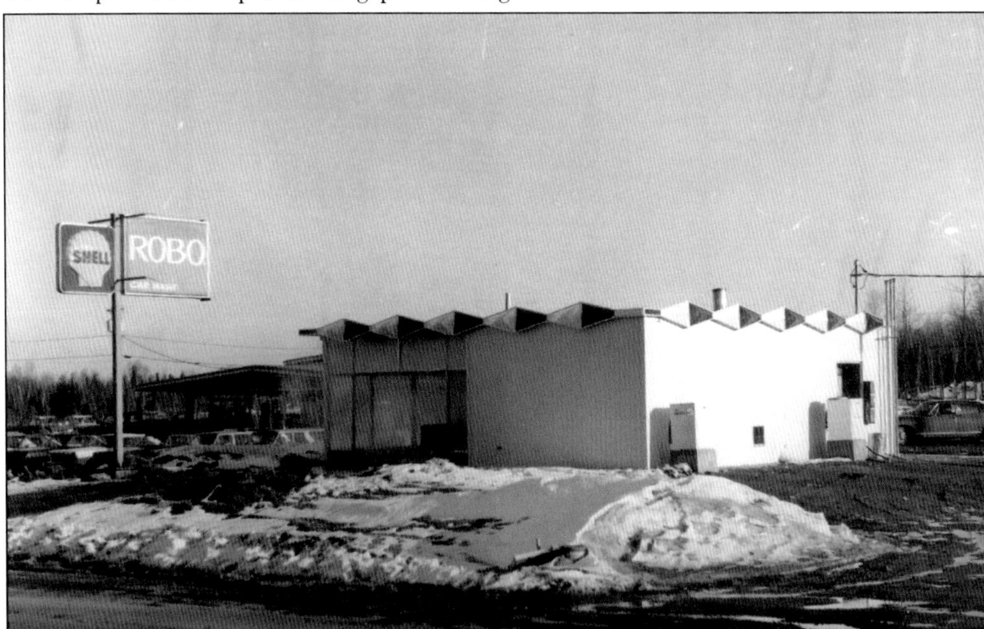

The Robo Car Wash was an early car wash in town. The car wash was on Balsam Drive next to Stearns Lumber. Automobiles were not very rust resistant, so the winter salt had to be washed off quickly. With the many logging roads around the region, automobiles collected a lot of mud that also needed to be cleaned off.

With the town being as compact as it is, it is possible for many kids to walk to school. With the crossing guard in place, these high school students cross Central Street after school lets out. The first school bus in Millinocket was purchased in the 1940s. When the area known as the new development was created, there was more of a need for school buses.

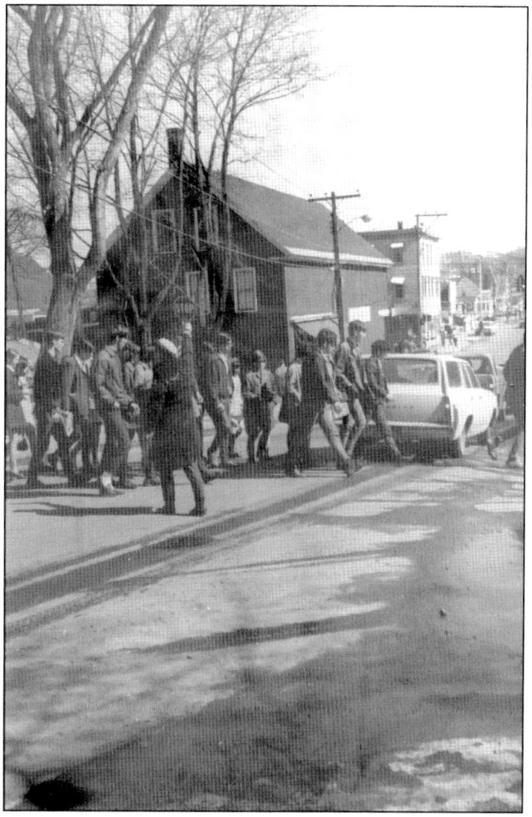

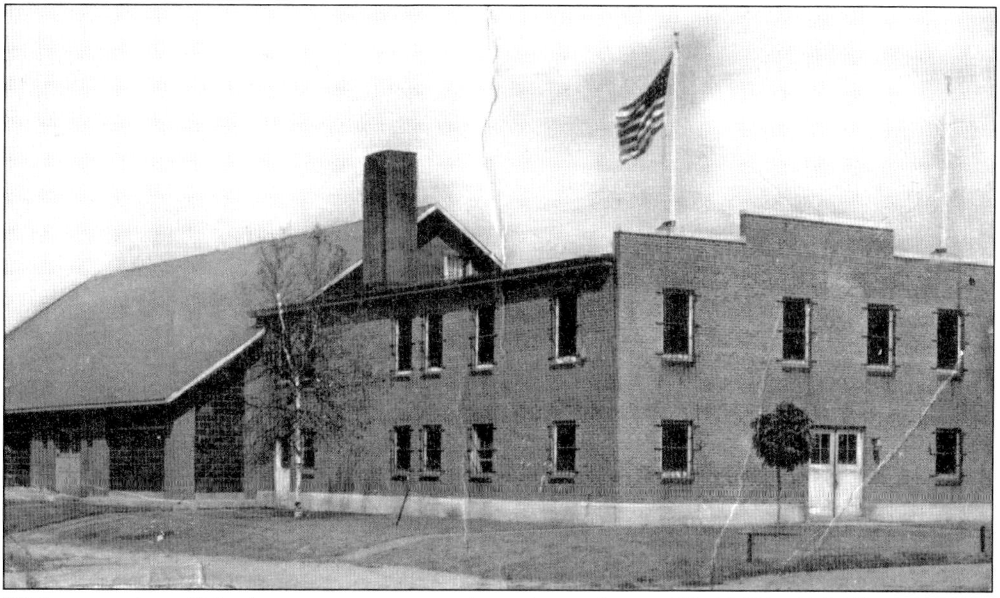

With more than 600 of its own serving in the military during World War II, Millinocket was well represented in the war effort. Company I of the 3rd Maine Regiment was headquartered in the new armory on Spring Street. A ballpark was once located on the site. Today the national guard unit is gone, and the armory serves as a religious outreach center for the community.

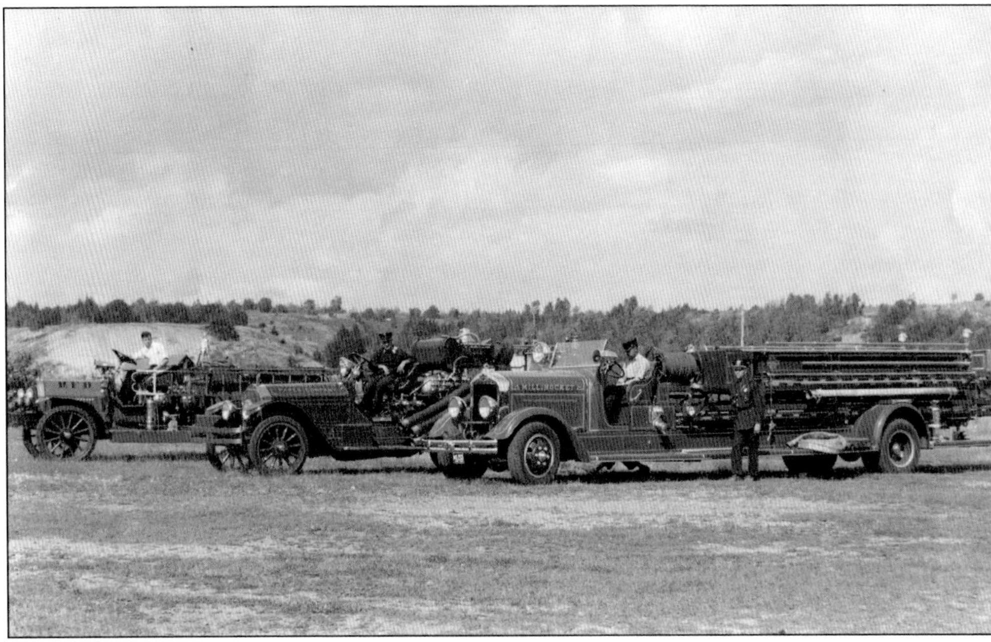

Pioneer Hose Company No. 1 was formed in 1901 in response to the fires that were a common occurrence in Millinocket. The first fire truck that was donated by the Great Northern Paper Company was a Knox combination chemical and hose motor truck. In 1920, a LaFrance combination pump, hose, and chemical truck was also given to the Millinocket Fire Department from the company.

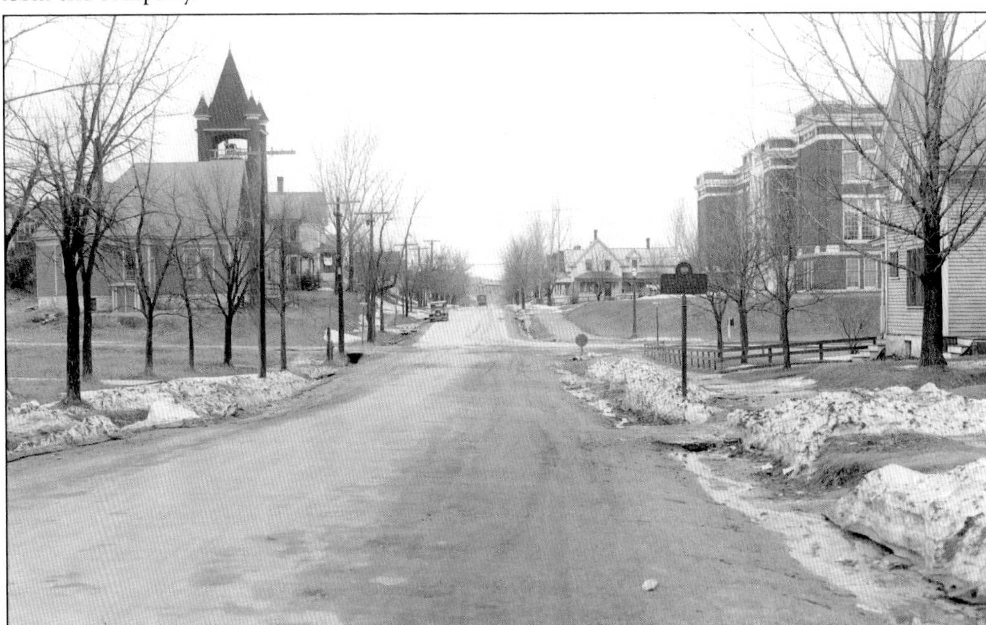

Katahdin Avenue was one of the first streets in Millinocket to be developed. The street stretched in front of the administration building for the Great Northern Paper Company and led directly towards Mount Katahdin. At the intersection of Katahdin Avenue and Central Street was the location of George W. Stearns High School and also the Katahdin Avenue School.

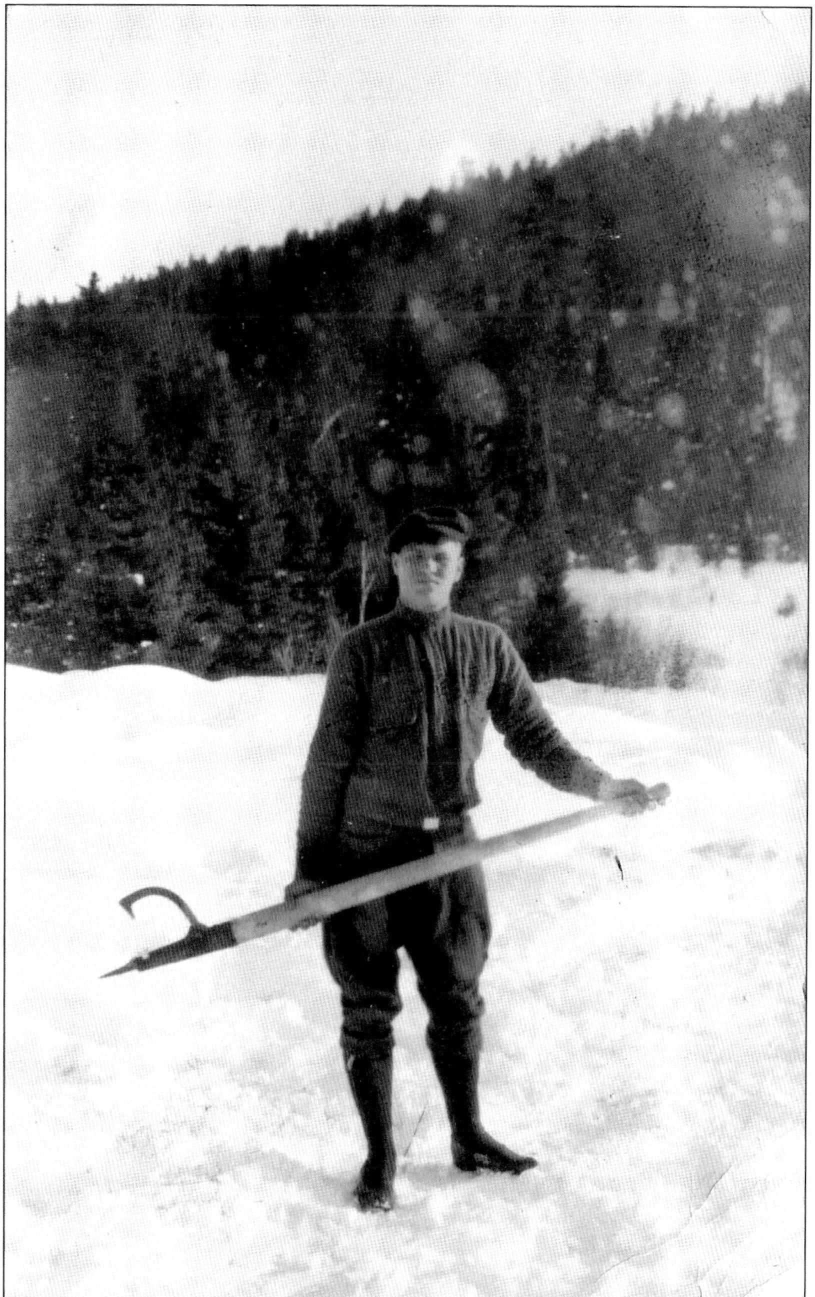

A tool that was used heavily by the lumbermen was the peavey. The peavey was a universal tool used to manipulate logs easier by hooking on to them and using the long handle as leverage. The peavey was named after Joseph Peavey from Stillwater, Maine, who invented it. It was sometimes referred to as a cant dog, which was a different tool. The peavey had a sharp point on the end; the cant dog had a blunt end. The peavey is a tool that is still in heavy use today and has proven its worth many times over. The work of men handling logs was a tough job, and they used a variety of tools to make it a little easier. With the axe, crosscut saw, and the peavey, the logs were moved from the far north to the mill.

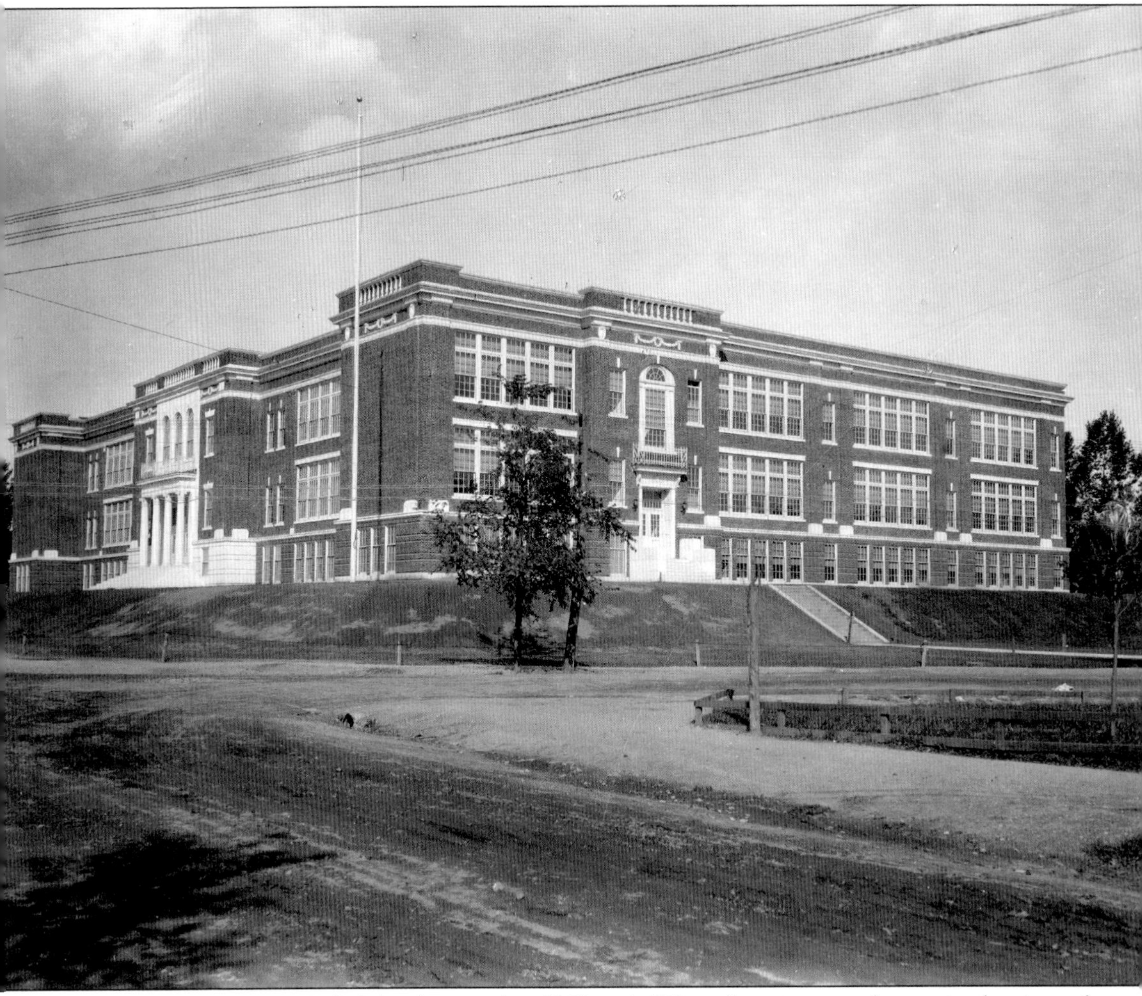

George W. Stearns High School opened in 1923 with 743 students in attendance. At the time of its completion, it was considered one of the most attractive schools in the state. The building is still thought to be one of the more impressive buildings in town. Although no longer a school, it is the home of Stearns Assisted Living. Built with red brick with a white Grecian-style trim, it was designed by Harry S. Combs of Lewiston. As a prominent citizen of Millinocket, George W. Stearns was honored to have the magnificent school named after him. Initially the school consisted of 24 classrooms, a music room, and a library. In 1926, another $50,000 was raised and a gymnasium was added. The building has served Millinocket well, and one can hope that it will remain a part of the town for years to come.

Three

PEOPLE OF MILLINOCKET

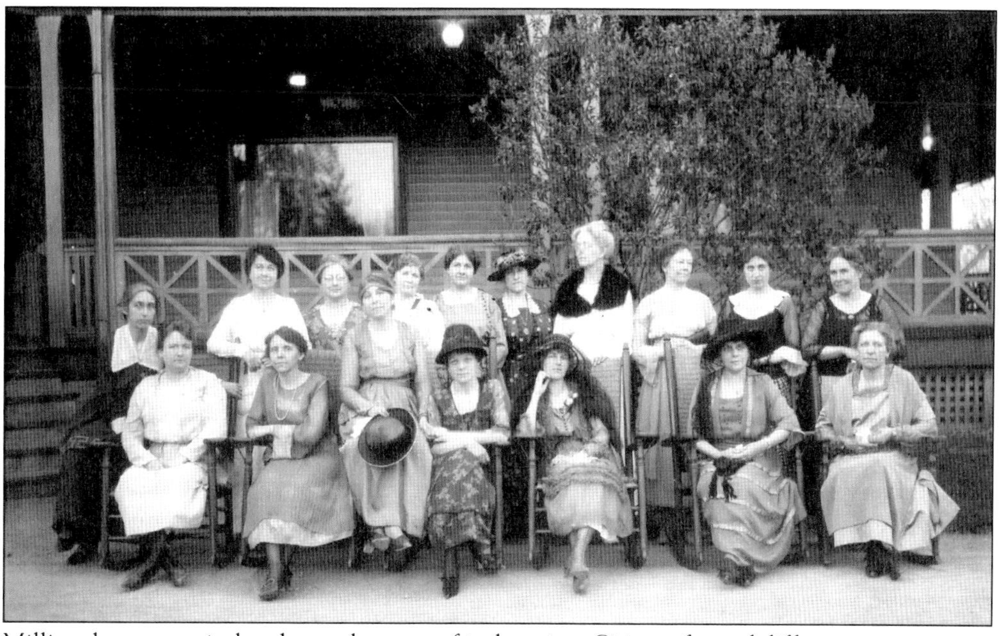

Millinocket was an isolated town because of its location. Citizens formed different organizations to provide entertainment for the town. There were a variety of locations to choose from to enjoy an evening or an afternoon of local talent. The Great Northern Hotel was one of the favored destinations that afforded an opportunity to be entertained. The Philharmonic Club was organized in 1920 and is seen here posing in front of the Great Northern Hotel. Although their locations are unknown, the back of the photograph identifies the following people: Jennie Walker, Minnie Felix, Mae Weeks Hilton, Bertha Walker, ? Currier, Mrs. Monahan, Mrs. Frost, Mrs. Jackson, Mrs. George W. McKay, Mildred Seaver, Elizabeth Stevens, Josepha Virginia Wheeler Evans, Dawn Bowler, ? Moore, and Myrtie Stearns.

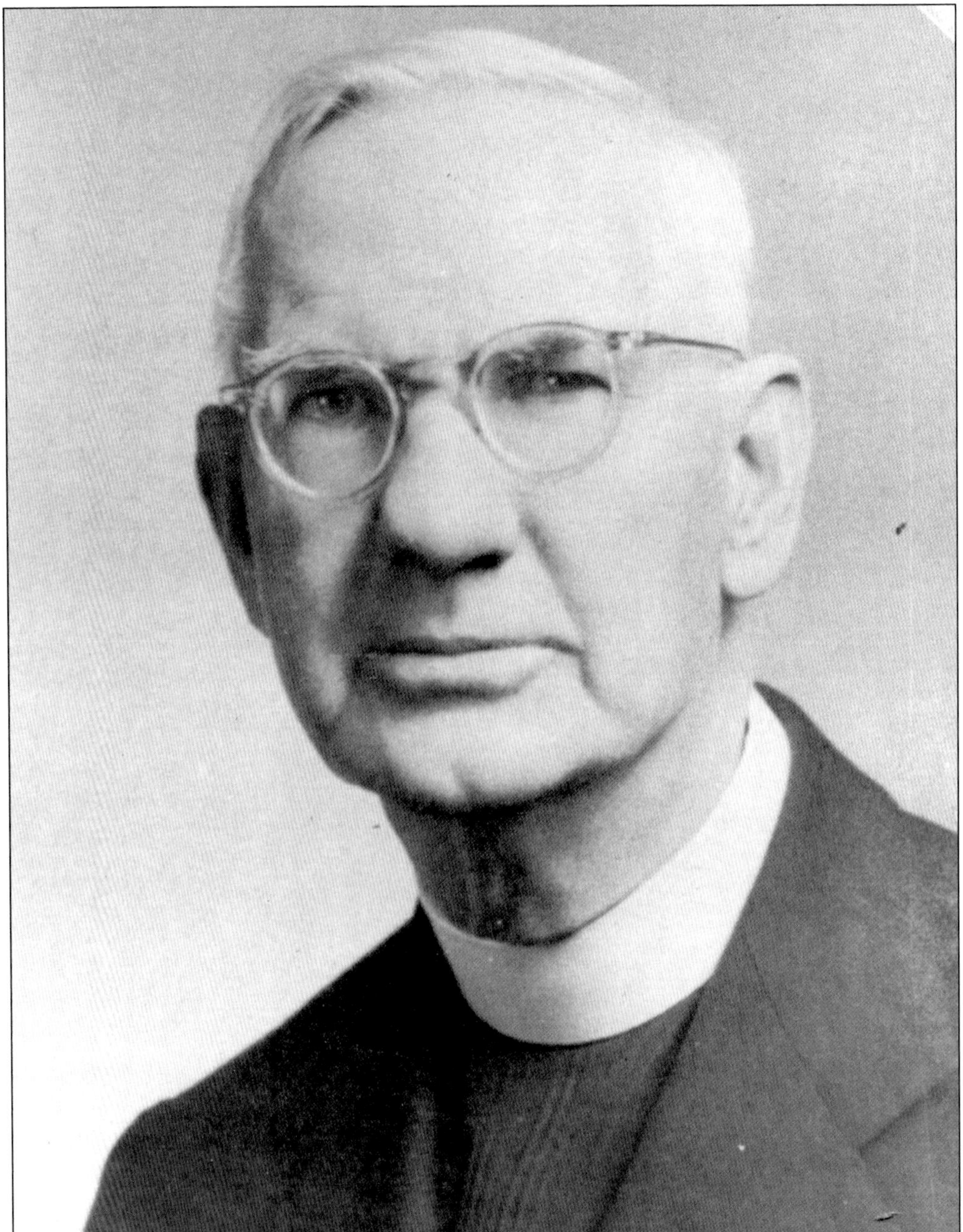

Fr. Joseph Quinn served the St. Martin of Tours Church from 1937 to 1955. During his time, Quinn saw the building of the St. Martin of Tours Parochial School near the St. Martin of Tours Church. The school was built on Maine Avenue just a short distance from George W. Stearns High School. Classes were taught by the Sisters of the Holy Rosary Order, and it graduated its first class in 1952. A large brick convent with a chapel was built for the sisters in 1958. The school was a welcome addition to the Millinocket education system, as it offered a high-quality religious school as an option for an education. Quinn was an asset to the community and to the church.

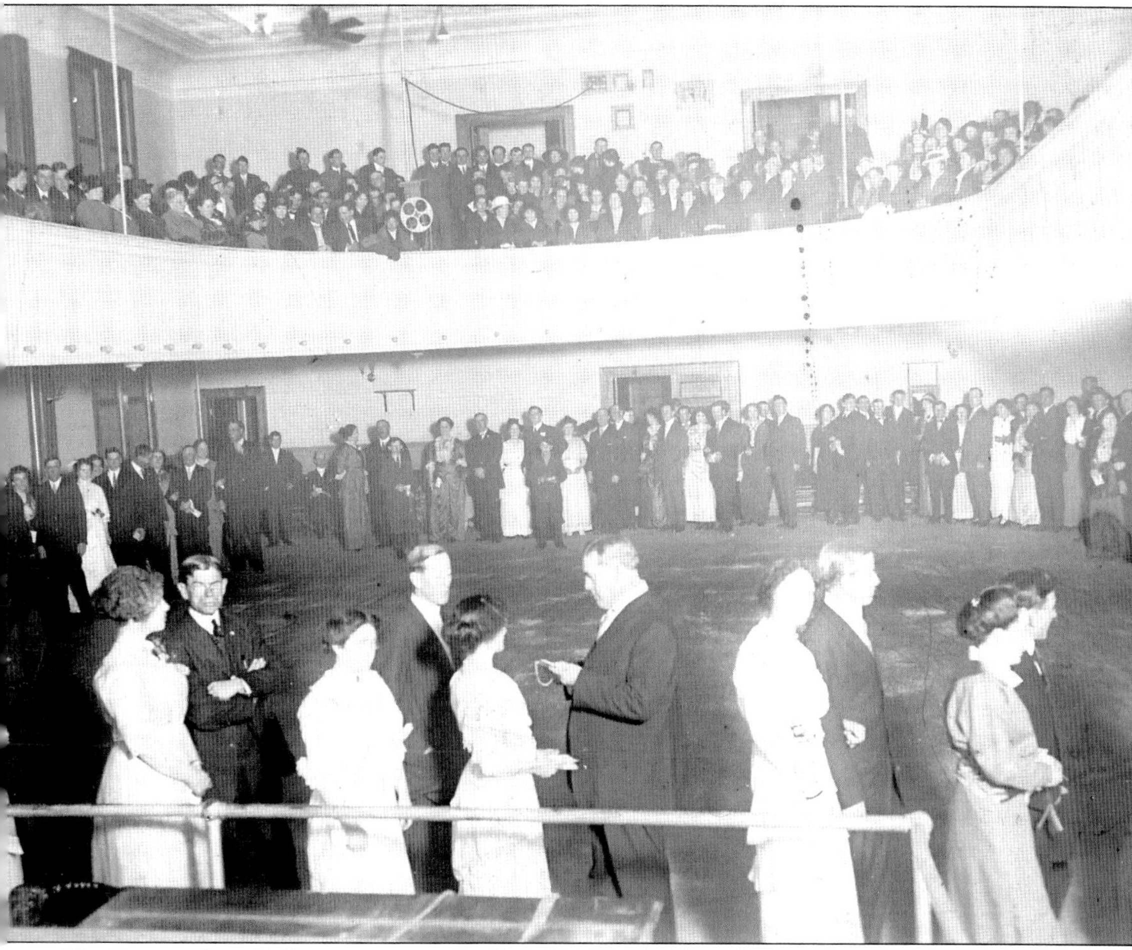

The Papermakers Ball was an annual affair that was held at the Millinocket Opera House. The patrons of this ball looked forward to attending it every year. With a band playing, the nicely dressed people danced the night away. Over the dance floor was a balcony that wrapped around the wall on the second floor. The Millinocket Opera House saw many uses and acted as the town civic center. Town meetings, school plays, and traveling shows were all held there. With an addition of a large screen and more seating, the Millinocket Opera House became the movie theater of the town. Not all the entertainment was to be seen in the Millinocket Opera House, because Andrew Davis operated a blacksmith shop next door, and many people enjoyed watching him shoe the Great Northern Paper Company horses when they came to town.

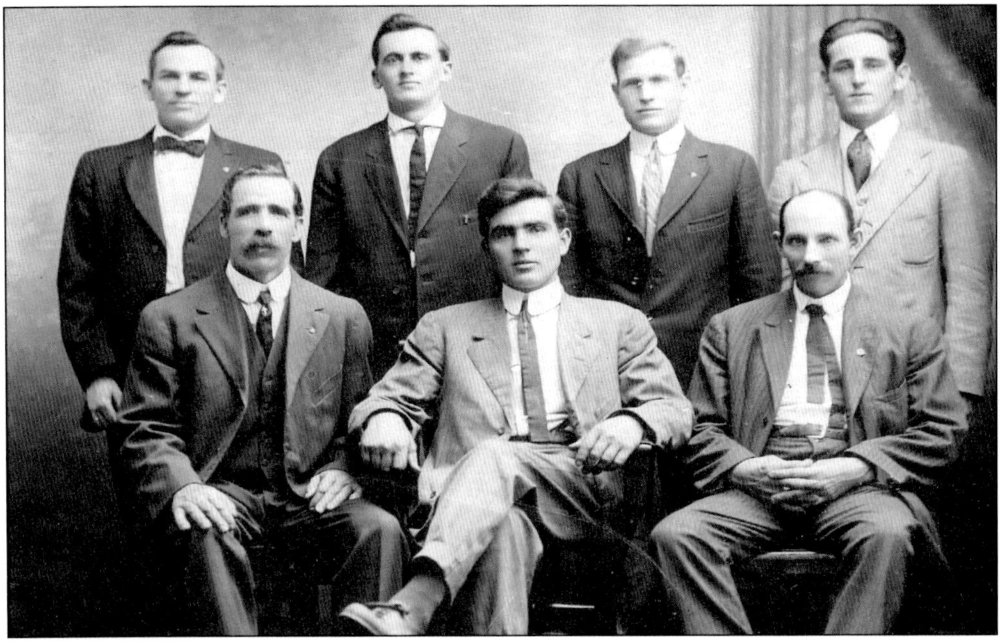

The federal labor union tug-of-war team is dressed handsomely and poses here as the winner of the tug-of-war contest on September 8, 1915. Labor unions were prominent in the mill and represented all the workers in every job. In addition to watching out for the workers on the job, they also sponsored athletic teams.

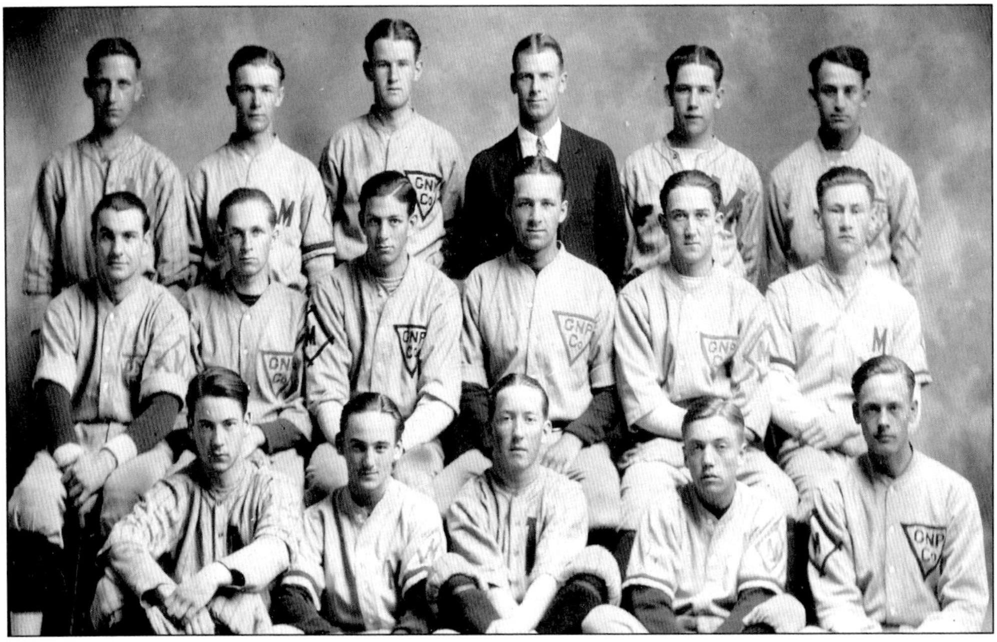

The Great Northern Paper Company provided the uniforms that this Stearns team wore. From left to right are (first row) Melvin Adams, James Stevens, Roy Brown, Eric Bouchard, and Clifford Gee; (second row) Daniel Daley, Richard Noyes, Harold Jones, Paul Noyes (captain), Fulton Daniels, and John Nutter; (third row) John Brunette, George Osborne, Gene McLean, coach Pearl Johnson, Lawrence Belodeau, and Simon P. Simon.

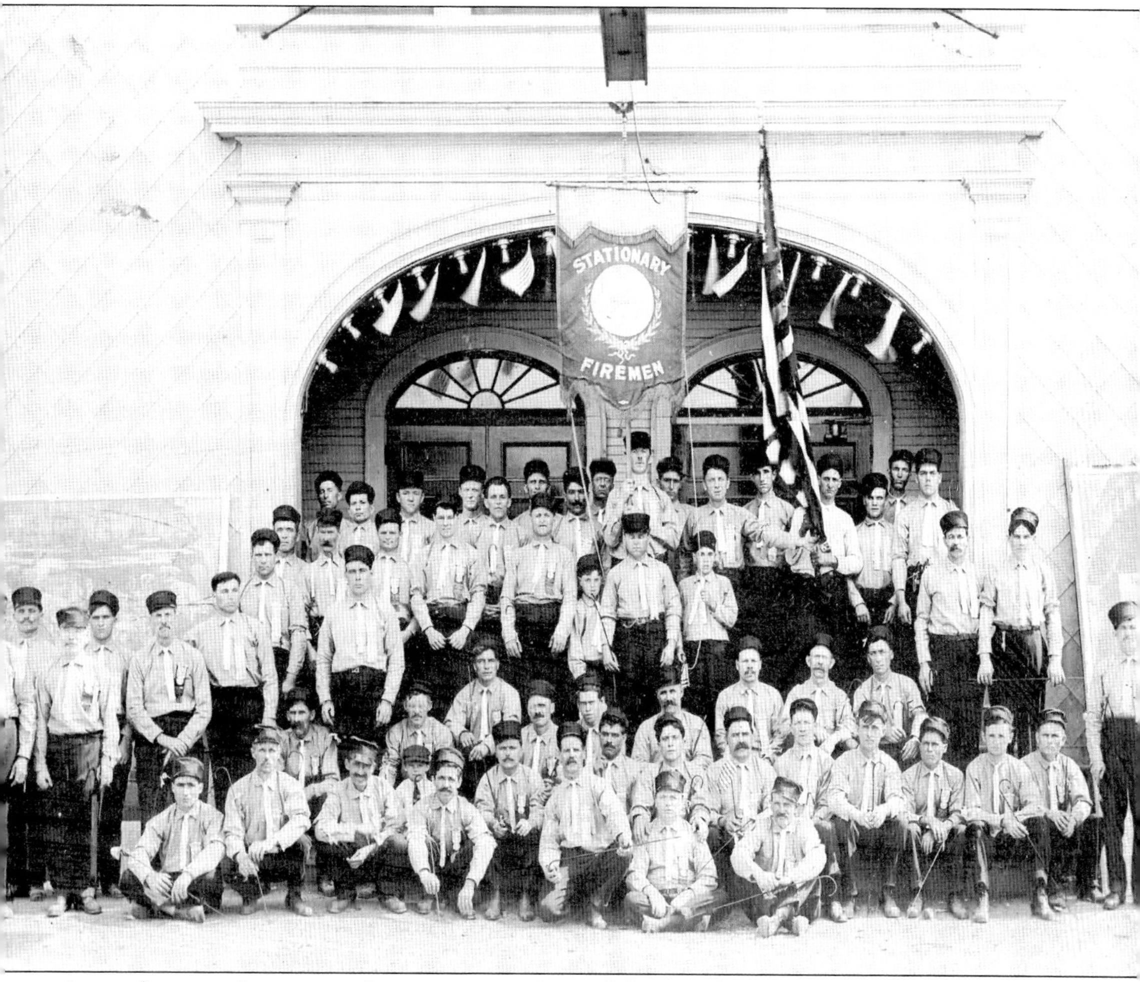

A proud group of stationary firemen pose in front of the Woodman Hall before a parade. The hall burned in 1912 and was replaced by the Millinocket Opera House. With the building of the Millinocket Opera House, the front entrance was moved to the Poplar Street side of the building. Millinocket Fire Department's beginning stems from the founding of Pioneer Hose Company No. 1 in May 1901, with William Heebner chosen to head it up. Fire was a constant concern in town. The type of construction materials used in home building created a tinderbox waiting to ignite at any moment. The paper mill, with its machinery and need for a heat source to produce steam, was also a prime spot for a fire. The paper mill had firefighters that were available to help the town when necessary.

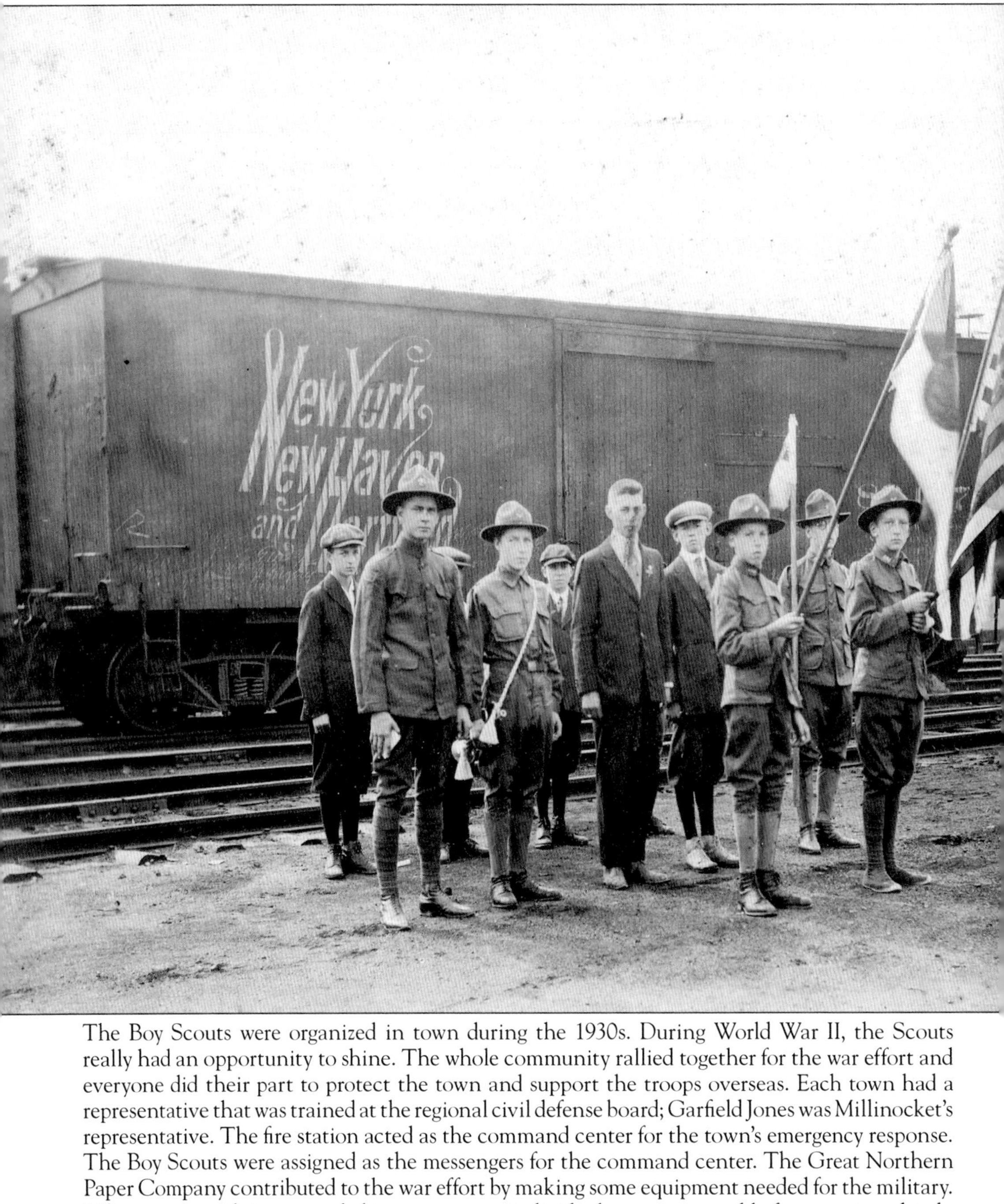

The Boy Scouts were organized in town during the 1930s. During World War II, the Scouts really had an opportunity to shine. The whole community rallied together for the war effort and everyone did their part to protect the town and support the troops overseas. Each town had a representative that was trained at the regional civil defense board; Garfield Jones was Millinocket's representative. The fire station acted as the command center for the town's emergency response. The Boy Scouts were assigned as the messengers for the command center. The Great Northern Paper Company contributed to the war effort by making some equipment needed for the military. When an air raid siren sounded in town, many individuals were responsible for an assigned task. Defense of the town was truly a community effort.

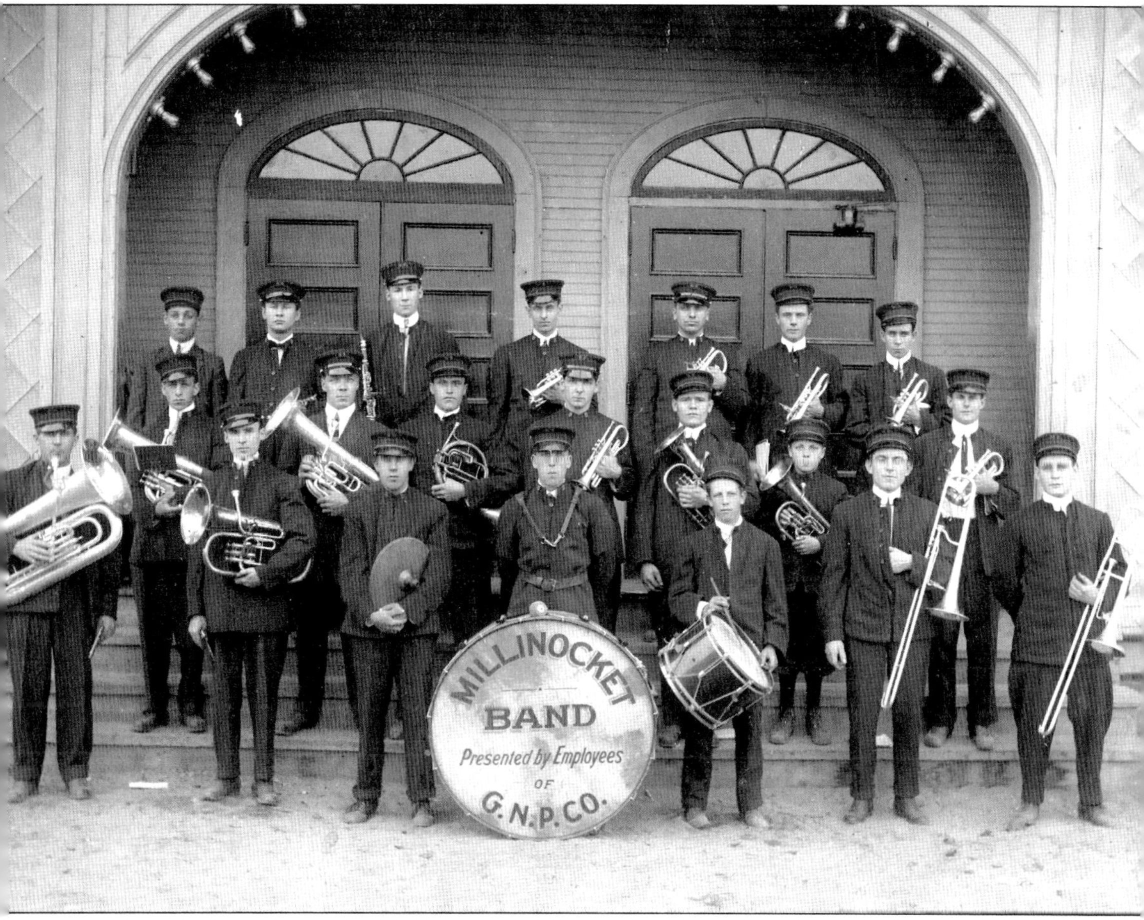

The Millinocket Band was formed in 1903 with Ray Harlow as its leader. From left to right are (first row) Charles Carter, Cecil Clower, Allen Carter, Shorty Bowen, Willis Gates, Sam Downing, and Royden Pratt; (second row); Fred Gates Jr, John Simpson, Halliburton Candlemire, James Simpson (director), Harry Carroll, Adam Simpson, and Clyde Folsom; (third row) John Galvin, Charles Morgan, Beverly Clowes, Eben Davis, Urban Mallet, John Cyr, and Walter Pratt. The Great Northern Paper Company provided the instruments for the band as well as the uniforms that the members wore. Many concerts were held at the pavilion behind the Bishop building and at the town bandstand. The band is standing in front of Woodman Hall on Penobscot Avenue. Some of the instruments are now on display at the Millinocket Historical Society Museum.

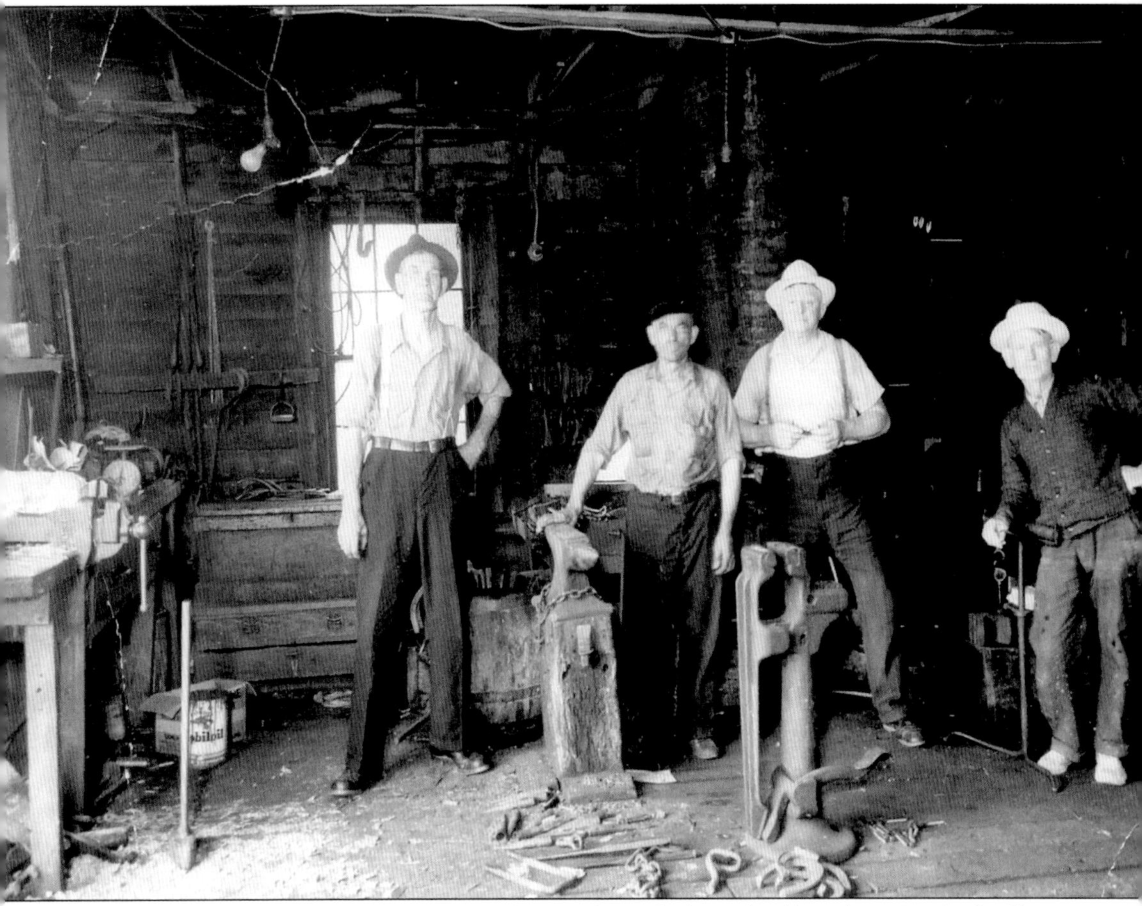

Blacksmith shops were a busy and noisy place in the early days of Millinocket. Hundreds of horses and oxen were used during the construction of the mill and a great deal in the woods operations. Martin George operated his blacksmith shop that was located in the back of Kimball's Store. Pictured here from left to right are Martin George, Bob Larrime, Wallace Noddin, and Tom Perrow. The blacksmith also kept busy by making tools that were used in the woods operations. Axes had to be made, chains needed to be linked, sled runners had to be run. The services of a blacksmith were always in high demand as so much relied on his knowledge of the trade. No more blacksmiths are doing business in Millinocket as their art is now a rare thing to see. Some of the tools made by these early blacksmiths are in the Millinocket Historical Society Museum.

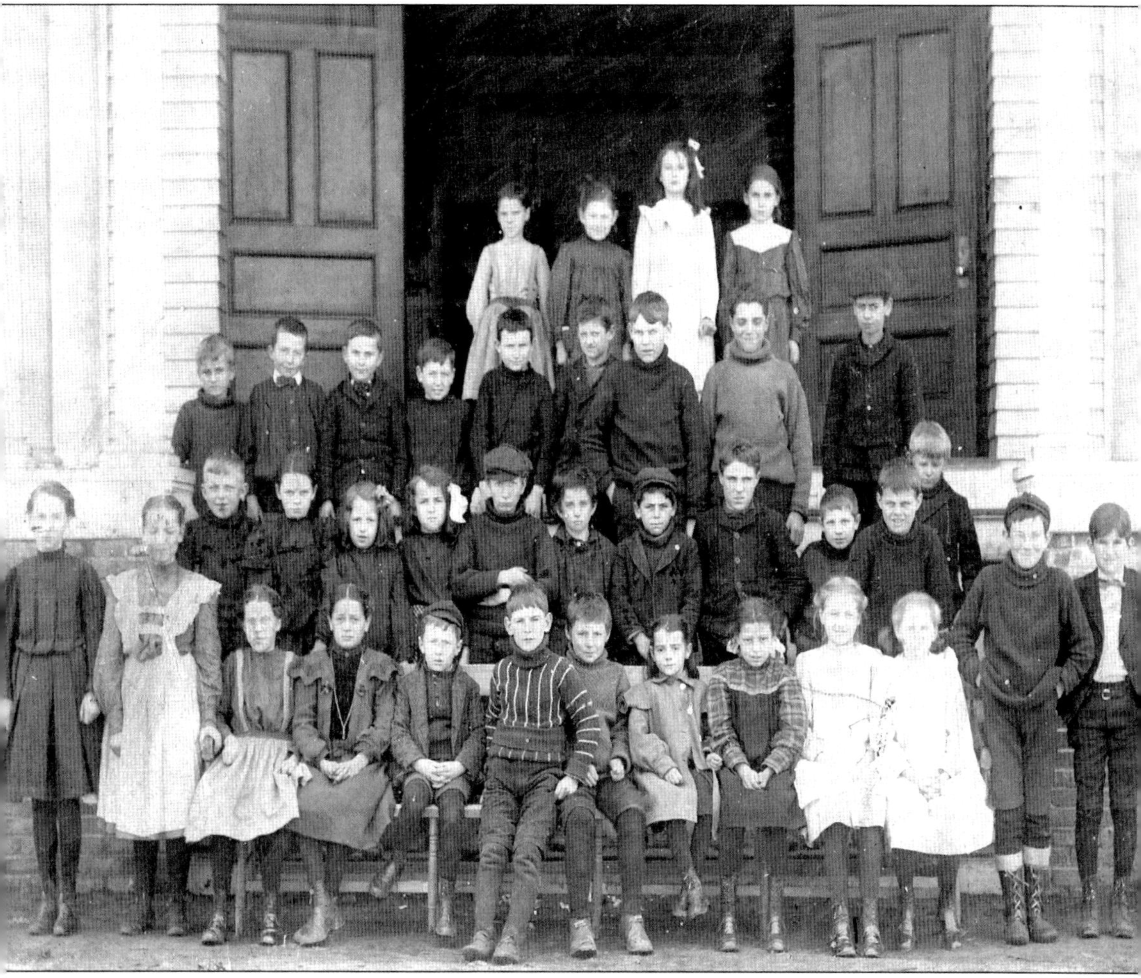

The Oxford Street School opened in 1907 and operated until 1943. A group of unidentified children poses on the front steps of the school in this early photograph. Teaching in the early schools was a challenge for the teachers. There were a large number of immigrants in the town, and English was not spoken in many homes. Proper hygiene in the school system had to be constantly monitored by the teachers to prevent outbreaks of diseases. Despite some of the hardships, with the help of fine teachers, the children were given a proper education. Although modified, the school is still standing and is now the headquarters of the VFW.

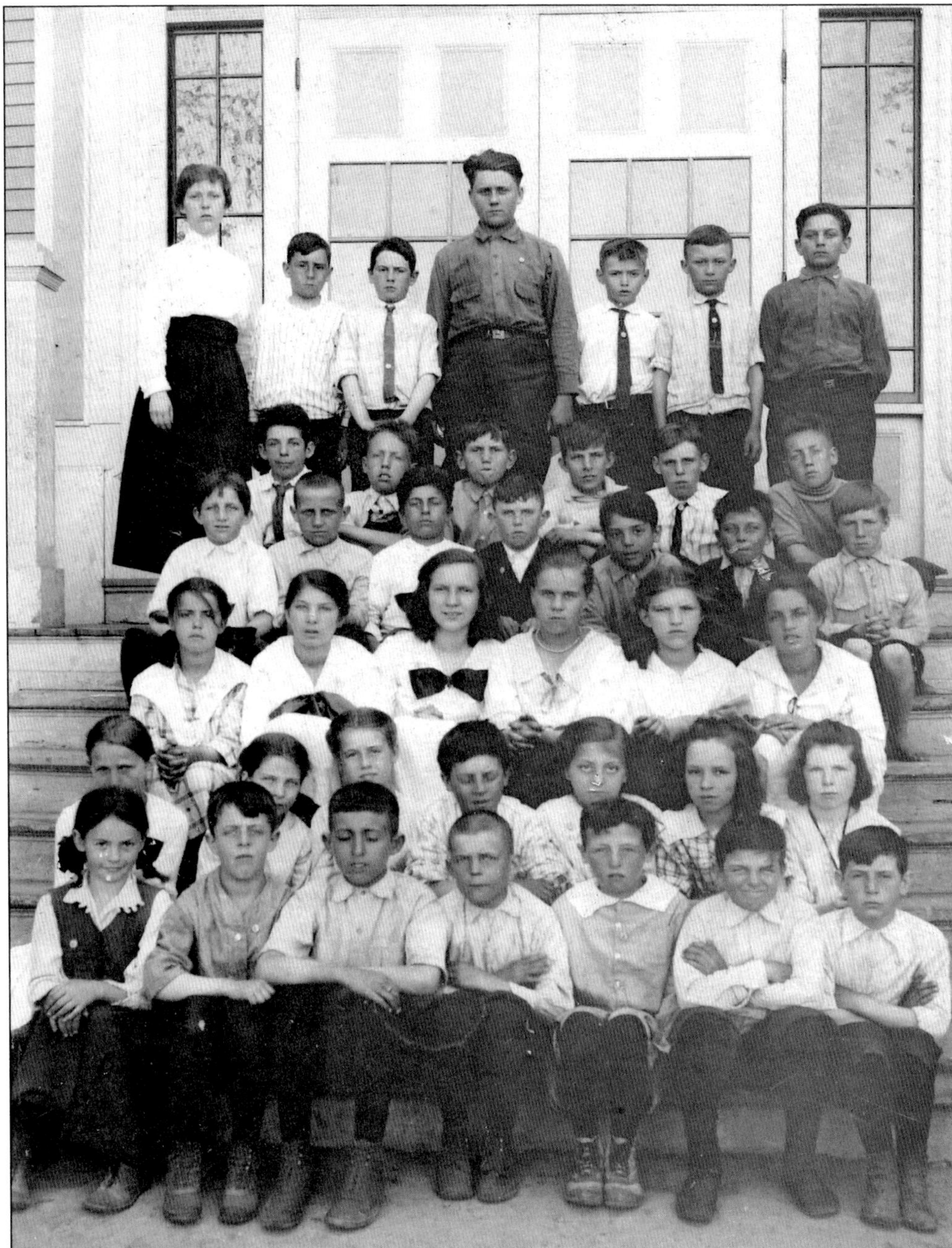

A group of students poses for a class picture on the front steps of the Oxford Street School. They include R. Wilson, R. Grava, R. Guy, ? McLain, ? Russell, A. Veronvi, G. Morrison, T. Decoursy, Dorothy Walls, A. Civiello, S. Garsia, E. Keith, J. Brunette, W. Boddy, ? Ferris, ? Gallant, C. Freeman, ? Gallant, and ? McMann. With the onslaught of winter, some families could not afford proper coats for their children to wear to school. One solution to the problem was to use some of the mill felt to make coats. Mill felt was a thick, stiff material that was hard to work with, especially for making clothes. When the children took off these coats, they were so stiff and hard that they stood up wherever they were placed.

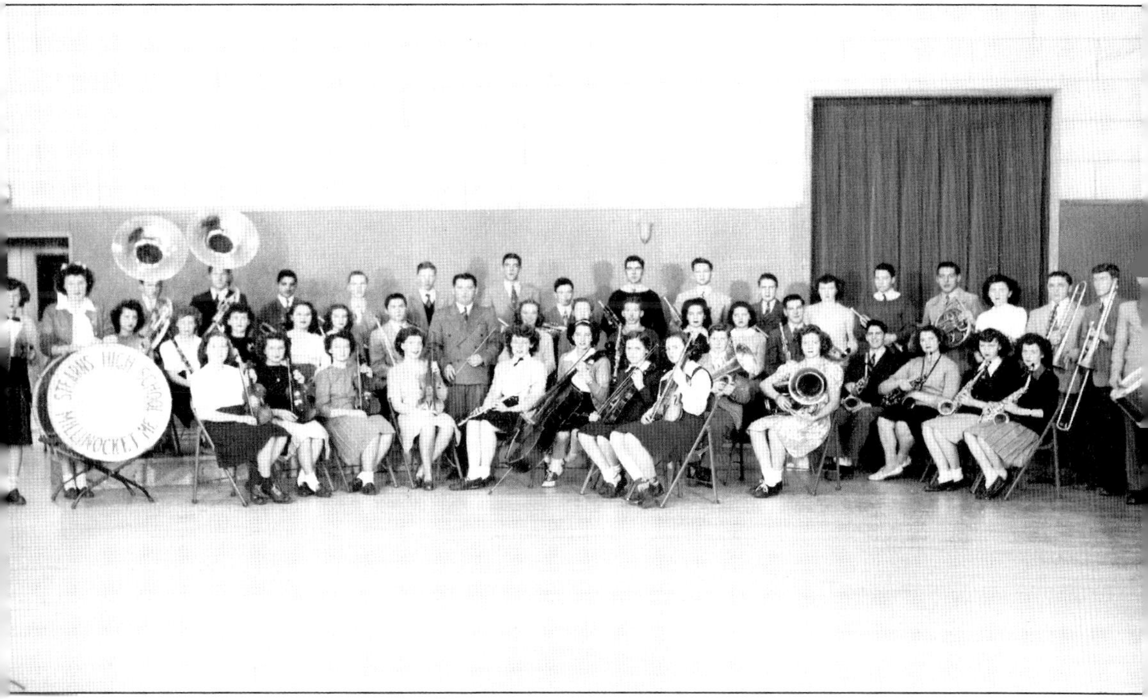

The George W. Stearns High School band was created with the help of Angelo Tsika in the late 1930s. It was a well-put-together band that was an added asset to the town. It was well known throughout the state as a top-of-the-line band. In 1954, it was chosen to march in the Cherry Blossom Festival in Washington, D.C. It was a proud day for Millinocket to see its children represent the town in such as way. Some of the students enjoyed playing instruments so much that they also played in the Millinocket town band during summer vacation from school.

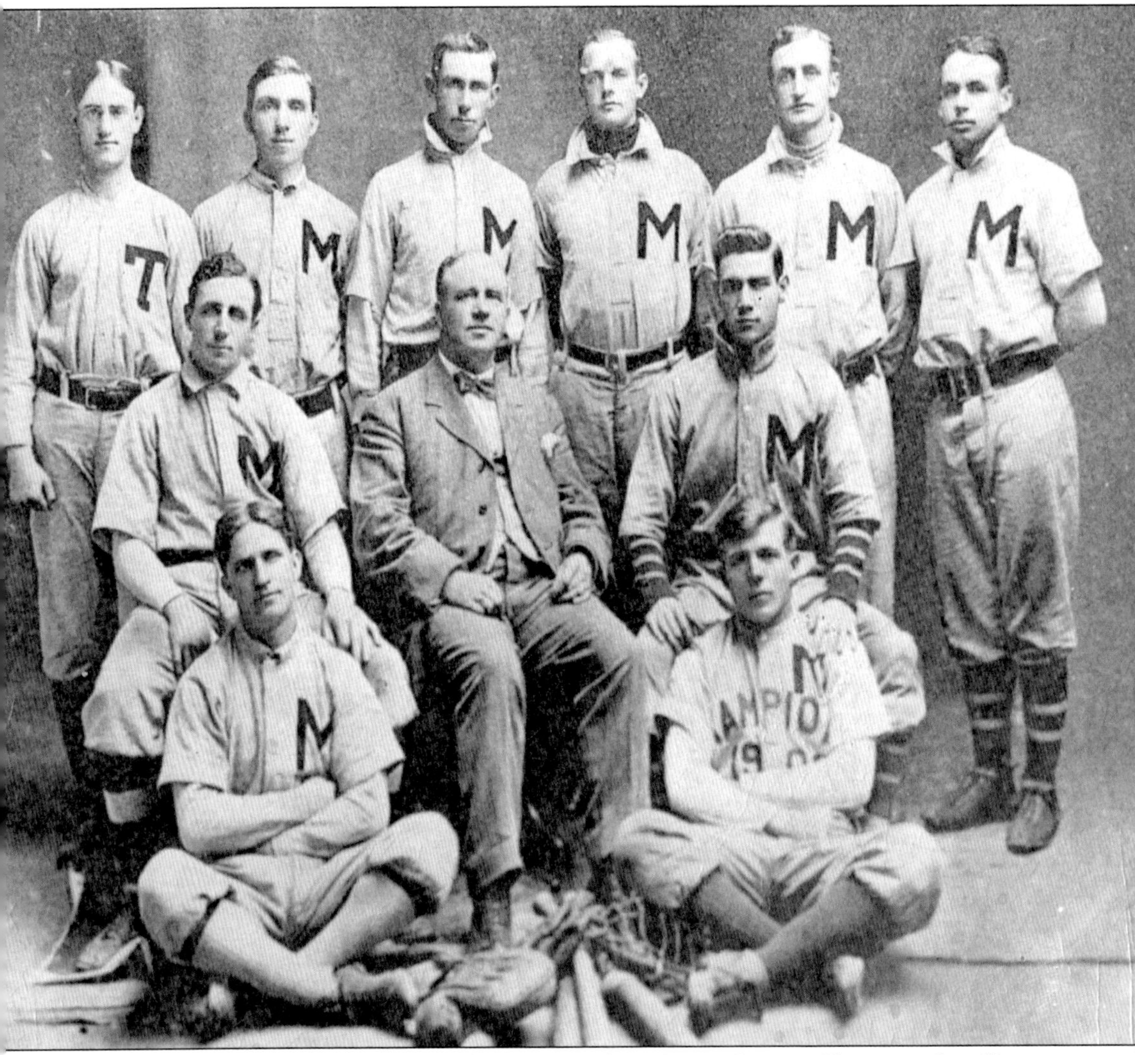

The Millinocket baseball club won the 1909 Northern Maine League Championship. Known as the Millinocket Tigers, the team was sponsored by Dr. Paul W. Cody. Pictured on the far right, Billy Jones played outfield for the Boston Braves from 1911 to 1912. In 20 games, his average was .226. Born in 1888, he was 21 years old in this photograph. Also shown in no particular order are Ralph Pond, Ralph Good, Harry More, Pete Willey, Ed Donley, Dick Breen, Jesse Lemeur, Joe Monahan, and Hammy Ordway. Baseball was played at the ball diamond that was built where the armory stands today. It was complete with a grandstand and a pavilion for the spectators. Baseball was a popular pastime in Millinocket and many games were played in town. The uniforms were often provided to the players by the Great Northern Paper Company and were made of heavy wool.

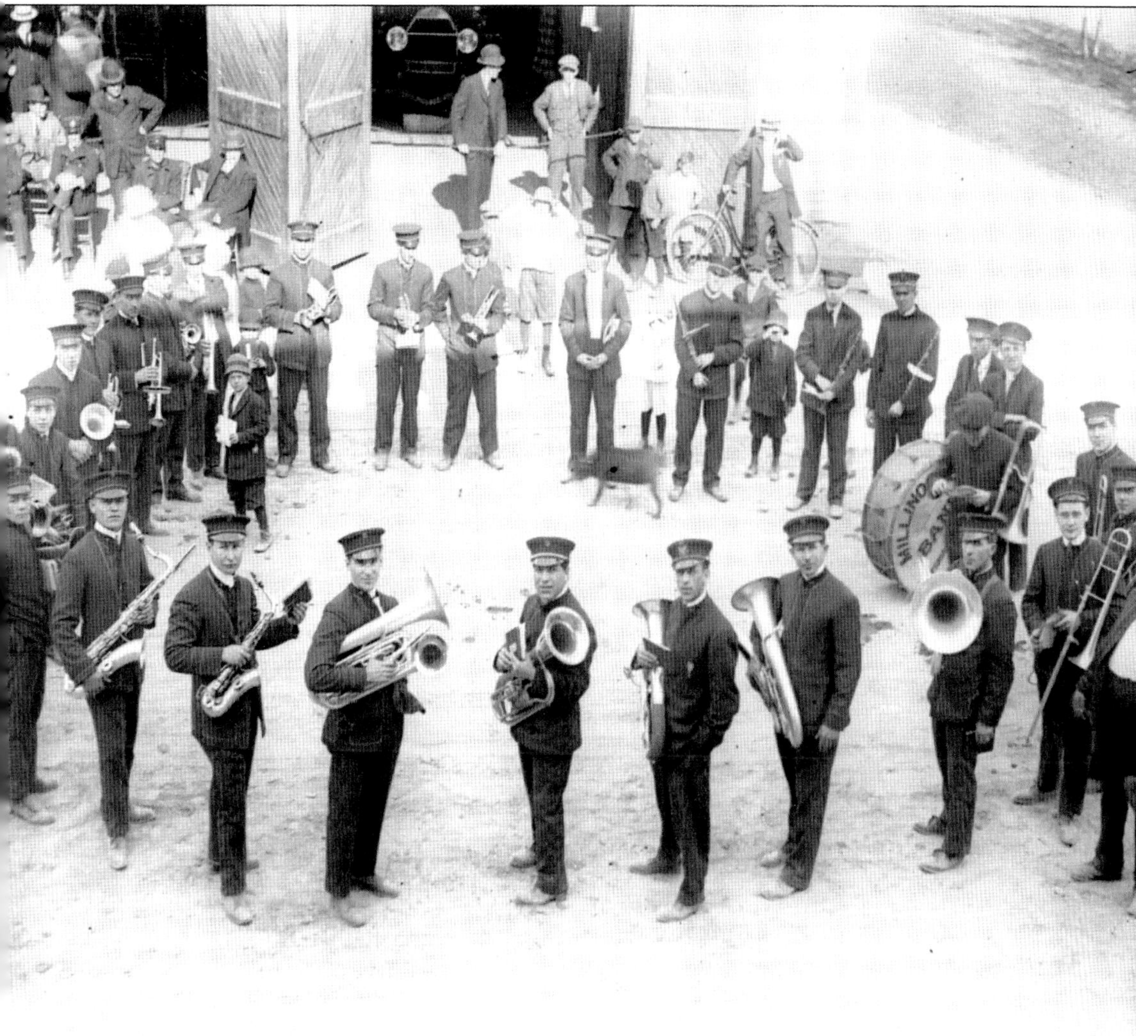

The Millinocket town band stands ready to make music and cheer up the day. When the Millinocket band was not entertaining at the local pavilion or Millinocket Opera House, there were still plenty of activities going on. When the medicine man came to town, he always attracted a large crowd in the hopes of selling some of his "magic remedy." Many customers fell for the sales pitch and purchased his products. By the time it was realized that the medicine was worthless, the seller had already moved on to another town.

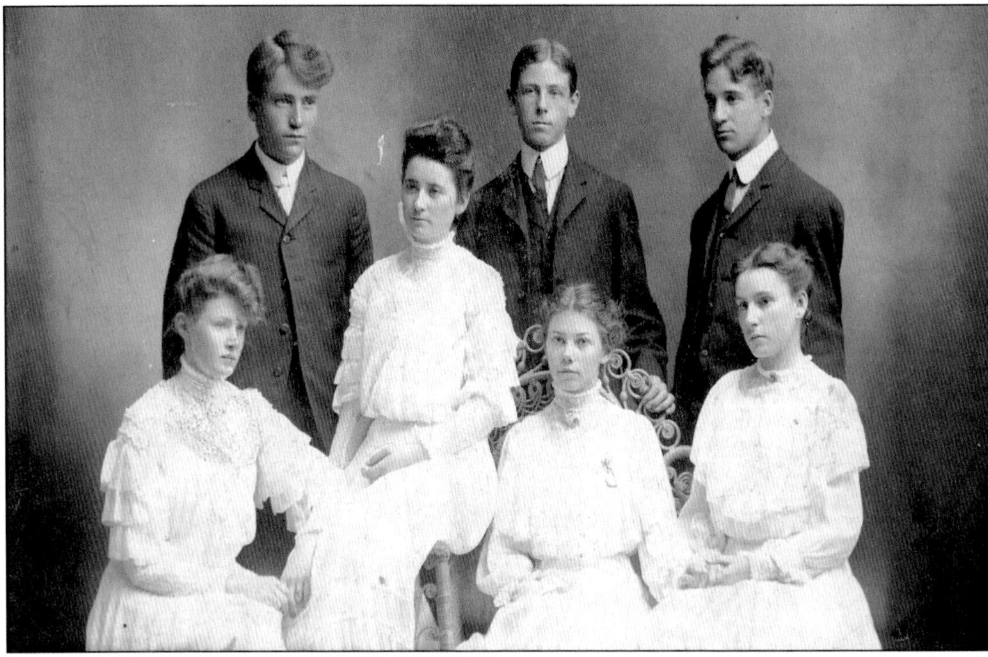

The Millinocket Hight School graduating class of 1905 poses for a picture. The students are dressed up in their fancy clothes. In 1901, a special town meeting was held and it was agreed that a common school and a high school should be set up.

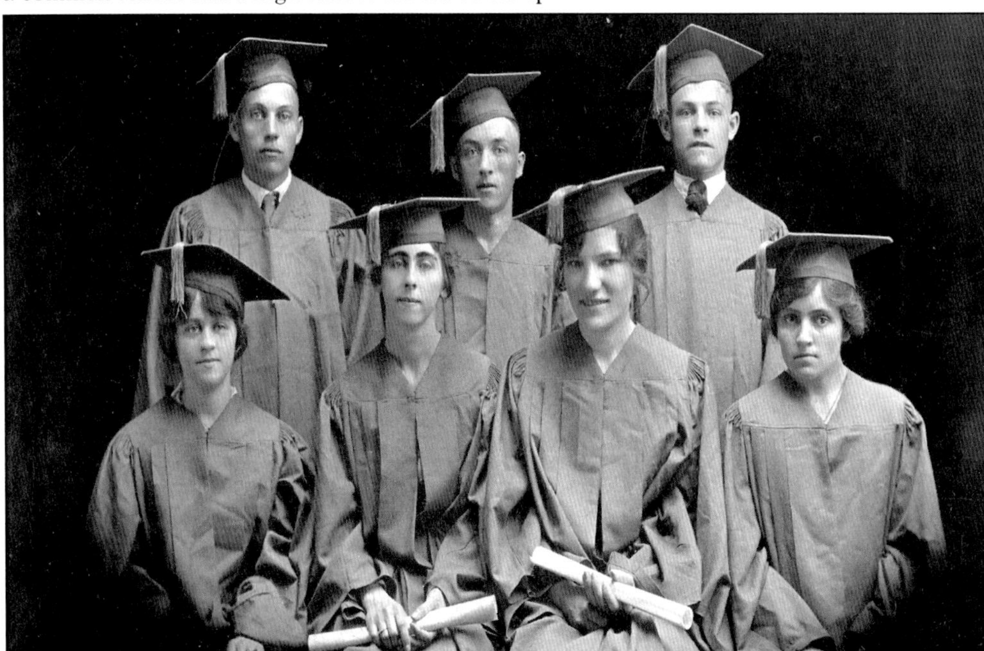

Dressed in their new gowns, the Millinocket High School class of 1913 is done with school and ready to head out into the workforce. The men that graduated from school were usually guaranteed a position in the mill immediately. The women would go on to be secretaries at the mill or perhaps nurses.

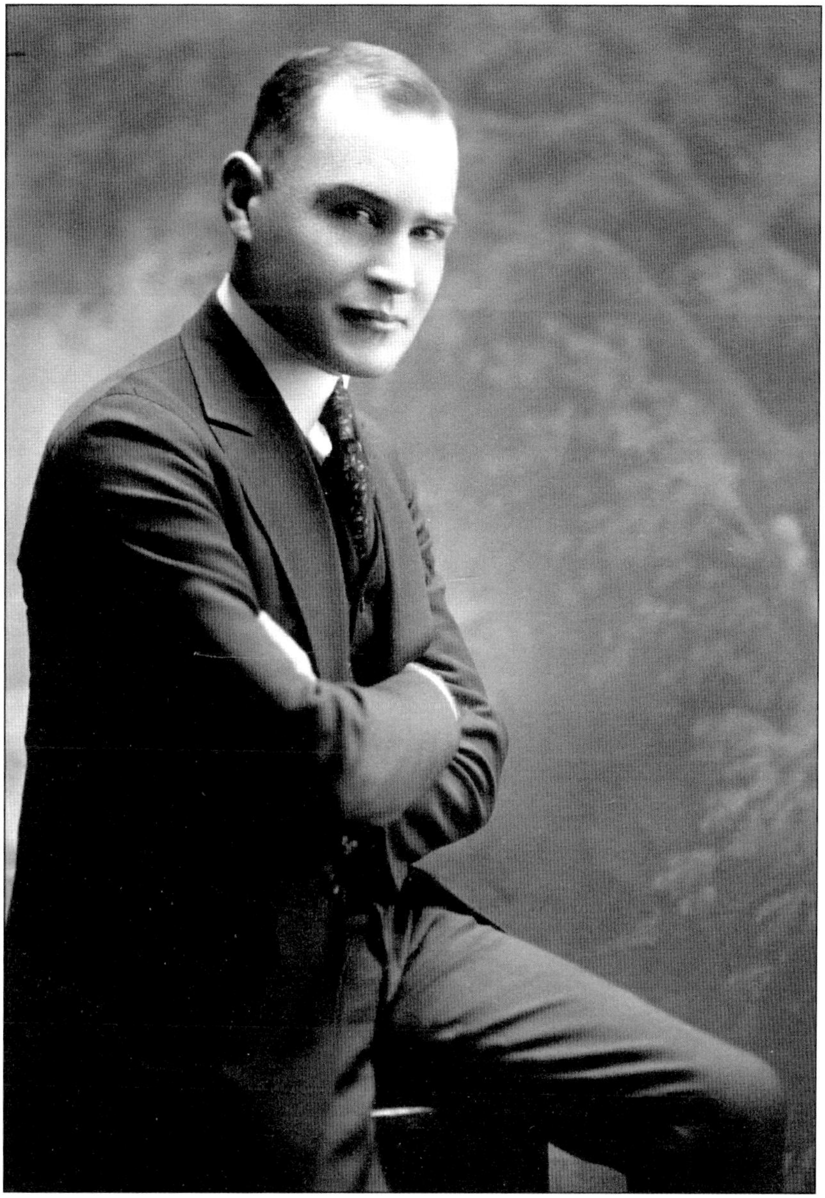

Dr. Martin Grumley operated the Millinocket General Hospital at the Curran House on Maine Avenue with Dr. Ernest Young. The Curran House served as the town hospital until 1955, when the Millinocket Regional Hospital was built. William Praught was the president of the office employees union and began the planning process for having a large hospital built for the town. Arranging all the finances that were needed was no easy task, and there were a number of entities that contributed to the effort. The Great Northern Paper Company generously offered a grant totaling $800,000. In December 1951, the board of trustees of the Millinocket Community Hospital met. The members included Robert Hume, president; Leslie Kewer, vice president; William Praught, secretary; Carl Stockwell, treasurer; and Charles Carrier and John Ward, both directors. Loius C. Stearns III was an attorney for the Great Northern Paper Company and helped set up the board as a nonprofit organization. By March 1955, Millinocket had the large hospital that it had longed for.

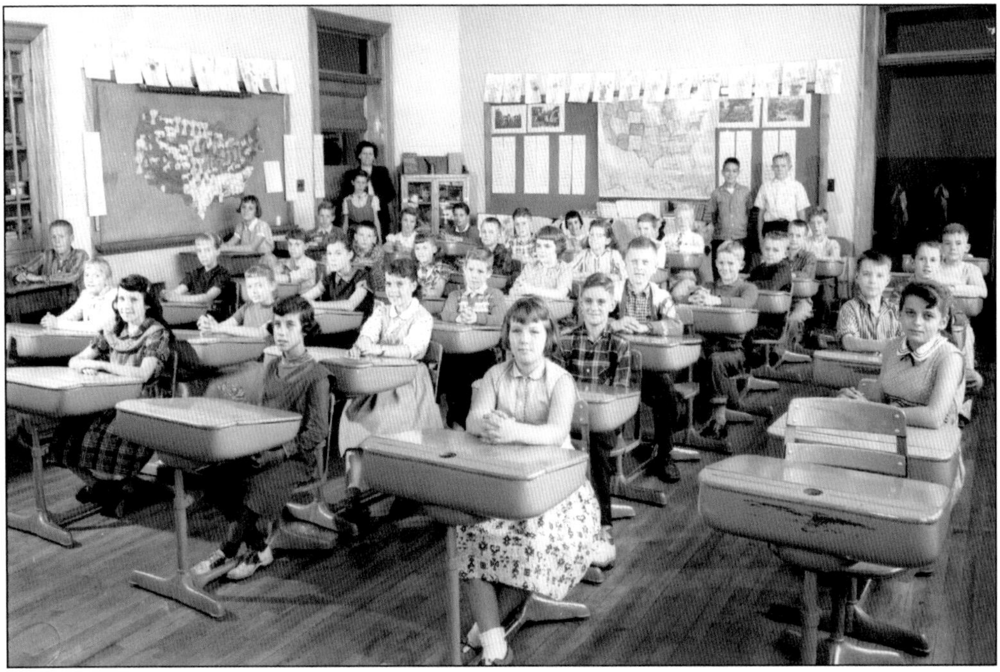

Annie Bear is standing by the door of her classroom (above), and Viola Bear is standing by the coat rack in the back of her classroom (below). Aroostook Street School was a brick school building that was located behind the Baptist church on Aroostook Avenue. It was built in 1914 and served as a grade school for many years. Before the school was complete, some students had to go to classes at Barbien's Hall on the Medway Road. The building is still standing today and is home to offices for various businesses.

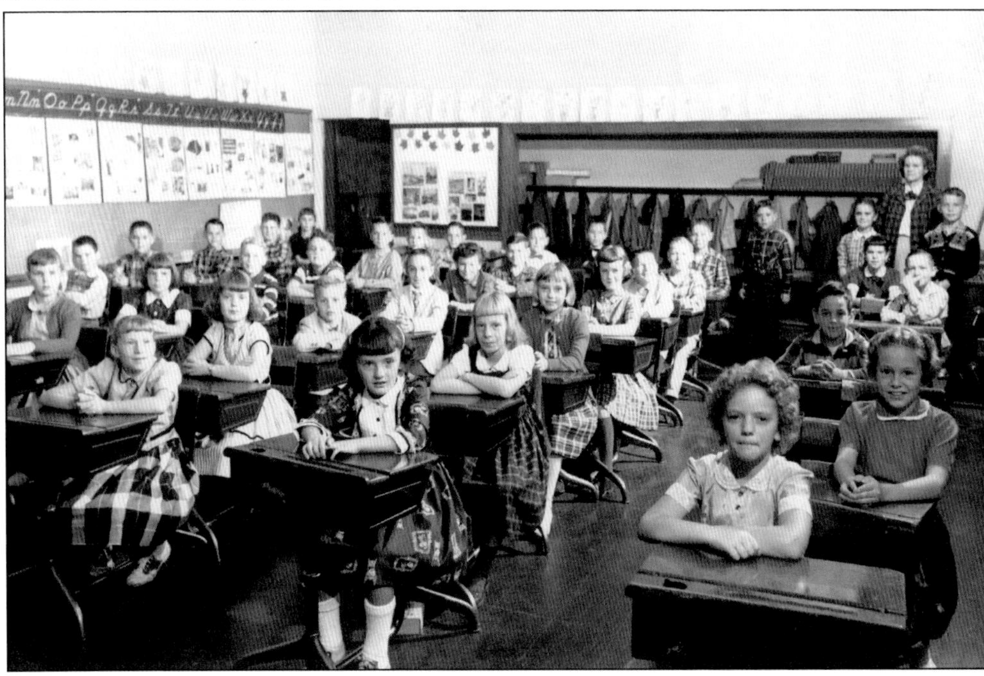

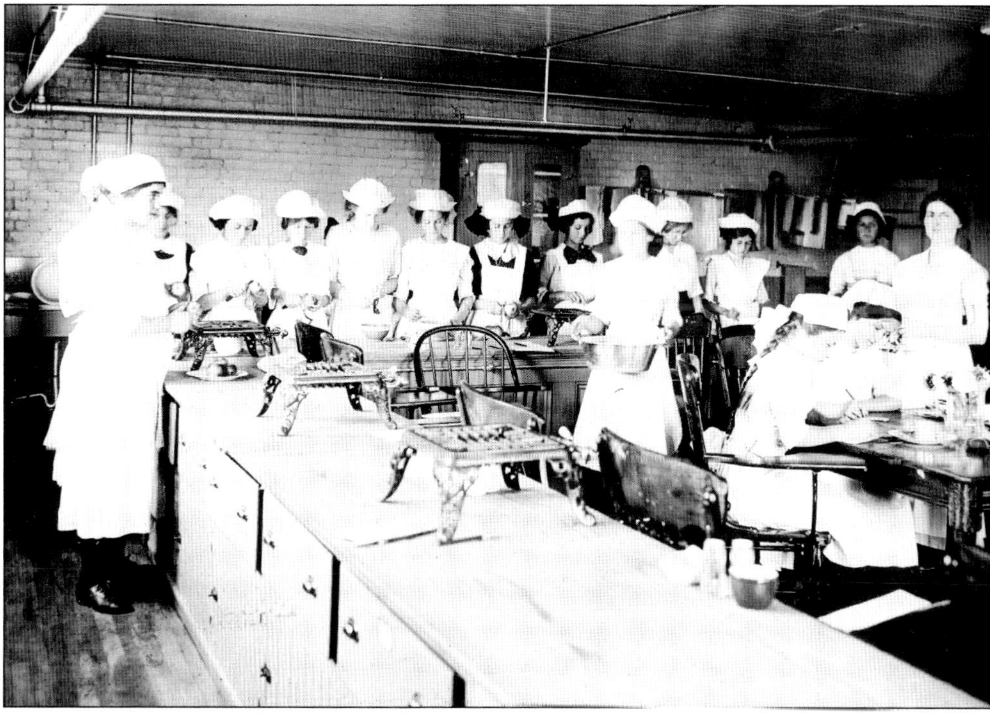

Young women were taught the art of managing a home in the home economics class of Grace Lufkin. Decked out in fancy outfits, the women standing are peeling apples to be used in cooking. Perhaps they are getting ready to make a dessert favored by many in the area, apple pie.

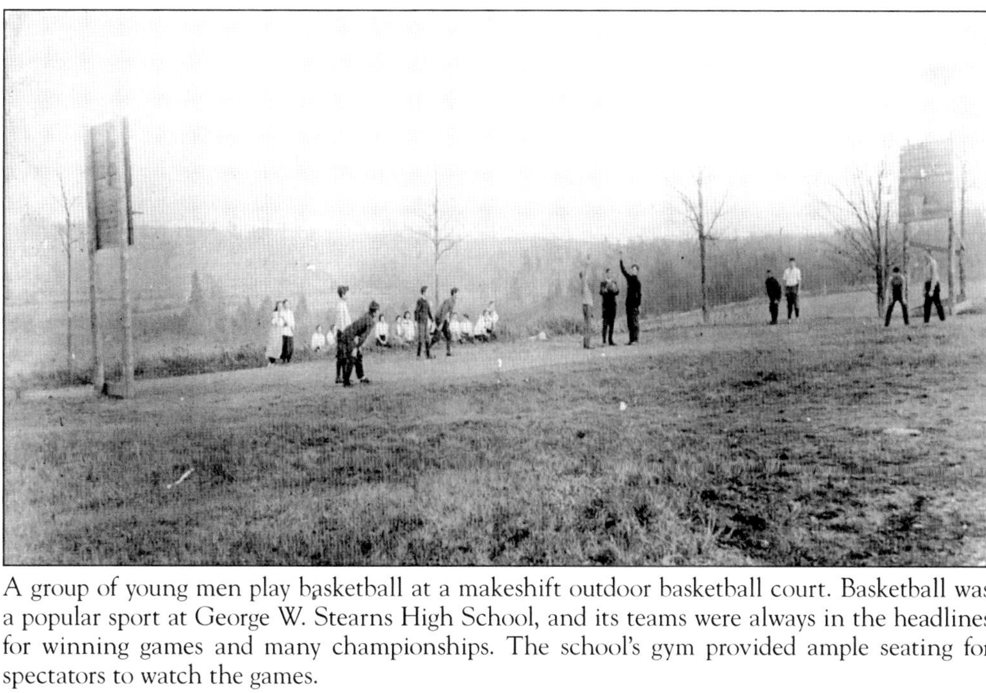

A group of young men play basketball at a makeshift outdoor basketball court. Basketball was a popular sport at George W. Stearns High School, and its teams were always in the headlines for winning games and many championships. The school's gym provided ample seating for spectators to watch the games.

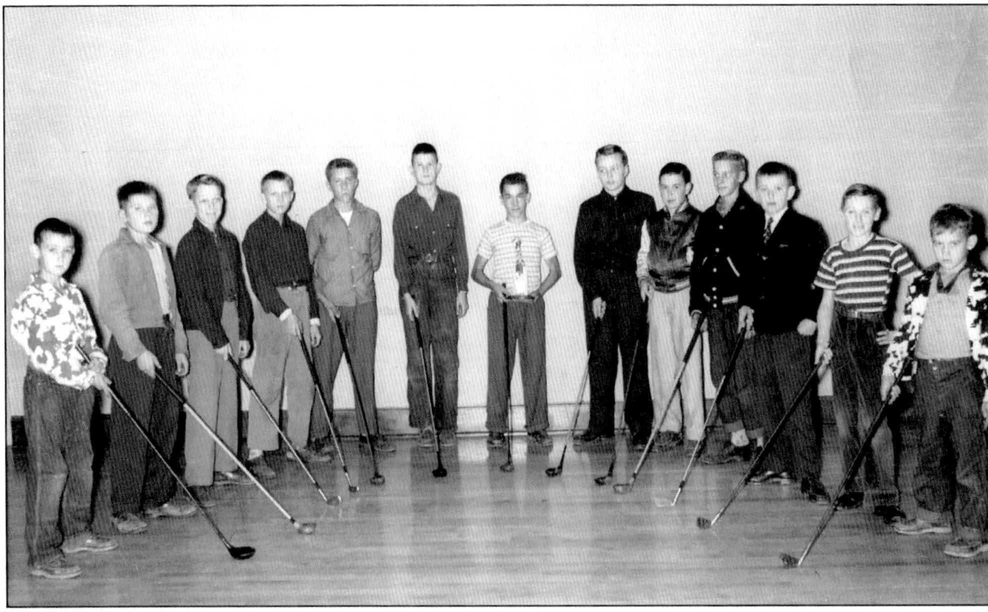

Hillcrest Golf Club had a golf course in an area that was known as Skunk Hollow. It got its start as a six-hole course in the late 1930s. For a short time beginning in 1949, it was taken over by the town and became a municipal golf course. Royden Pratt took over its operations, and it reverted back to a private course once again. Golfers came from all over Maine to play a round there. Various teams were formed that played in tournaments held at the course, and many trophies were won.

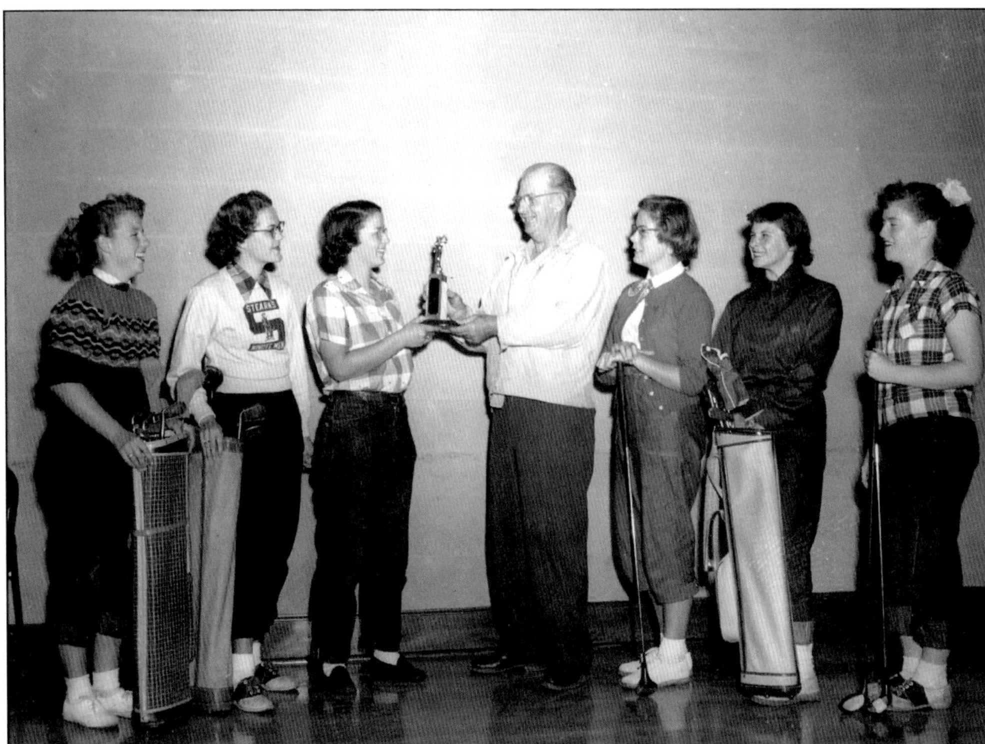

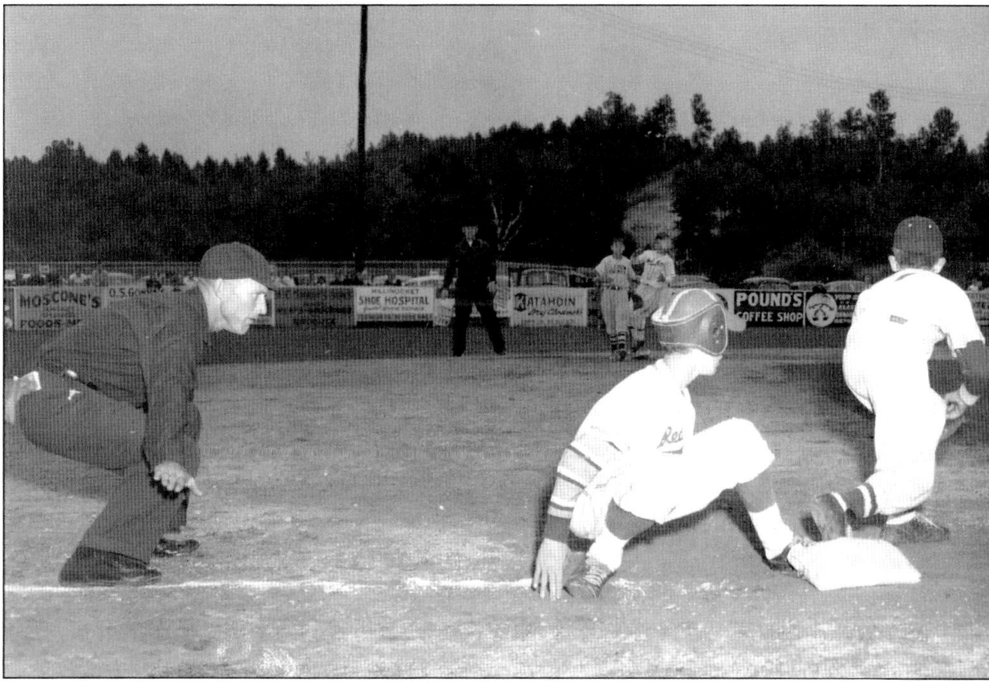

Baseball occupied young people and kept the adults entertained. With the large recreational complex offering a variety of sports activities, there was always an opportunity to play on one of the local teams. The recreational area has been a huge asset to the town of Millinocket.

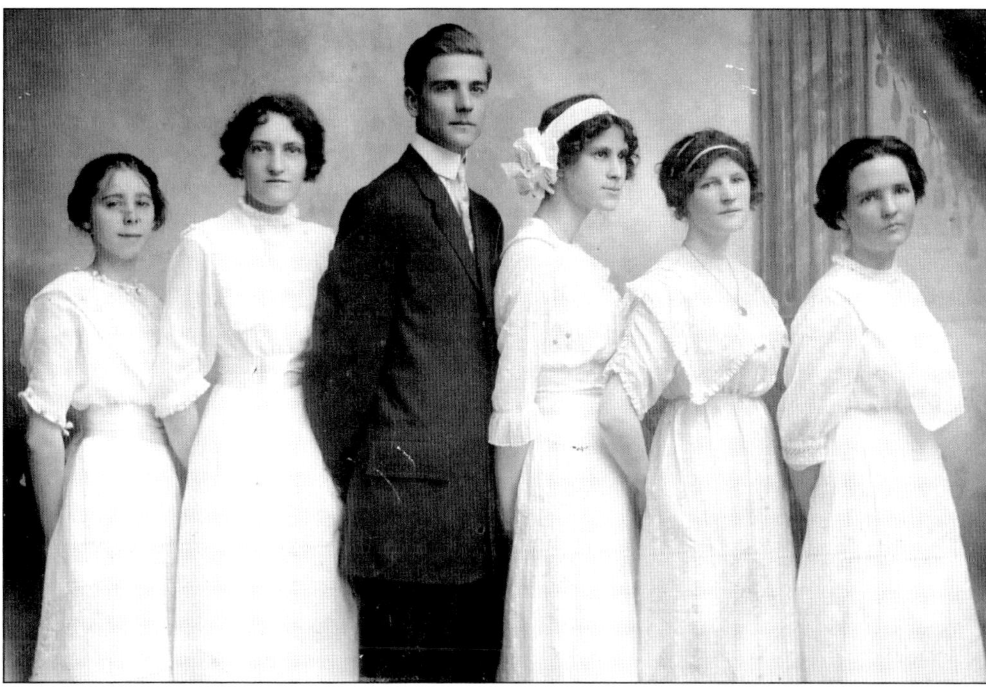

Millinocket's remote location provided a harsh existence for the early settlers, but that did not mean they were unsophisticated. They looked forward to dressing up and enjoying a social event at the Millinocket Opera House or one of the boardinghouses.

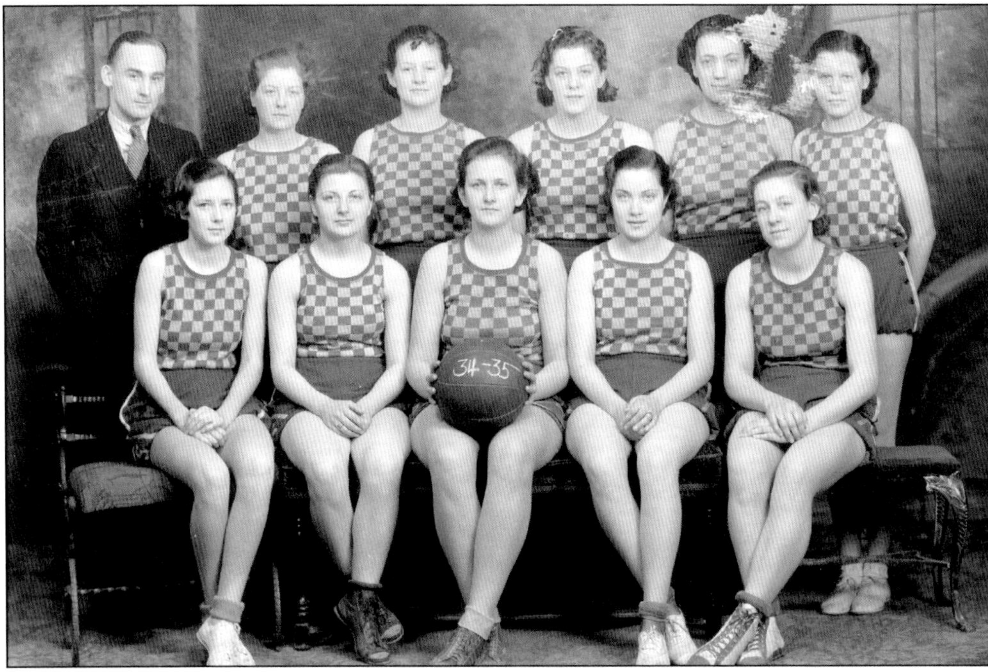

The girls of George W. Stearns High School have an impressive history of being an award-winning team. These girls are showing off their conservative attire in the early days of female basketball. Note the high stockings that were the uniform of the day in the 1927–1928 basketball season. Often times the uniforms were also made of heavy wool to add to the discomfort. The girls of Stearns today carry on the tradition of fine sportsmanship and have maintained the record of being a high quality basketball team. Unfortunately there were no names on these pictures to identify the players here.

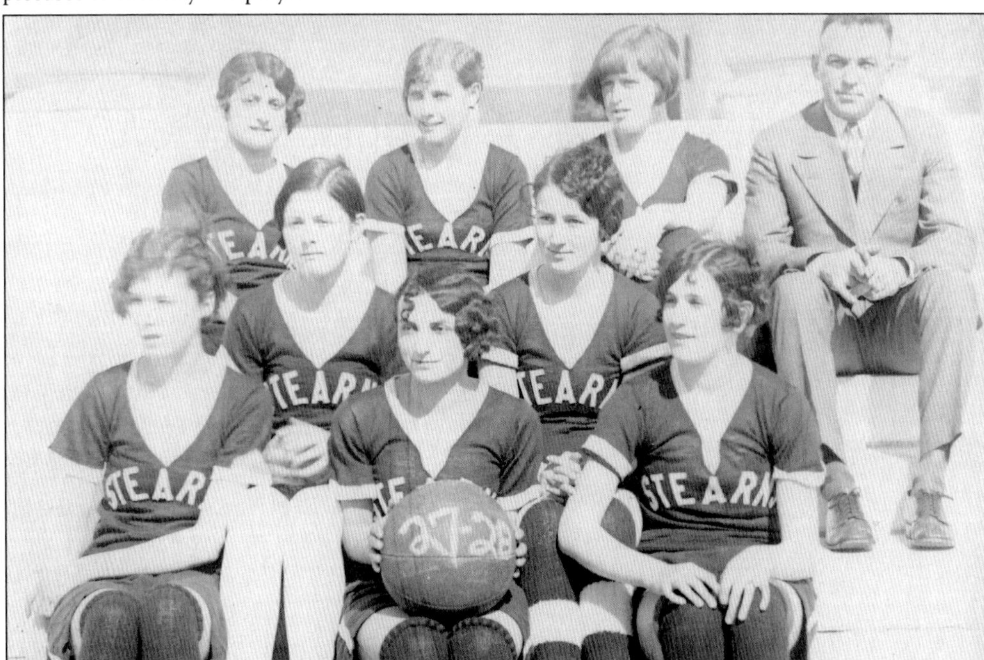

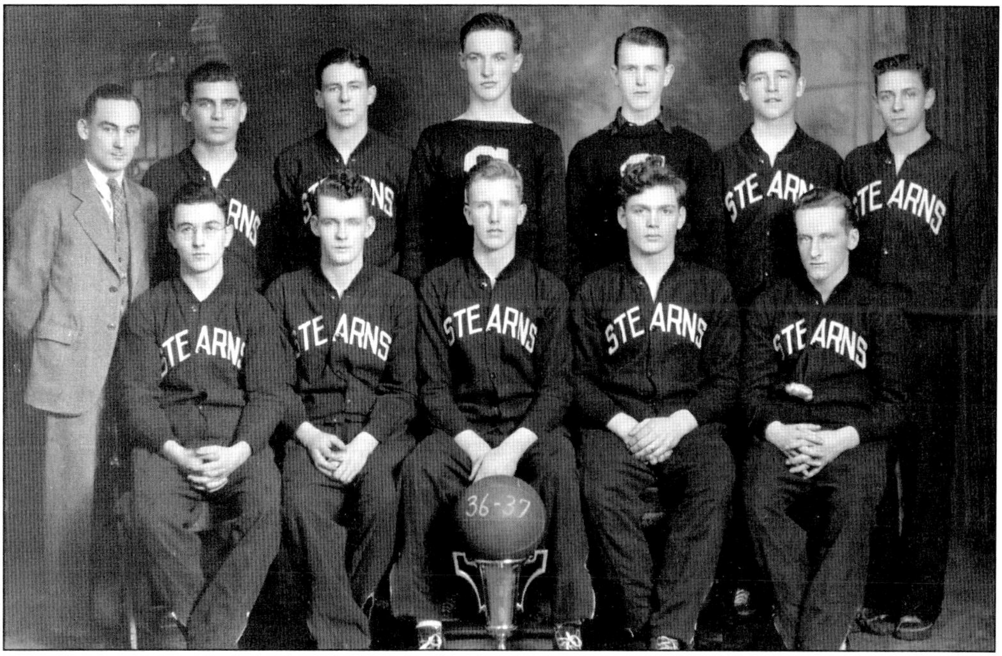

The Stearns High School boys' basketball team has evolved into a state championship team and has won many tournaments. The 1936–1937 team already has a trophy to their credit. Coach Jimmy Stevens is pictured standing at left. Team members include Lloyd Pound, Murry Benjamin, Rip Brown, George Ferland, and Ted Boynton.

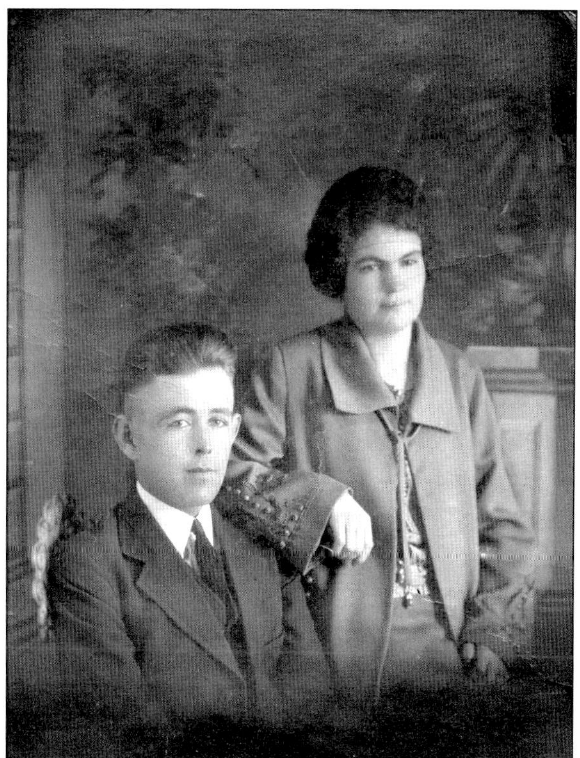

Millinocket attracted people that were looking for a good life and the promise of a good-paying job. For workers that were loyal to the Great Northern Paper Company, the mill treated them well. Elias and Amanda Gagnier, pictured here, moved to Millinocket to start a family. Elias worked in the mill as an electrician. (Courtesy of Kathy Gagnon.)

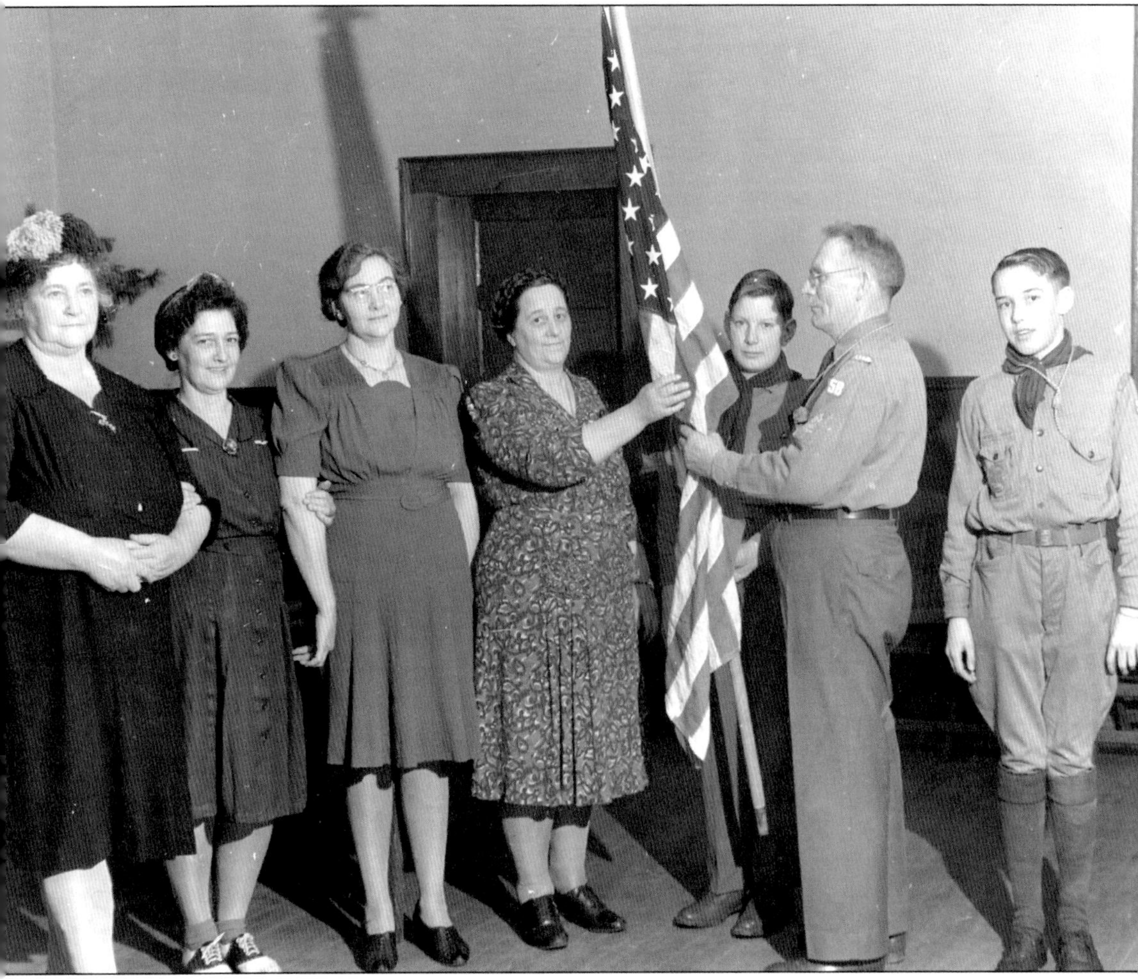

Boy Scout Troop 58 of Millinocket presents the American flag to the Navy Mothers Service Club. It is estimated that one out of every seven people in town served in the military during World War II. A majority of the men who joined the service enlisted in the navy and served aboard a ship. The Navy Mothers Service Club made sure that letters were written to the servicemen and that packages were sent to them. The club also did their part supporting the war effort by helping the Red Cross with sewing and bandage making. Pictured from left to right are Elizabeth Garvin, vice president; Ruby Segee, secretary; Birdie Ireland, treasurer; Wauneta L. Chase, president; Eugene Jones, scout; Frederick A. Tippins, scout master; and Lawrence Barnes, scout.

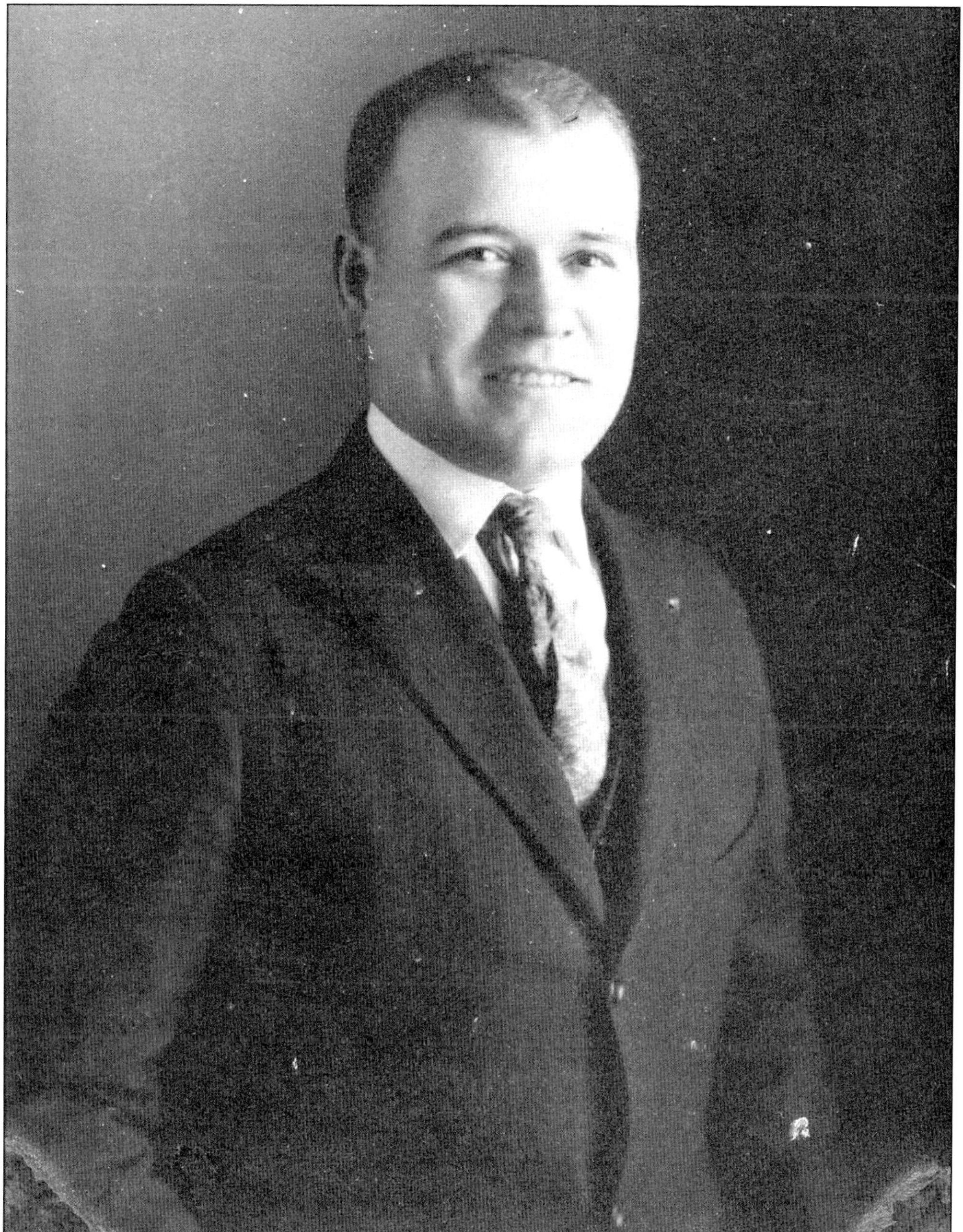

Harry Carroll was a citizen of Millinocket from 1914 to 1980. He loved the town and wanted to see it become a better place in which to live. He was actively involved in the community for many years. He was a charter member of the Millinocket Fire Department in its early days and a charter member of the Hillcrest Golf Club. He also joined the Donald V. Henry Post No. 80 of the American Legion. He operated the first bowling lanes in Millinocket and was a member of the Eastern Maine Bowling League. He joined the Millinocket band as a charter member and was also a part of the Donald V. Henry Drum and Bugle Corps. As an active member of the community, he contributed a great deal to the town and was a positive influence.

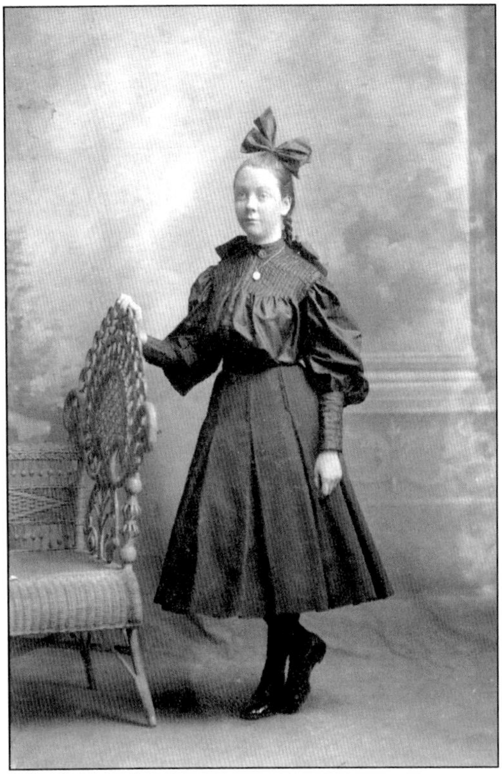

Beulah Atherton Carroll came to Millinocket in 1898 and lived here all of her life. She was a devote Baptist and was a founder and charter member of the Millinocket Baptist Church where her father was a deacon. The Millinocket Baptist Church is a large colonial-style church that is on the corner of Penobscot Avenue and Spring Street. Its first service was held on October 23, 1903, and the Reverend C. E. Young was its first pastor. The building was originally designed as a Victorian-style church, but after a fire destroyed it, the design was changed to the Colonial style it is today.

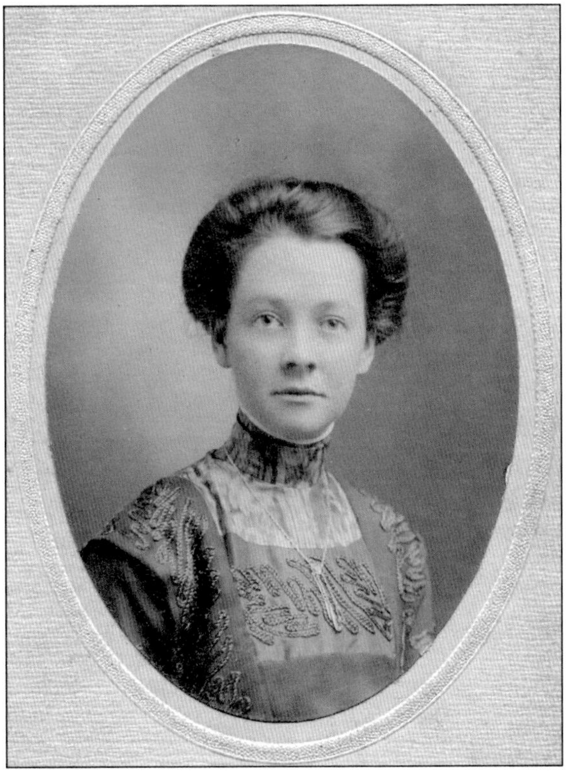

Four

AROUND MILLINOCKET

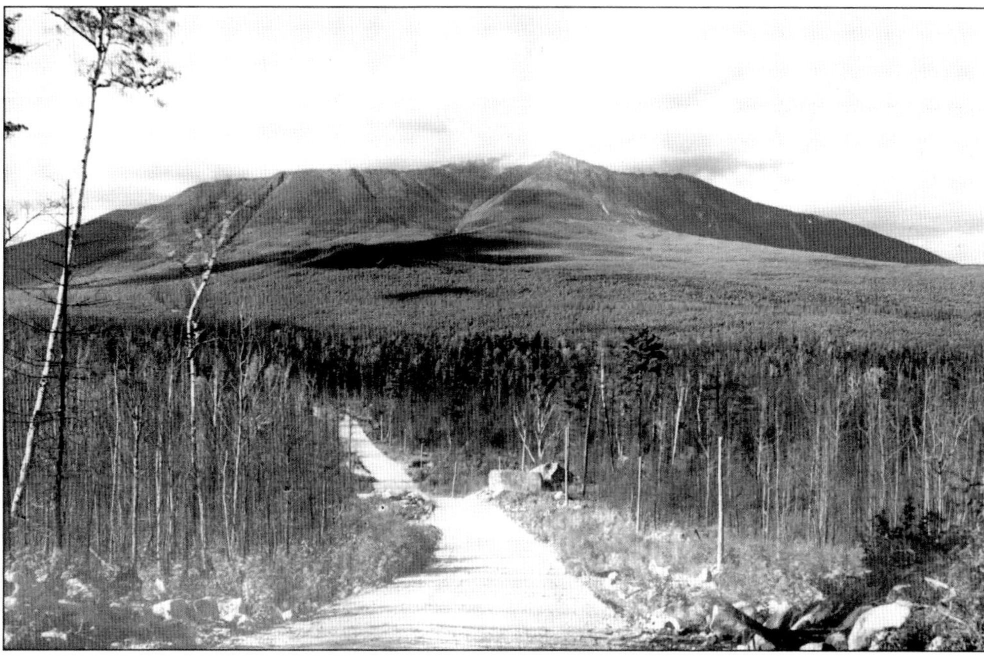

Mount Katahdin is the highest mountain in Maine. Percival Baxter had enough forethought to purchase large sections of the north woods of Maine to be forever preserved as a wilderness park. When he was going through negotiations with logging companies to buy the land, he was in a race against time. Logging operations had already started setting up camps on the mountain. In the Basin Pond area, there was a small town being built. There was some talk going around about building a large hotel on top of the mountain, much like what was built on Mount Washington in New Hampshire. Once Baxter acquired the land, he created the park and deeded it to the people of Maine. The park encompasses nearly 205,000 acres of prime pristine wilderness for all to enjoy. The view from Pockwockamus Hill is a pretty sight to see with the peak of Mount Katahdin covered in white clouds.

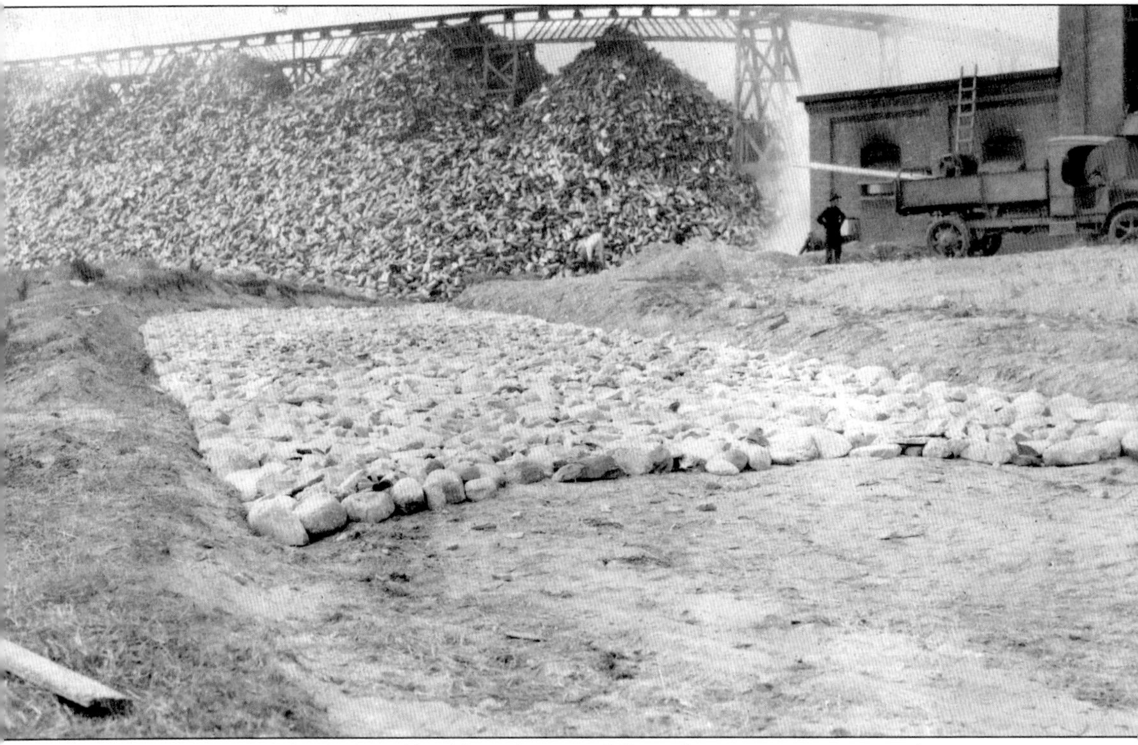

By utilizing the method of road building that was followed since ancient times, there were many miles of solid roads built in the Katahdin region. The roads were surveyed out and graded with the proper slopes. Once the roads were graded to specifications, rocks were carefully laid out as a foundation. Dirt was then spread over the rocks, which created a very strong road. The roads held up well and made traveling in the muddy spring a little easier. Another form of road building in the area was called a corduroy road. This type of road was built by laying logs side by side across the ground. Once the logs were laid down, they were covered with gravel. This was done extensively in the woods, as it was an effective way to build roads in swampy areas.

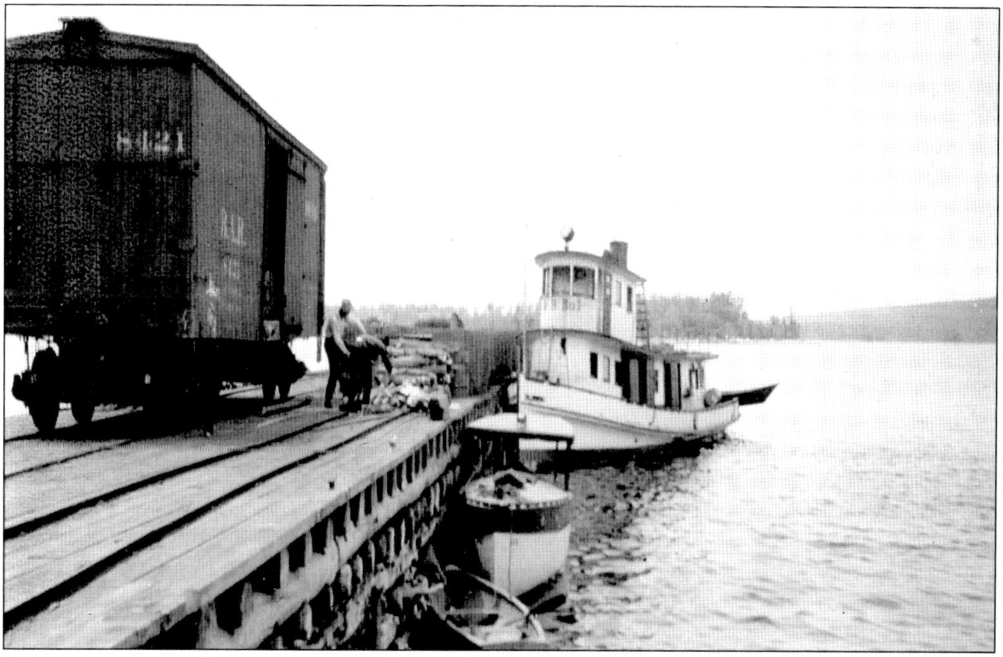

The community of Norcross sat on the banks of the chain of lakes of the West Branch of the Penobscot River. It was a major jumping off point from the Bangor and Aroostook Railroad for sportsmen coming to the area known for its excellent hunting and fishing. Fred Peasley's Norcross Supply Store offered the sportsmen a chance to purchase all the outdoor gear that they needed for their excursions to the Maine wilderness. The Norcross House was a sportsmen's resort that was operated by F. A. Fowler, a grandson of Thomas Fowler who was an original settler of the Millinocket area. The Great Northern Paper Company maintained boat docks there in order to have easy access to the railroad by water for their boating operations.

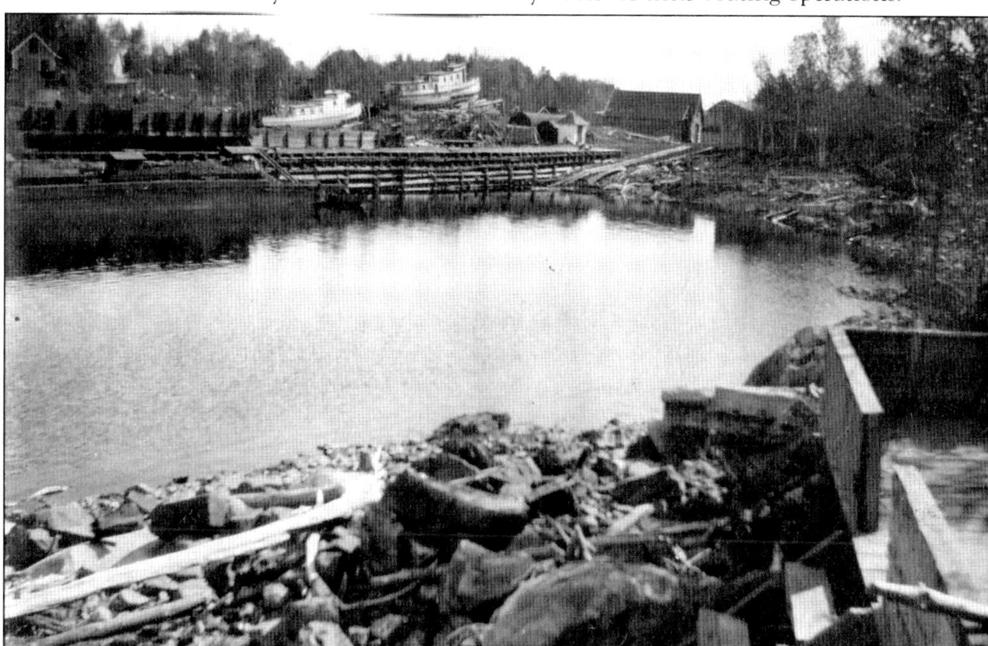

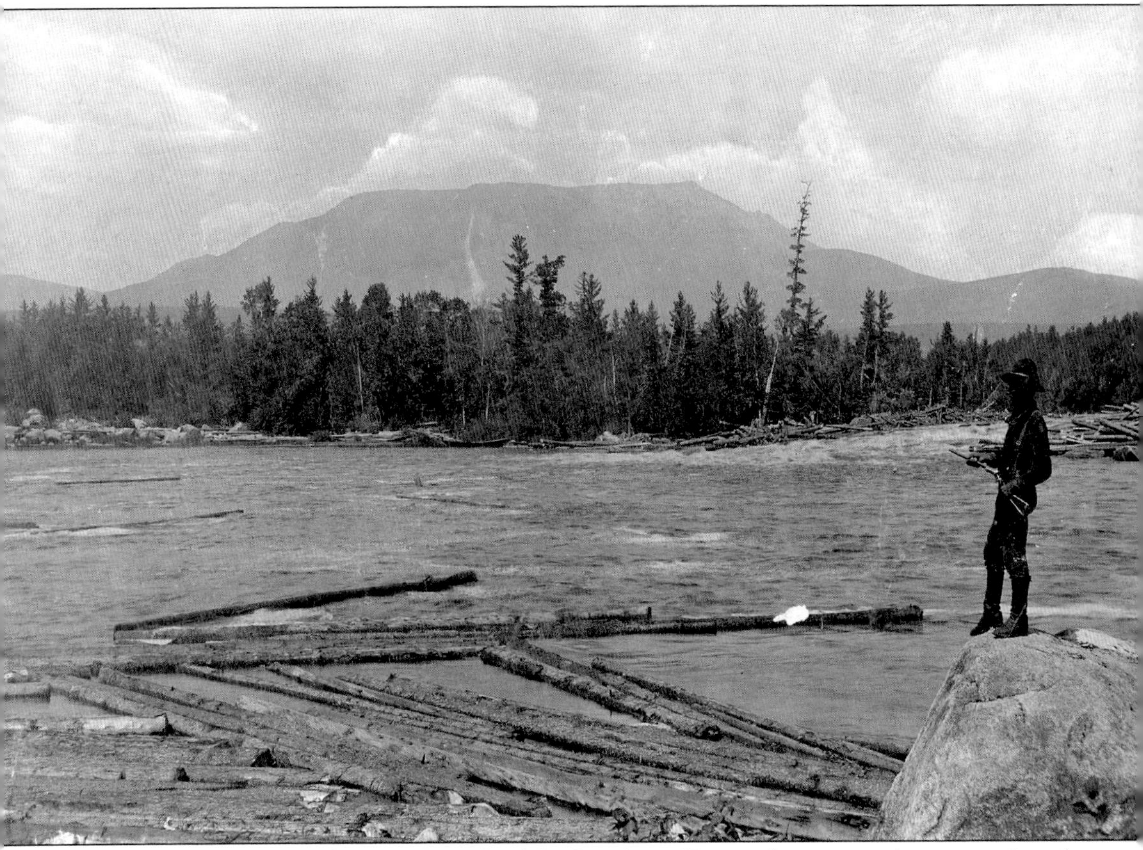

Standing on a rock in the West Branch of the Penobscot River, a hunter watches as tree-length logs float downriver heading to the mill. The Penobscot River flows strong along the foot of Mount Katahdin and provides for some spectacular views along the river of the mighty mountain. The Native Americans thought that Mount Katahdin was home to the god Pamola and would not venture on the mountain itself out of fear of running into the god. The Penobscot River was an important waterway for the Native Americans, allowing for access to the traditional hunting lands that had been used for generations. Today the river is favored for white-water rafting and kayaking. The waterway is also well known for its salmon and trout, and many anglers will travel here to master the fly rod in an attempt at a prize catch.

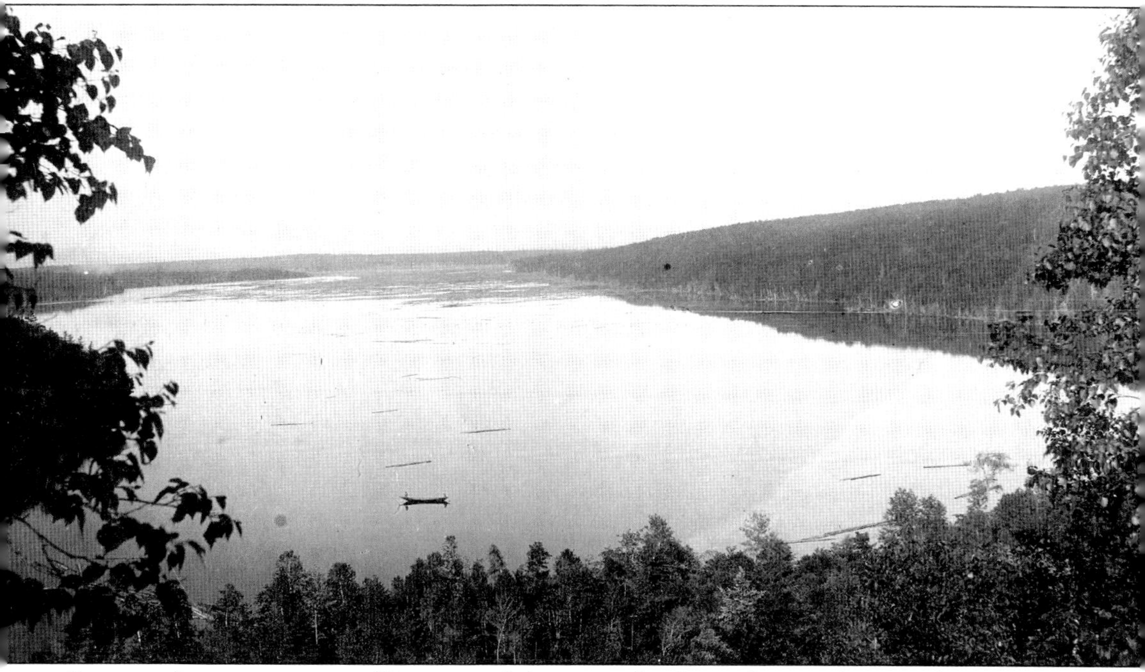

Enjoying the quiet serenity of Ripogenus Lake, a couple of men float on the smooth surface of the lake. The bateau was a heavy wooden boat that was favored by the woodsmen that worked on the rock-strewn rivers of Maine. It was a strong boat that could withstand a great deal of pounding on the rocks and logs during the drive. It took a strong man with a good knowledge of the river to expertly pole the bateau around the rapids of the Penobscot River. The boat was heavy and hard to move around on dry land, and the job of portaging from one waterway to another was no easy task and was avoided when possible. Looking like toothpicks thrown out on the water, a number of logs can be seen on the lake making their way to the outlet to head down the river.

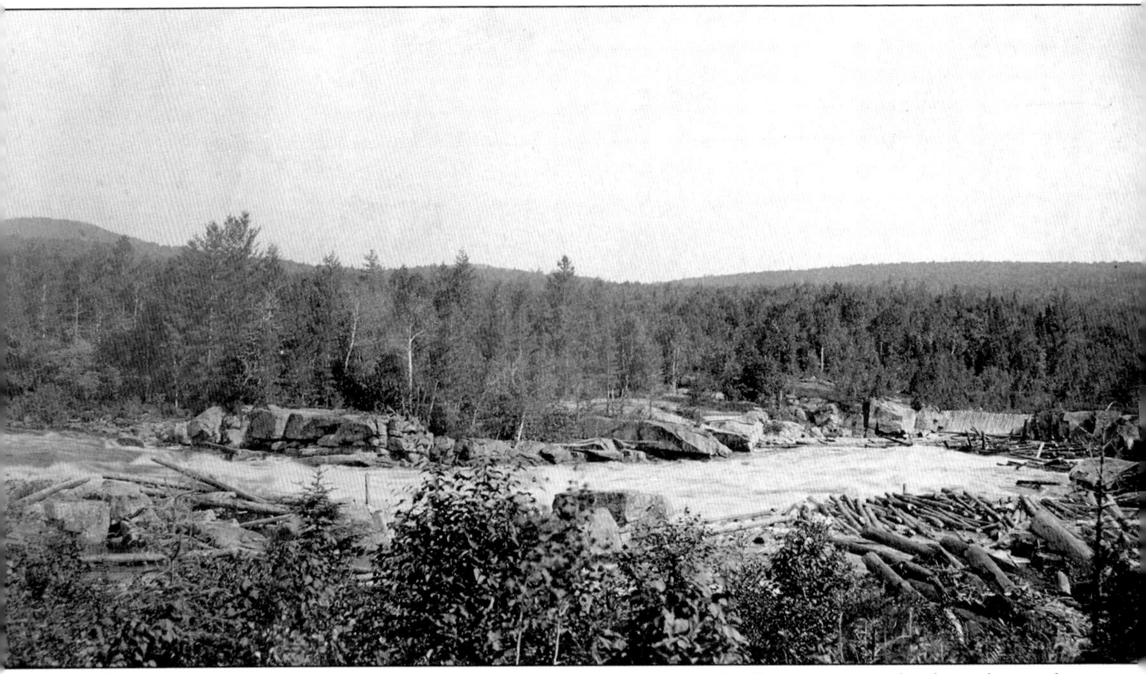

The Penobscot River is a rough, rock-strewn river. It was a challenge to get the logs down the river without them getting hung up on the rocks or caught up in an eddy. The work of the river driver was a nonstop job of undoing the numerous logjams that hindered the process of getting the logs to the mill. In order to untangle a logjam, a river driver had to go out on the log pile. With a great deal of finesse and strength, he had to wrestle the logs loose so they floated free to continue on. The tools of the trade included a long pole, a peavey, and often times a stick or two of dynamite. The dynamite was used to deal with the hard jams. A common accident involved the river driver being caught on a log pile as it let loose, resulting in an unpleasant fall into the grinding and churning logs as they thrashed over the rocks. There were an untold number of men lost this way, never to be found.

Frank Speed presented the idea of a road linking Millinocket to Brownville in 1926. It took over 20 years for it to be completed, and in 1948, the bridge over the West Branch of the Penobscot River was finished and the road was opened. The road provided a much-needed link between Millinocket and Brownville. For the first time, it also allowed a road to go to Norcross as it passed right by that small community. Supervising the building of the Brownville to Millinocket road are, from left to right, sub-foreman Earl Lancaster of Milo, foreman Harold Edgerly from Sangerville, sub-foreman Ora Kelly of Milo, and shovel operator Harold Finson.

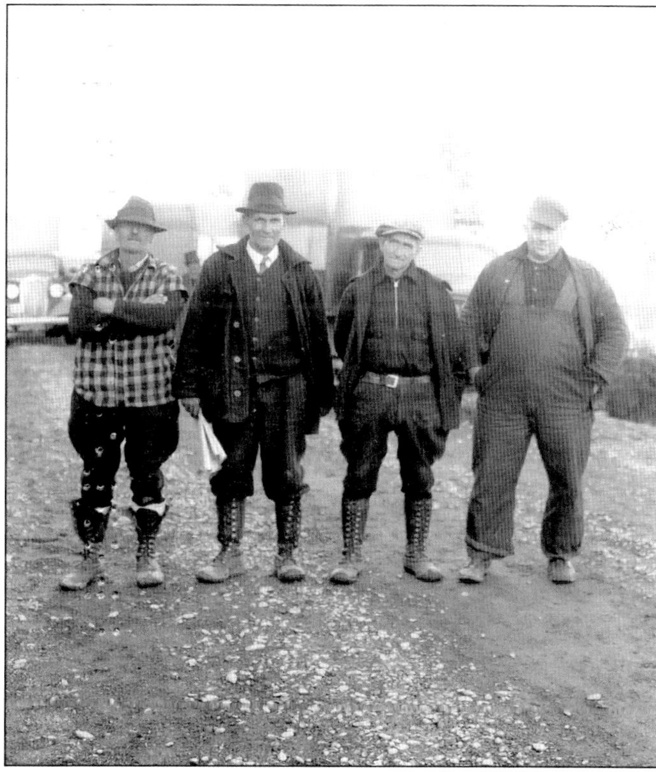

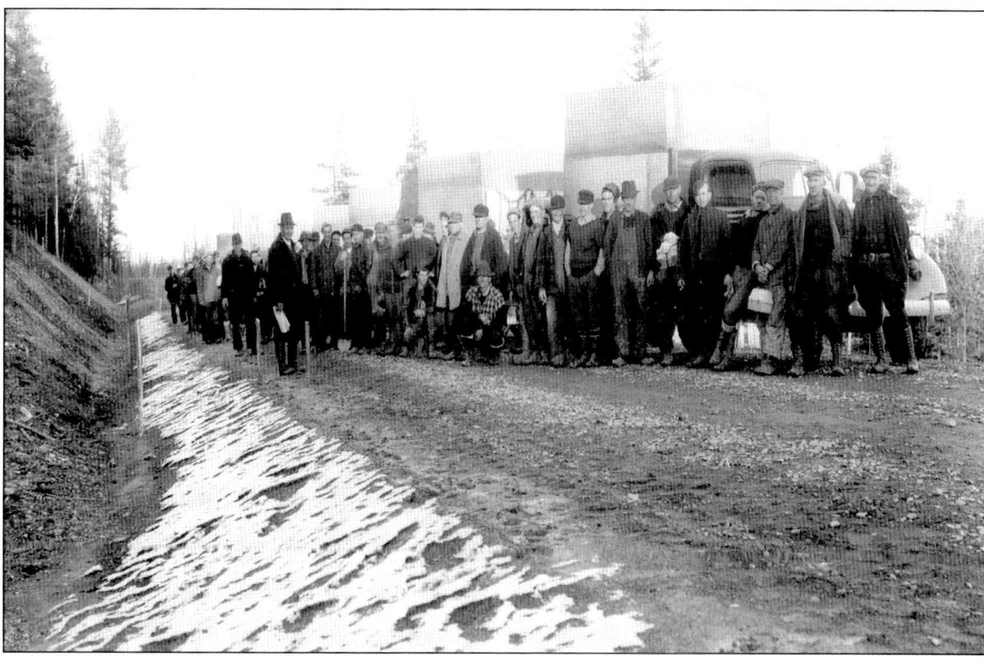

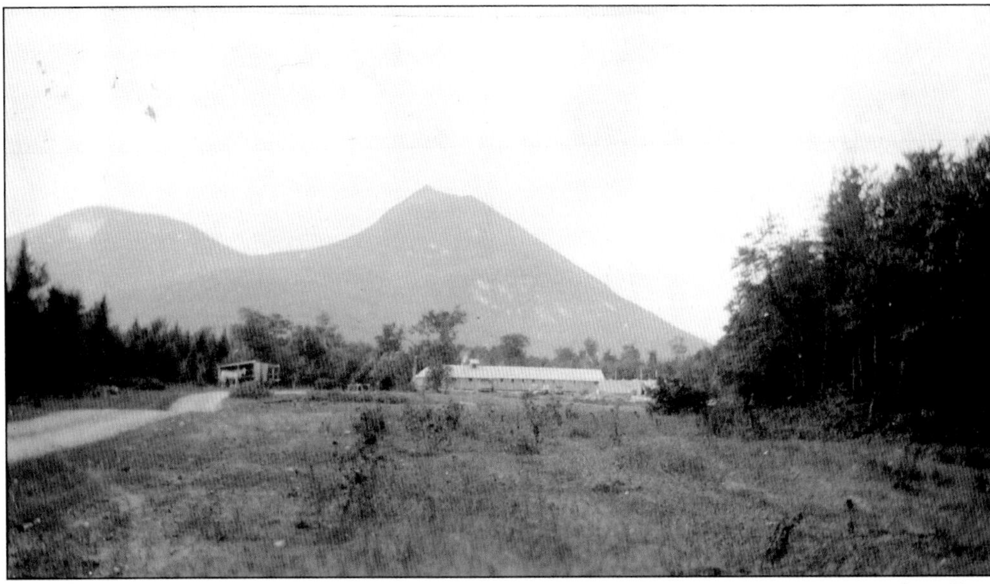

In the 1930s, Pres. Franklin D. Roosevelt created the Civilian Conservation Corps (CCC) as a way of providing jobs for people during the Depression and allowing them the chance to be trained in another job specialty. The Katahdin region was home to several hundred men from the CCC. Some of the men were housed in the area of the airport in Millinocket. Others were housed at Foster Field in Baxter State Park. The labor provided by the men of the CCC built the road leading from Millinocket Lake to the entrance of Baxter State Park.

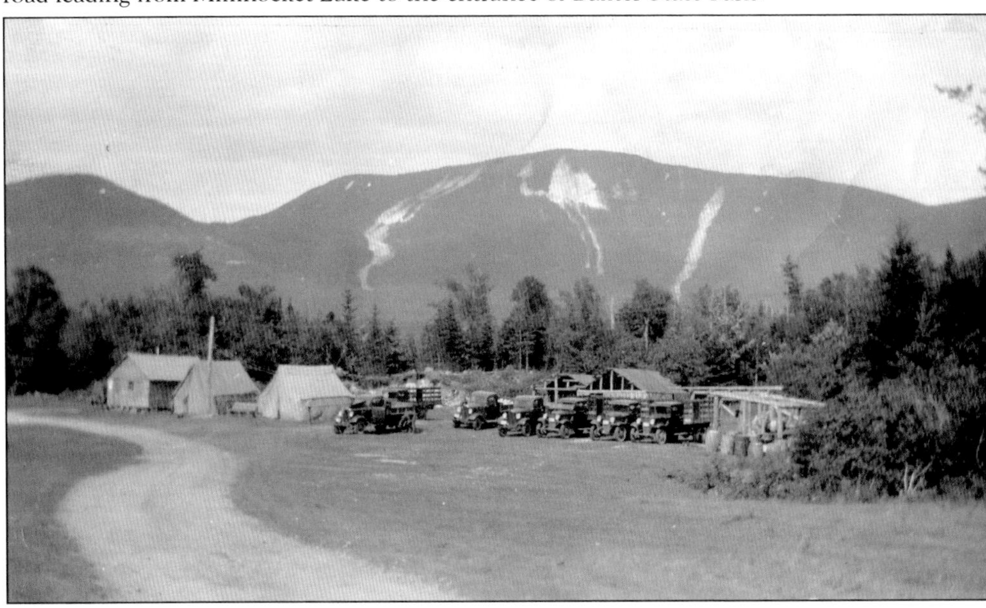

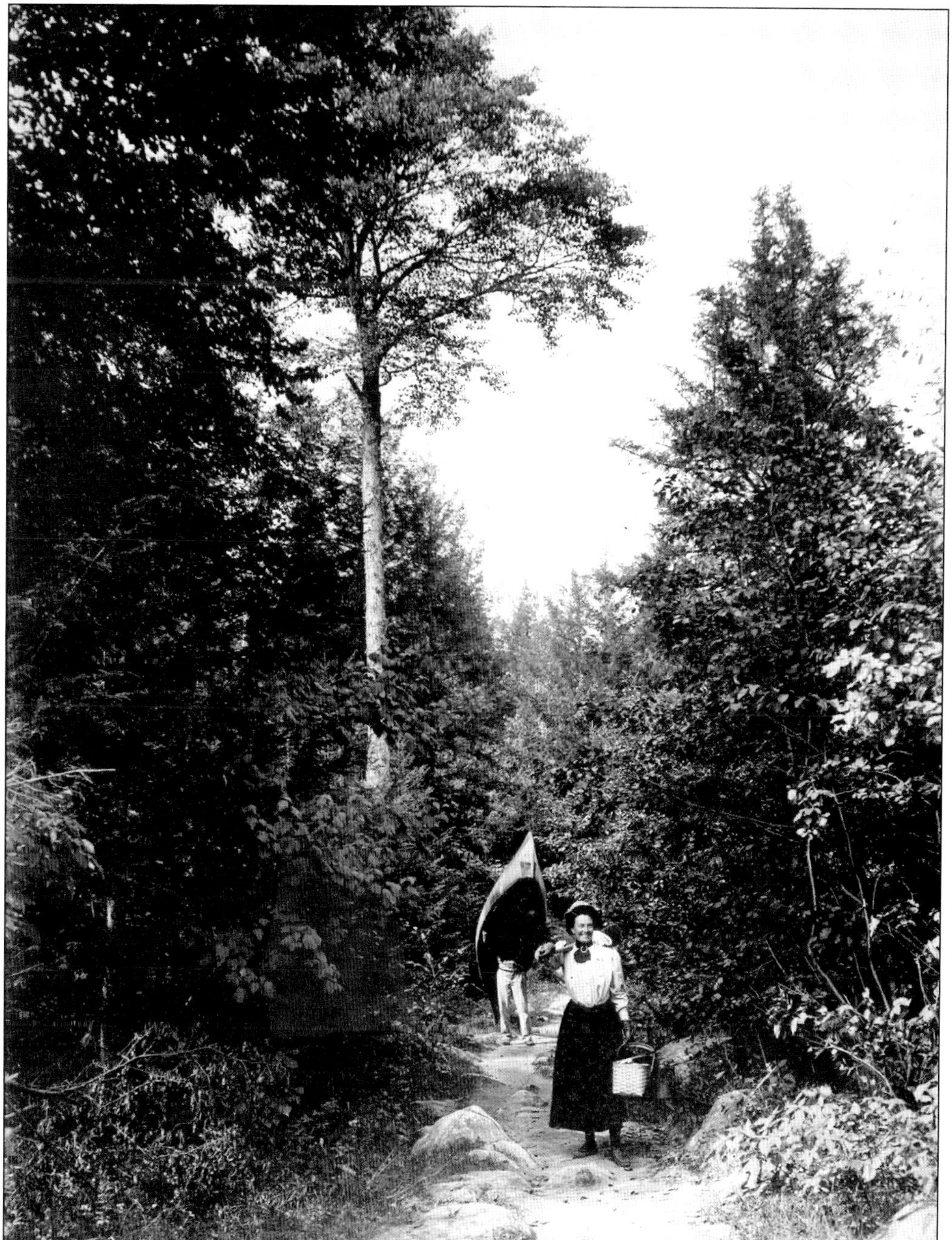

Recreational opportunities in the Mount Katahdin area are abundant. The vast waterway system allowed the brave to explore the region by canoe. Henry David Thoreau vacationed here, marveled at the area's beauty, and returned here for other trips. Using an old Native American trail, a couple on an outing portages to another waterway. A portage was made to get around one of the many waterfalls in the area or to get from one body of water to another. The canoe was especially suited for the area, as it was light and easy to handle. The early canoe was made with birch bark and tree pitch and could be carried with ease.

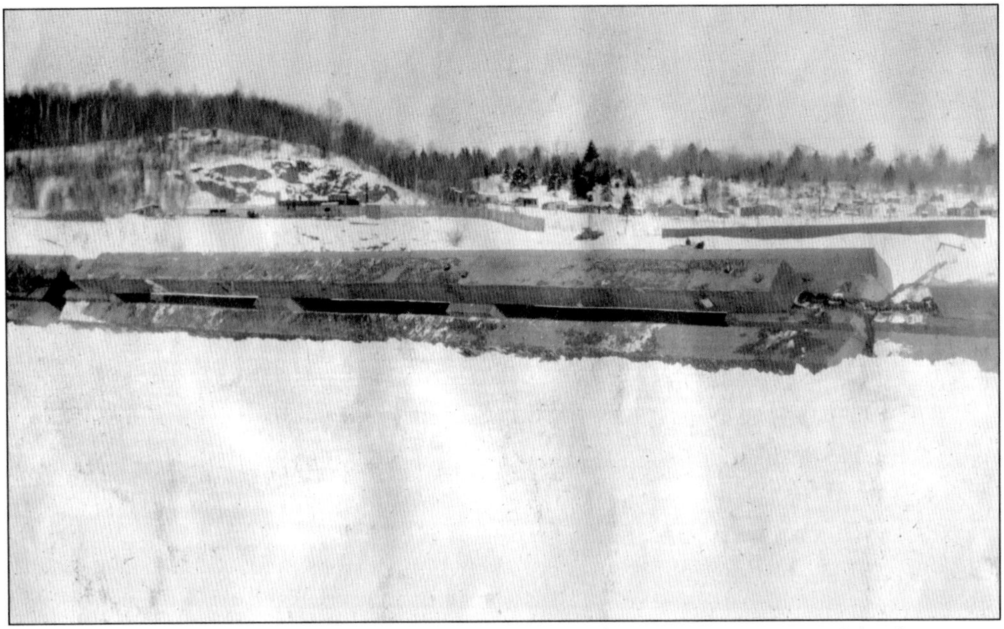

Large logs were cut square and bolted together to create floats. Many sections of the floats were then chained together to create the boom that was used on the lakes to coral the logs into one area. Thousands of feet of these boom logs were needed throughout the region. An easy way to deploy the boom was to wait until enough ice formed on the lake and then place them on top of the ice with teams of horses. By doing it this way, the boom was in place for the spring run of the log drive.

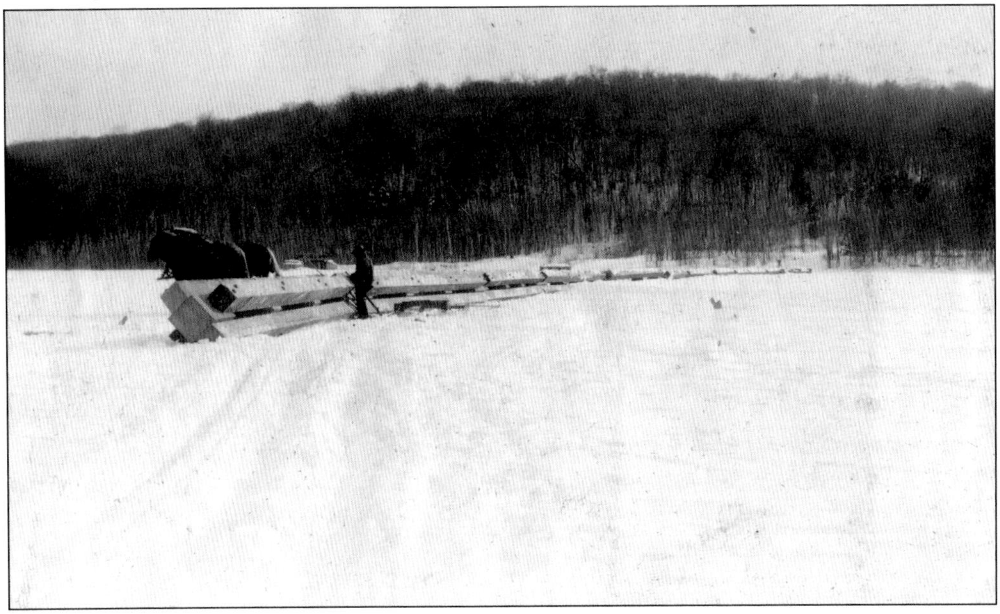

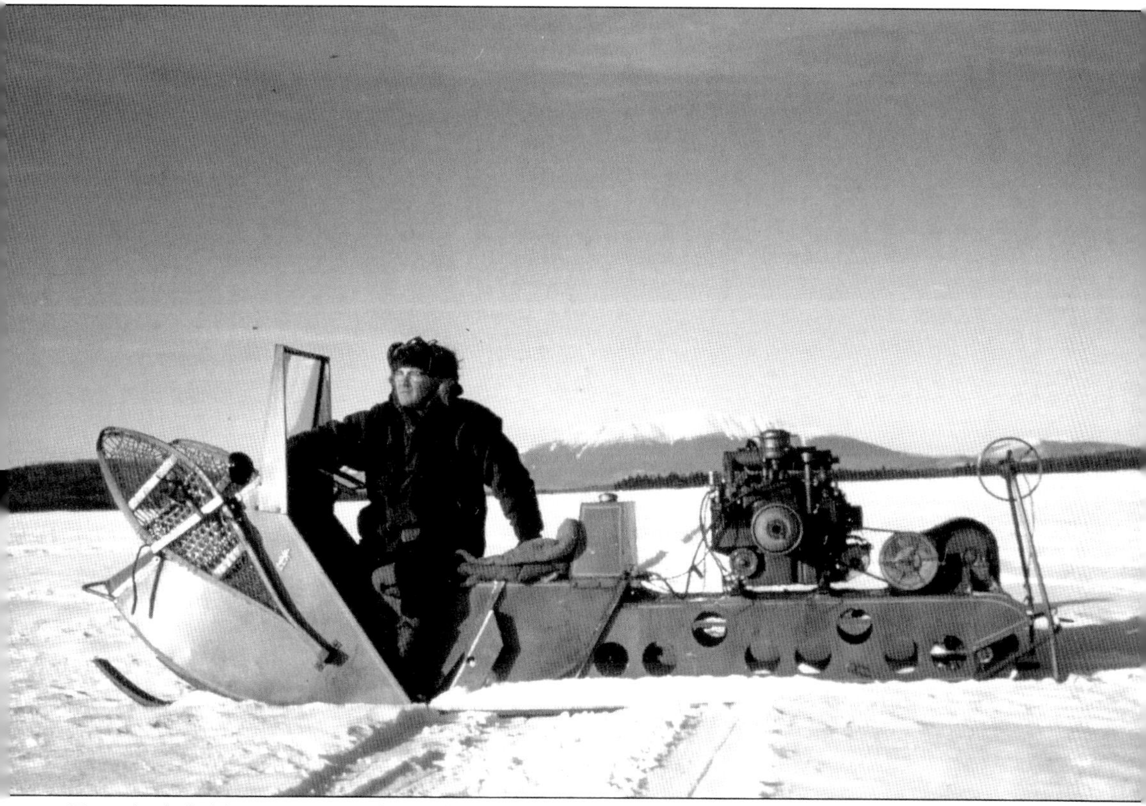

Tom Archibald sits on an early model snowmobile on South Twin Lake with Mount Katahdin standing tall in the background. The snowmobile provided the transportation needed to travel longer distance in the winter with more ease than one could have with snowshoes, and it opened up a whole new winter sport. The early ones were big, noisy, and unreliable contraptions, but they had strong roots in Millinocket. Earlan B. Campbell became the first Polaris dealer in Maine, and by 1960, he was a good friend to the founders of Polaris. With the help of Earlan, Polaris was using the Millinocket area to develop and test various models in an attempt to improve the sled. Many of the early prototypes that were tested here are housed in the only snowmobile museum in Maine, directed by Steve Campbell. The museum is located at the Northern Timber Cruisers clubhouse just outside Millinocket. In 2006, Earlan B. Campbell was inducted into the Snowmobile Hall of Fame. Today there are many trails leading from Millinocket providing opportunity for winter sportsmen to explore the Mount Katahdin region.

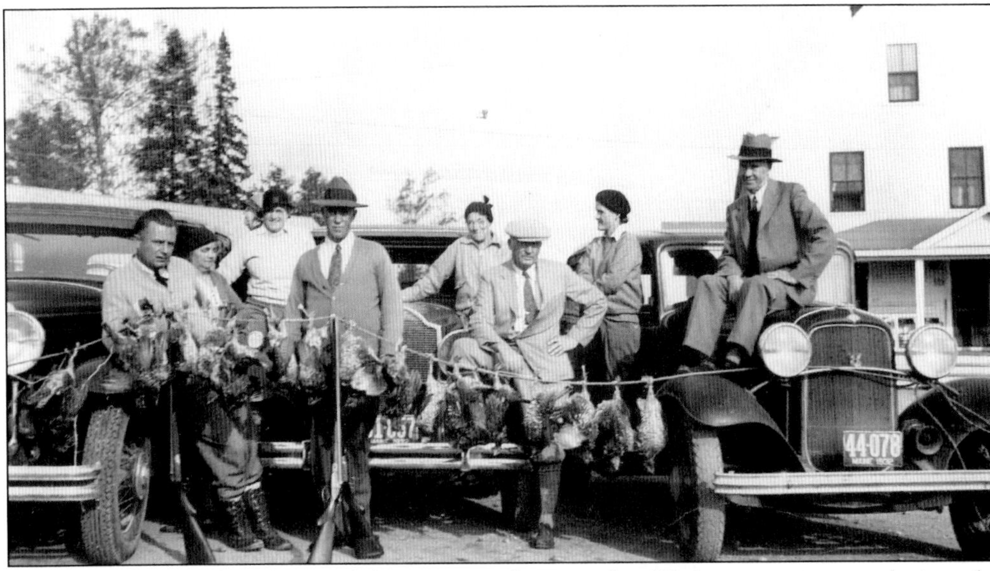

A popular game bird in the Katahdin region is the partridge. With its notorious explosive take off, it is a fun bird to hunt. The building of more roads and the development of the automobile made it more convenient to go farther in search of more game. The white meat of the game bird is a cherished dish in the area.

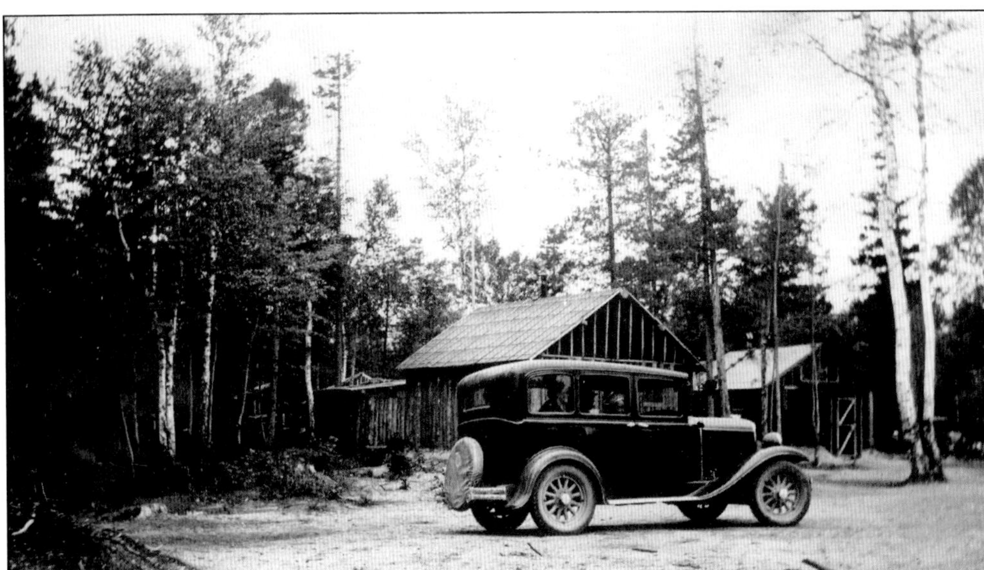

As seen in this 1935 photograph of Togue Pond, camps sprang up around the region after more roads were built. The main entrance to Baxter State Park was built between Lower Togue Pond and Upper Togue Pond. Now the many waterways are dotted with camps that sit on land leased from the many logging companies that make up the north woods of Maine.

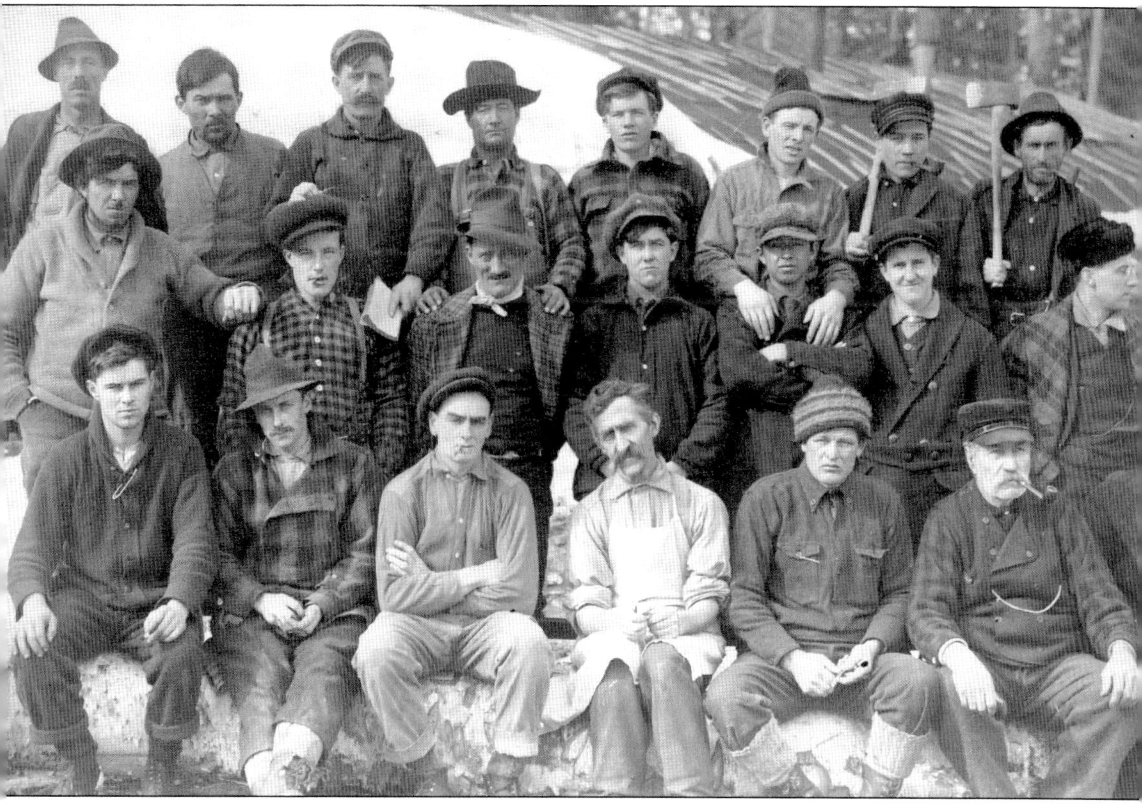

The lumberman of the day was an interesting fellow. Lured to the area with a promise of work, many of the lumbermen came from up north over the border. French-Canadian men were able woodsmen and many of the logging camps resounded with the French dialect. The camps that were built for the men were dark and dingy. Built out of spruce logs and complete with a low roof covered in shingles, the buildings were heated by a central fire and vented with a hole in the roof. Wet wool clothes that stunk of sweat and pitch hung from the low roof around the fire in order to dry. In order to save on building more dwellings than needed, often times the horses and oxen were housed with the men. There were no rooms in the low building, being all open on the inside. Sleeping arrangements were made by making the bedding along one long wall and all the men slept together in one long bed.

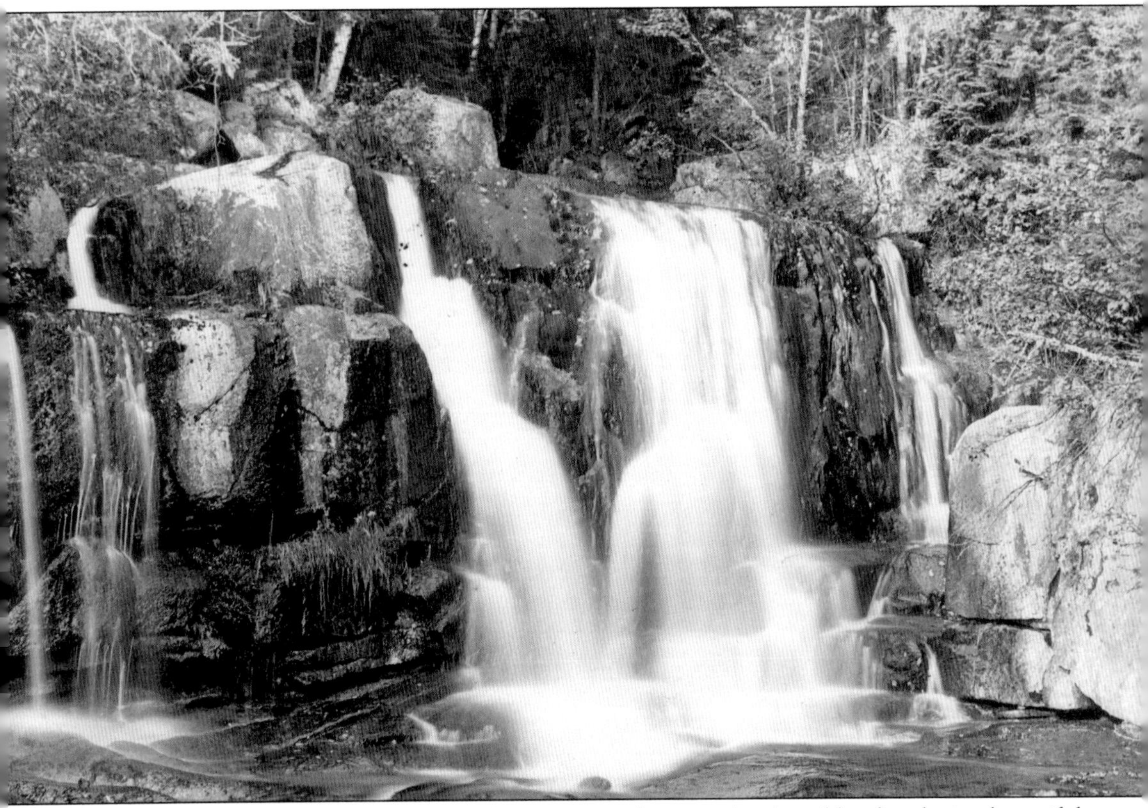

The Mount Katahdin region's crystal clear water, and vast undeveloped land make it a beautiful place. With hundreds of square miles of forestland, one can find little niches of natural beauty and while away the time staring in awe at it all. Katahdin Stream Falls is such a place, with its cold, clear water coming off the mountain. Located in Baxter State Park, it is a short hike up the beginning slopes of Mount Katahdin. The trail takes the hiker along the left bank of Katahdin Stream through the mixed forestland where the roar of the stream can be heard. Small turnout spots along the way allow for the hiker to peak over the steep embankment to the stream below and marvel at the pink and white granite in the streambed that was washed off the mountain. It is a treasured place and a sight to see.

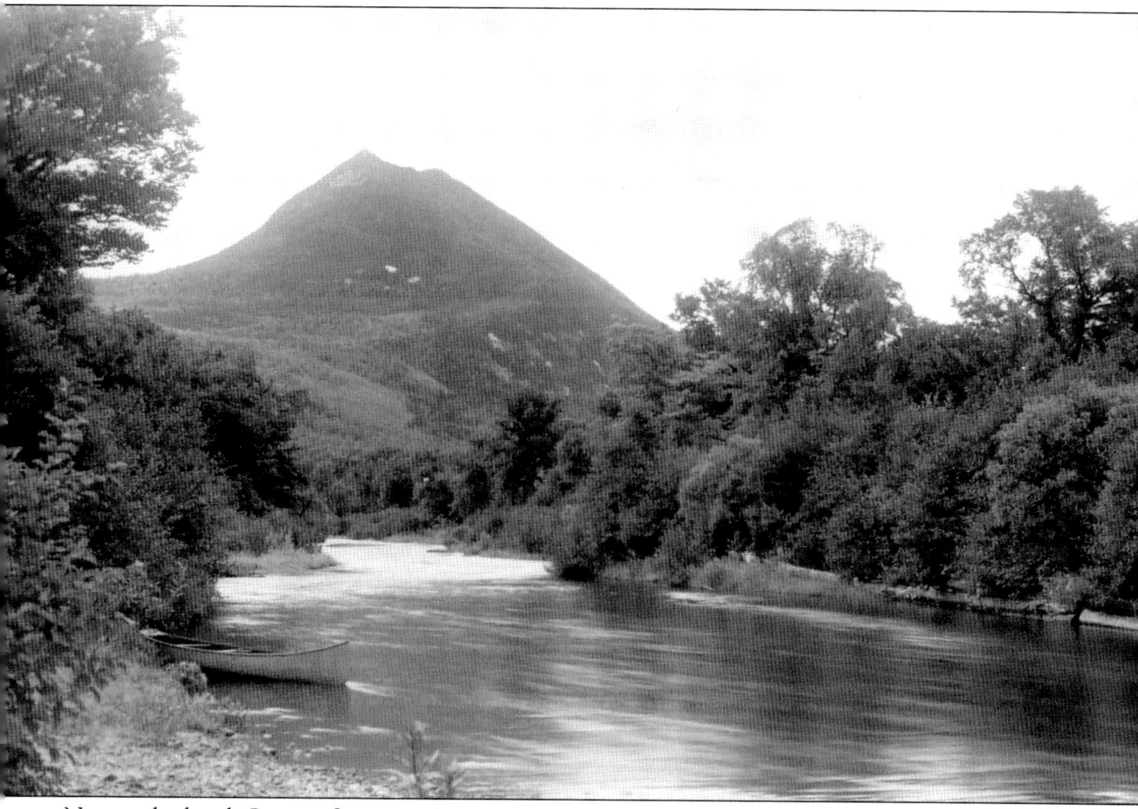

Nesowadnehunk Stream flows gently over colorful fist-sized granite stones as it passes the twin peaks of Double Top Mountain. Brook trout are abundant here and can be taken readily with a fly. Further down the stream the water roars over the breathtaking Little Niagara Falls and the Big Niagara Falls. With its impressive drop and the beautiful scenery, it is easily accessible by trails that are well marked. A relaxing lunch while overlooking the falls makes for a memorable day. Enter through the main gate of Baxter State Park, follow the signs to the parking area, and the well-marked trails will lead here. The massive granite boulders still bear the scars of the log drives when dynamite was used to clear a smooth path for the logs. The stream eventually flows into the West Branch of the Penobscot River where the logs joined the main drive to the mill.

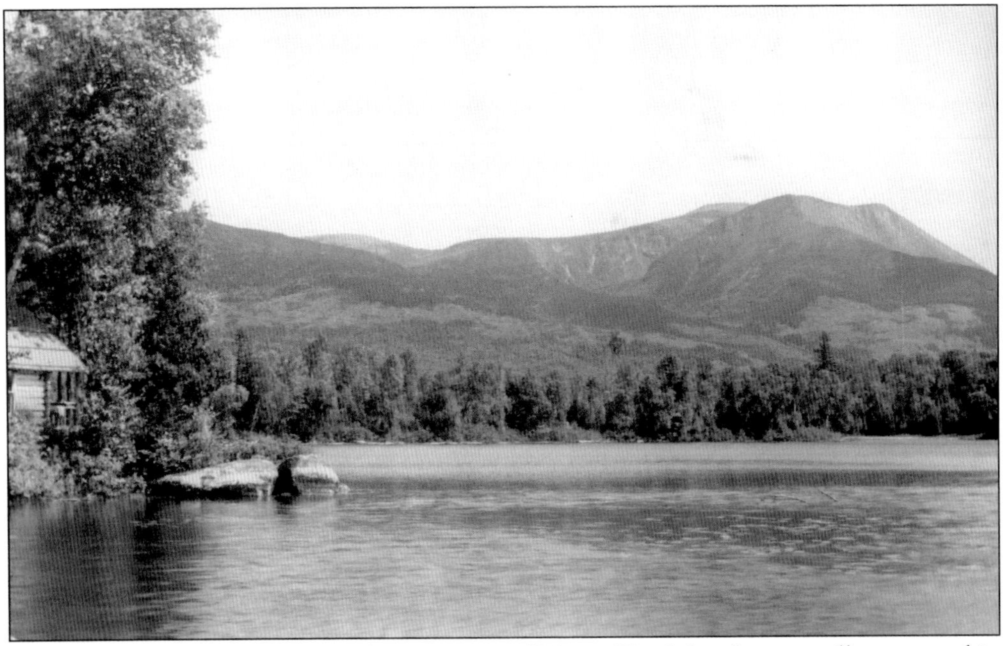

Kidney Pond is located at the southwest corner of Mount Katahdin. It is a small trout pond in Baxter State Park that still has some of the old log cabins built many years ago. Guests to the park can stay in the log cabins and enjoy a good day of fishing on the pond.

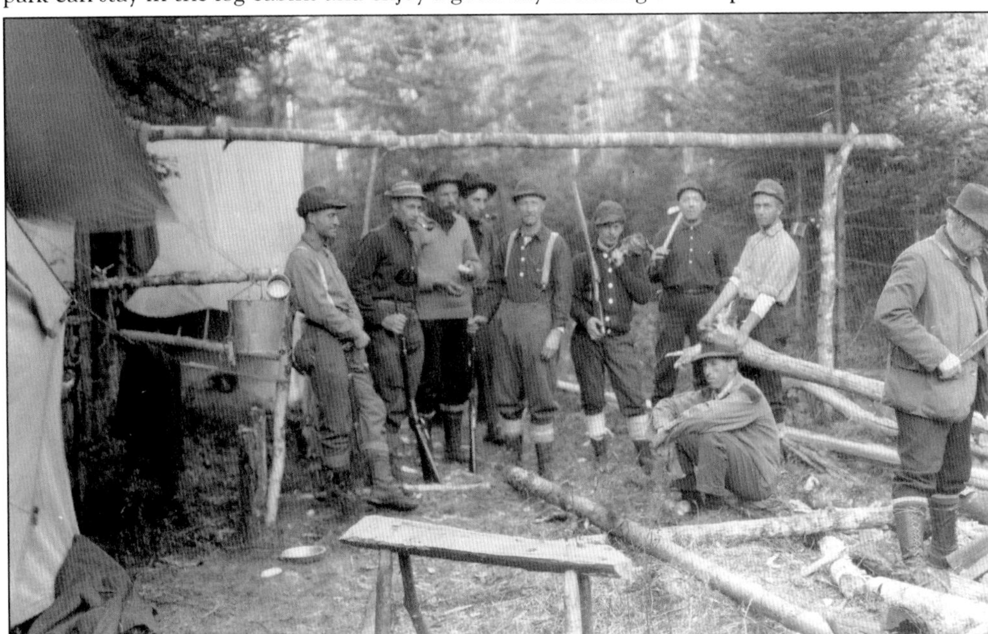

Taking a rest after building their crude campsite, a group of men prepare to go hunting. Outfitted with hunting boots or moccasins and clad in wool pants and shirts, they are ready to take on the elements. A much-hated pest in the outdoors is the black fly, humored to be a set of jaws with sharp teeth and wings. It puts the mosquito to shame and can drive one insane if it were not for proper precautions. Bug repellent in those early days was whatever home recipe one might be able to dream up that kept the bugs away.

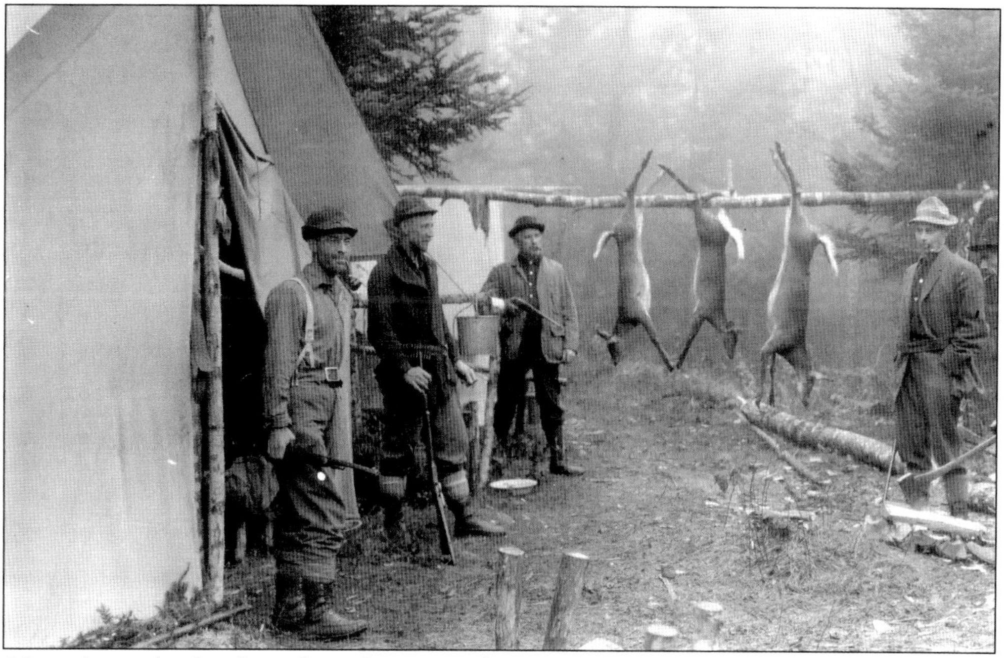

After a hunt, the deer hang from the game pole. Deer were so heavily hunted that, by the early 1900s, their numbers were severely reduced. It is through proper game management that the deer herds are coming back. The hunter of today stands more of a chance of bagging a mature deer that would be more of a trophy than can be seen here.

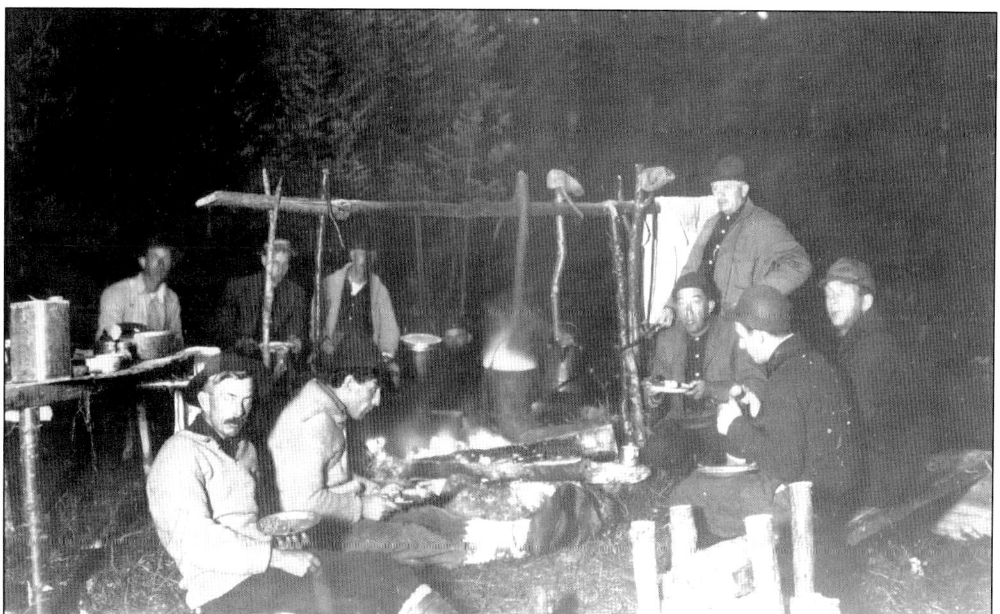

Resting by the campfire on a chilly night, the hunters enjoy a plate of baked beans and strong coffee. A pole is suspended over the fire to hang cooking pots from. Traditionally one person, who started the fires and prepared the food, was designated as the camp cook. With a group of hungry men ready to eat, the cook better be good at his job. Hunting today is done more for sport rather than for survival, as it was done in the early days.

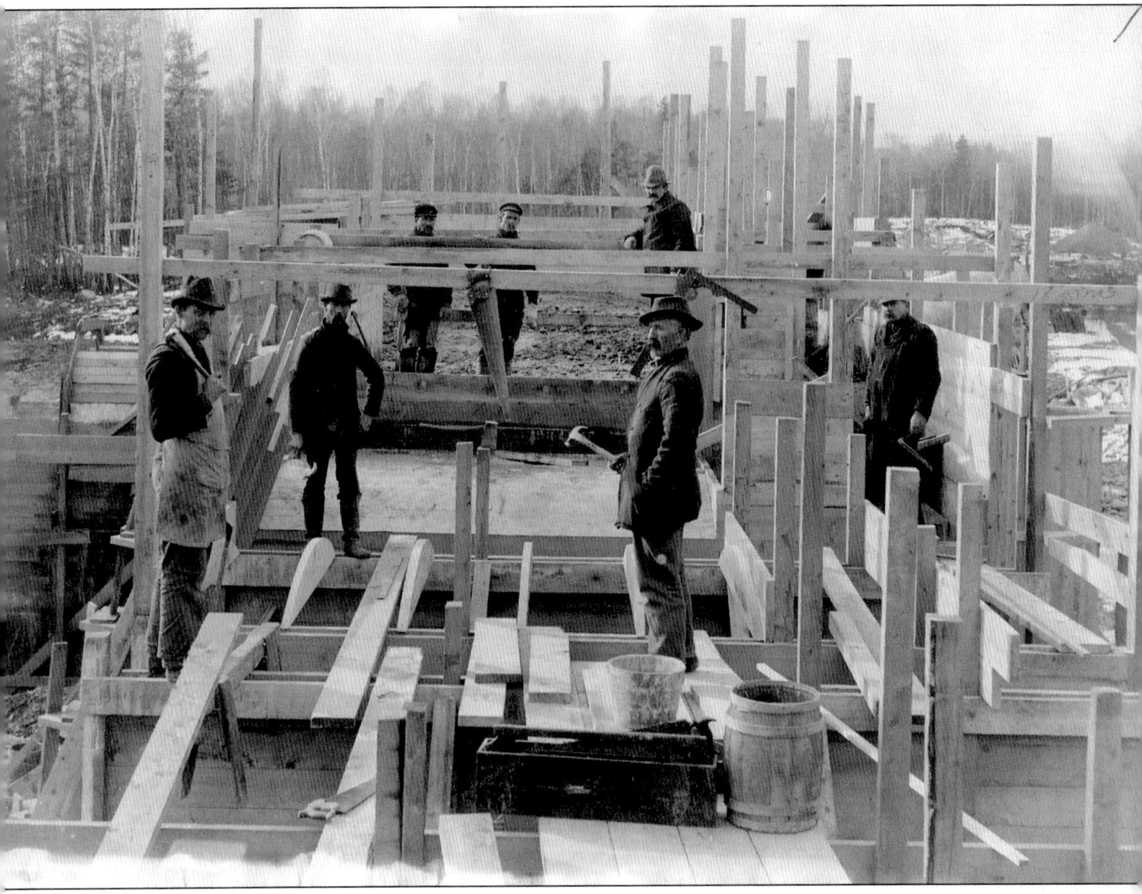

The Great Northern Paper Company always supported its organized labor; however, it had a change of heart in 1934. A new dam was needed in order to generate more power. It was during the height of the Depression and the company took the opportunity to direct-hire 250 to 300 men for the construction of the North Twin Dam. Utilizing unorganized labor allowed the company to have a more direct say in the work without having to go through a union. The wages were low, but the men needed the work, so they accepted the conditions. The dam was complete in a year at a cost of just over $1 million. The dam is still in use today and sits at the outlet of Elbow Lake on the West Branch of the Penobscot River.

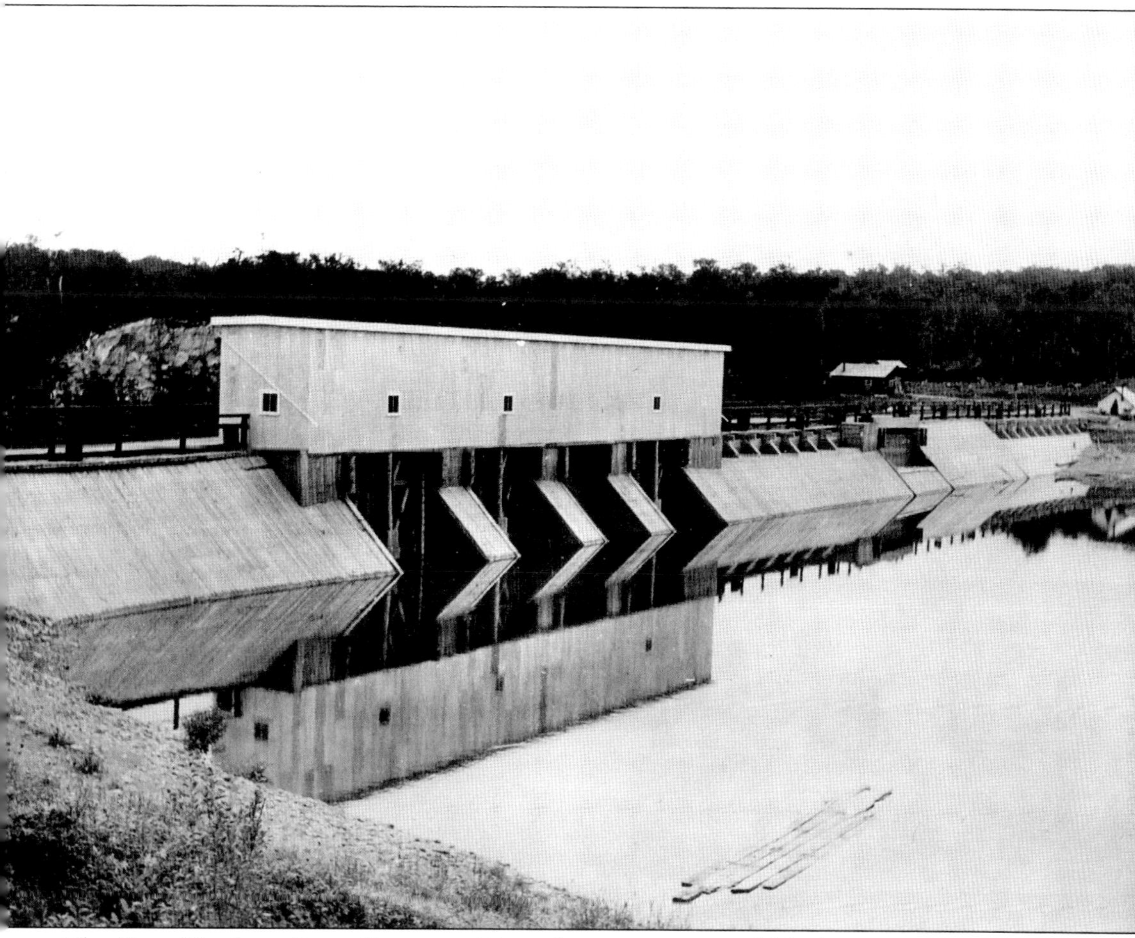

The Great Northern Paper Company did not become so successful by being extravagant and careless with money. The management was always looking for ways to save money and still put out a good product. The Canadian market was heavily subsidized, and it was a challenge to keep costs down and remain competitive in the market. To make matters worse, the federal government passed new laws regulating the paper industry and creating numerous hurdles for the Great Northern Paper Company. For the company, the building of the infrastructure that was needed to do business was perhaps the biggest cost it had. In 1926, Garret Schenck convinced the directors that a new dam could be built out of wood to save $350,000. The company needed new paper machines to replace aging ones, and the savings helped pay for them. The Seboomook Dam was built out of wood and it became the largest timber crib dam ever built.

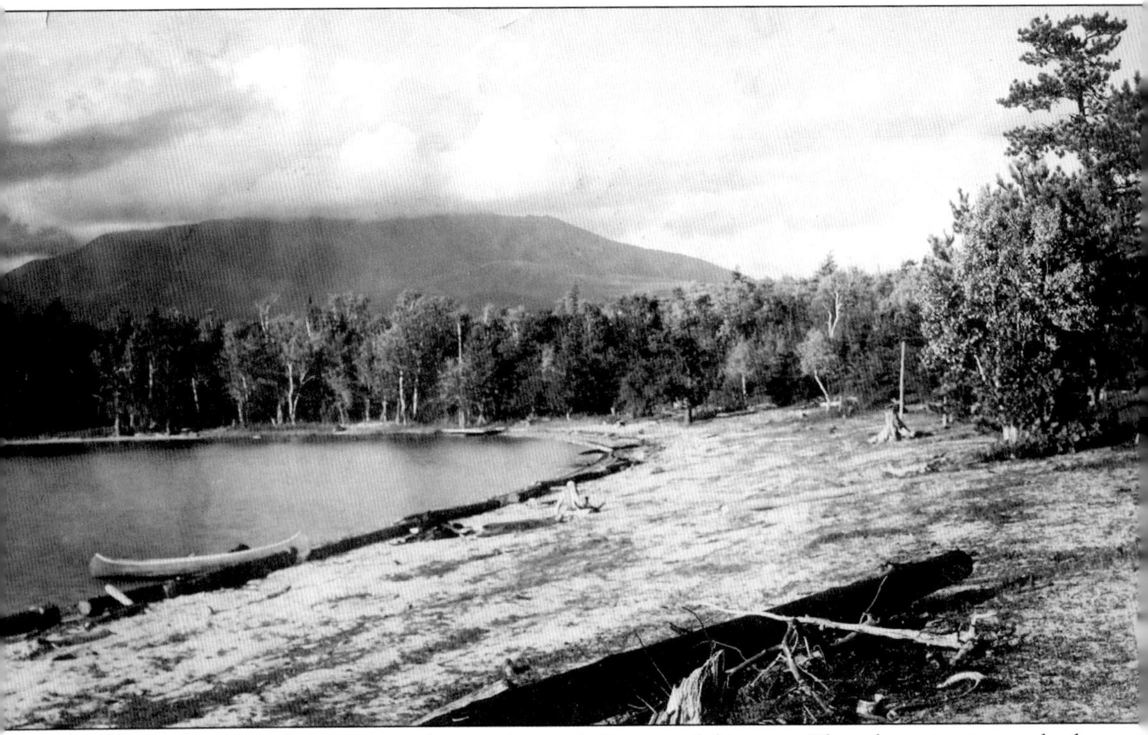

The Ice Age played a big role in the carving and shaping of this area. The advancing ice pushed up the mountains, and the valleys were dug out. There was a tremendous amount of force involved to create what was left behind. From the grinding of the glaciers to the erosion caused by the rivers, the granite was ground down to course sand. While not the fine sand found on the ocean beaches, it serves its purpose and the beaches around Millinocket are well appreciated. This beach area is known to the locals as Omaha Beach and is on the Debsconeag Deadwater on the Penobscot River about four miles in from the Golden Road. Mount Katahdin has its top shrouded in the clouds in the background.

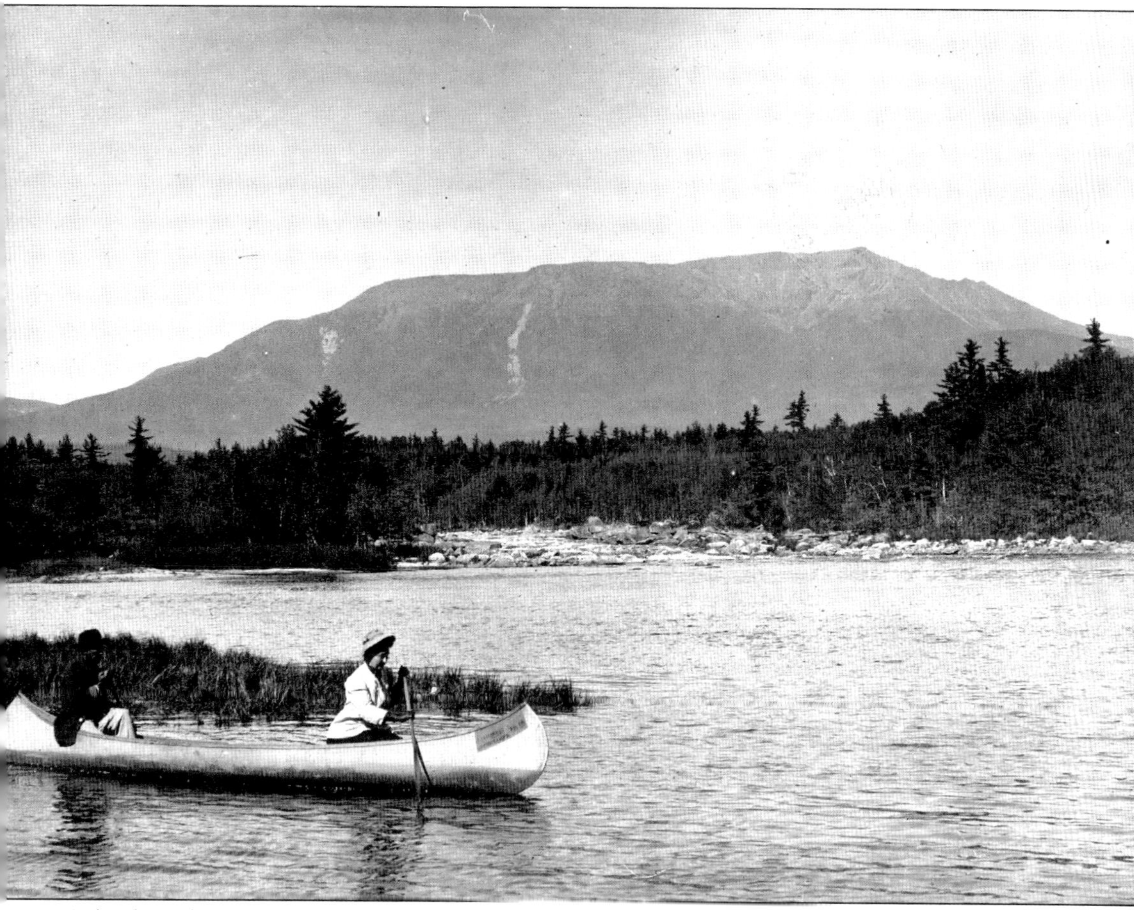

A lot has changed around Millinocket over the years, roads are in place to ease the travel deep into the woods, all terrain vehicles can go in other areas not easily accessible by car, and snowmobiles can zoom through the trails and over the frozen waters of the north woods. One thing that has not changed is the satisfaction of paddling a canoe slowly along a secluded stream. Just a short distance from Millinocket there are no sounds of traffic and the hustle and bustle of everyday life is left behind. A glance in the sky and the contrails of a jet quietly passing overhead is a reminder of the realities of the modern day. It is almost possible to hear the far-off echo of an axe as some long-ago lumberman chops a tree down. The quiet serenity is only enhanced by Mount Katahdin, overlooking the river as it flows past the enormous expanse of the great mountain.

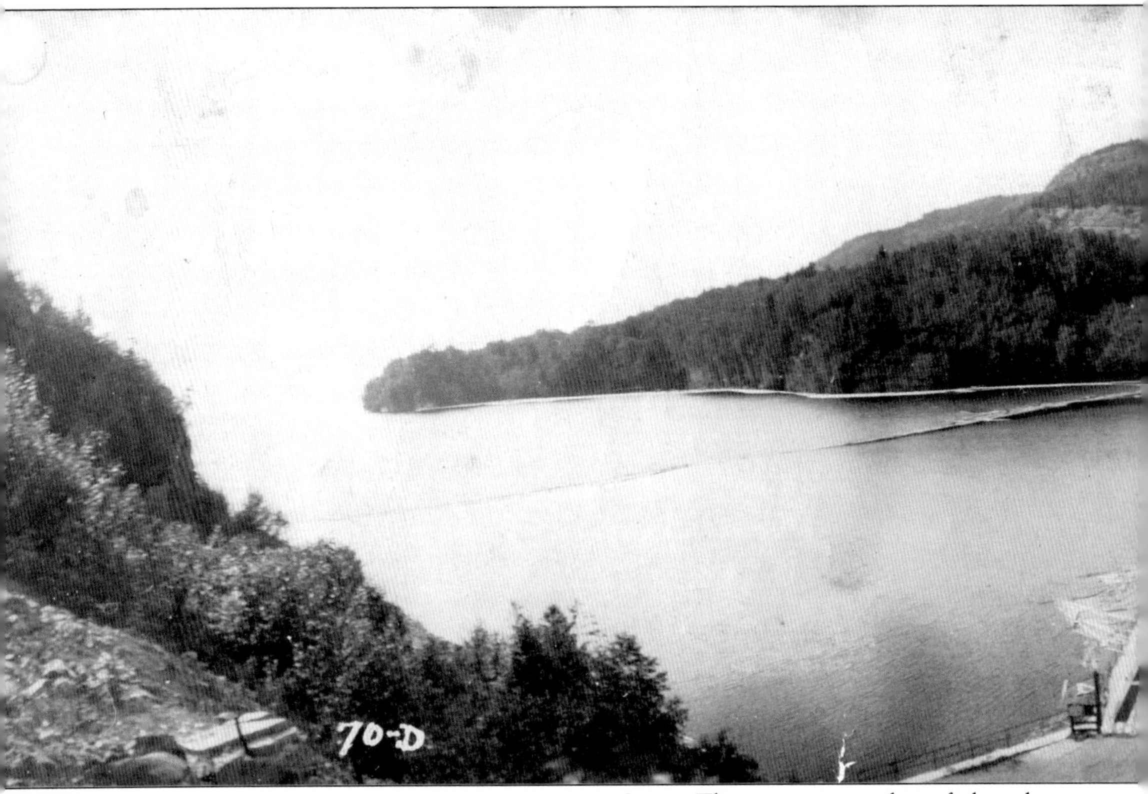

Ripogenus Dam was started in 1915 at Ripogenus Gorge. There were a number of obstacles to overcome for the construction of this dam. The biggest obstacle was that there were no roads or railroad tracks within 45 miles of the gorge. A new road had to be built from Lily Bay on Moosehead Lake. Sias Hill was partway between Lily Bay and the work site. Sias Hill was so steep

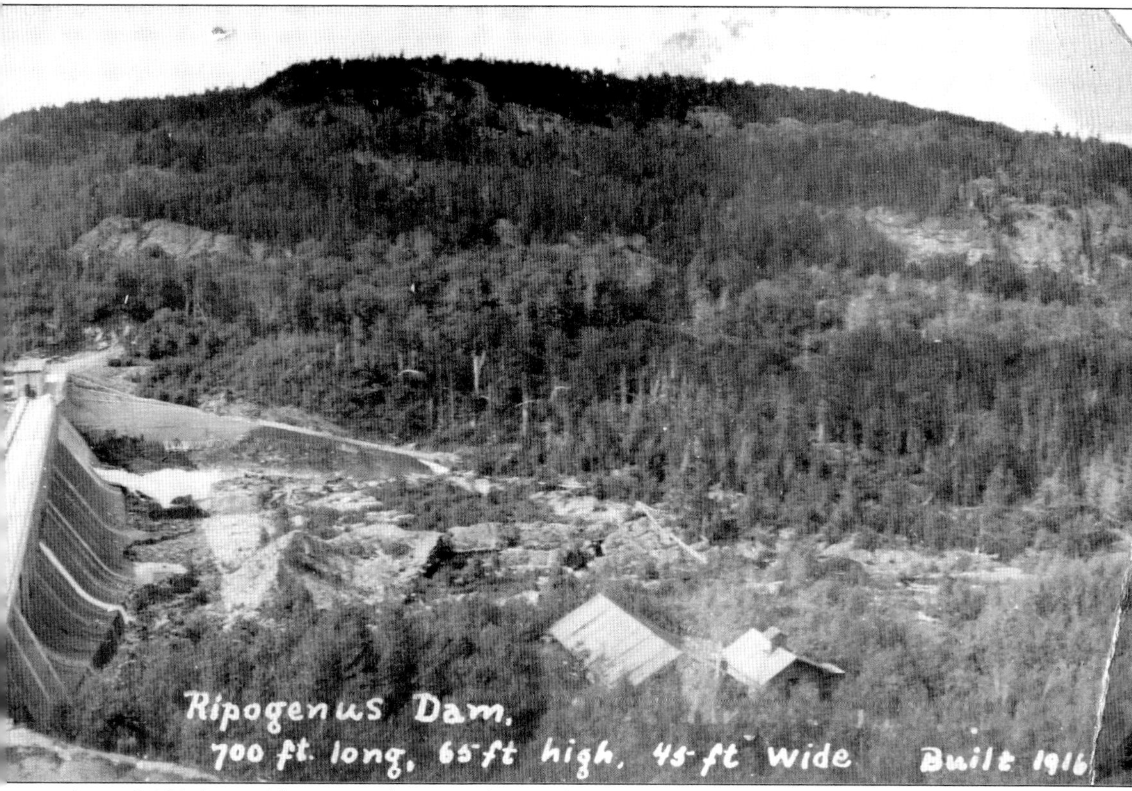

that a 2,200-foot cable was used to ease the trucks over the hill. Despite the numerous problems to overcome, the dam was built. When it was complete, it was considered the largest privately owned storage dam. It measures an impressive 704 feet long and is 92 feet above the ledge. It still stands today and is in use. A road runs the length of it, allowing for automobile traffic.

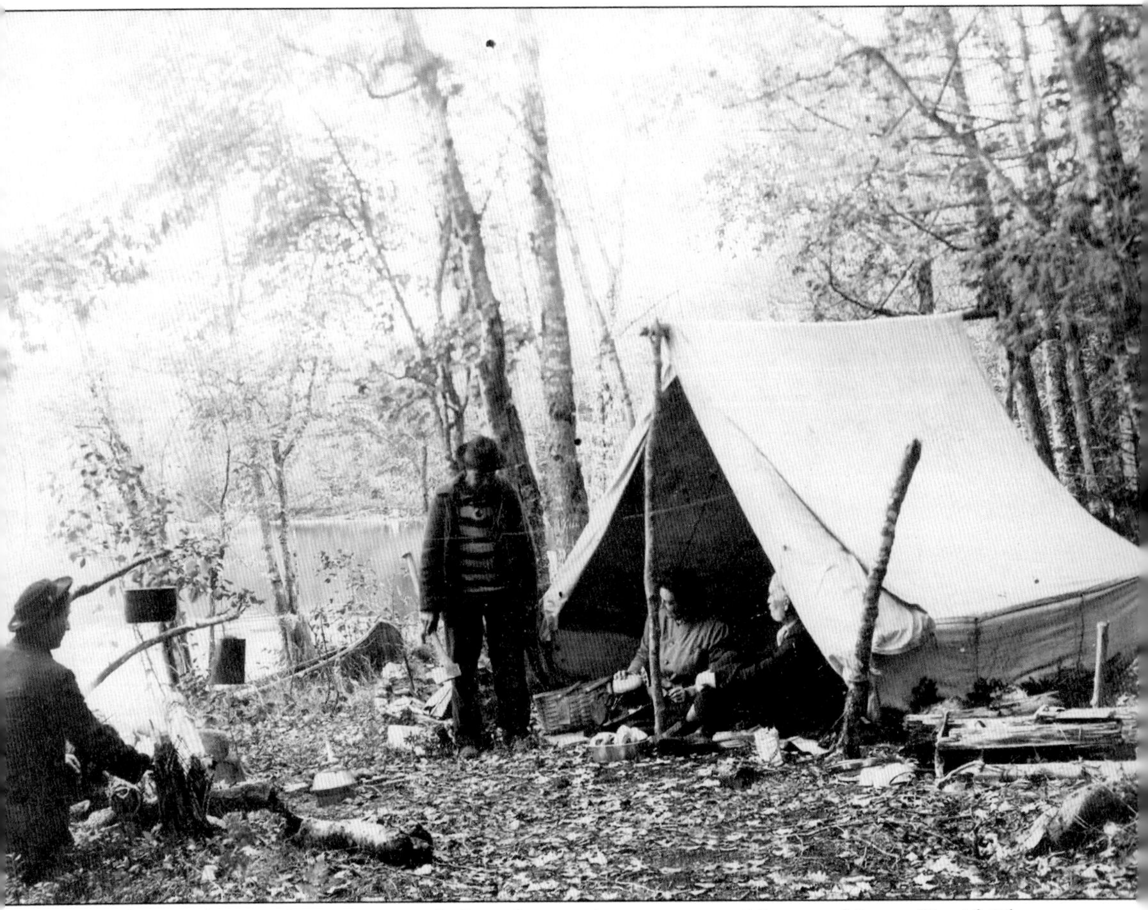

Early travelers to the area marveled at the area's vastness and beauty. Henry David Thoreau ventured here and carefully documented his travels in his writings. He spoke often of the area to his friends on his return trips back to Boston. An excursion to the area in those days involved significant travel time, as there were no roads. Few had climbed Mount Katahdin, so there were no trails to follow. Early mountaineers picked their way through the clouds, hoping to not come to an impassable spot that would block the way and force backtracking. It was formidable land that was hard to get to.

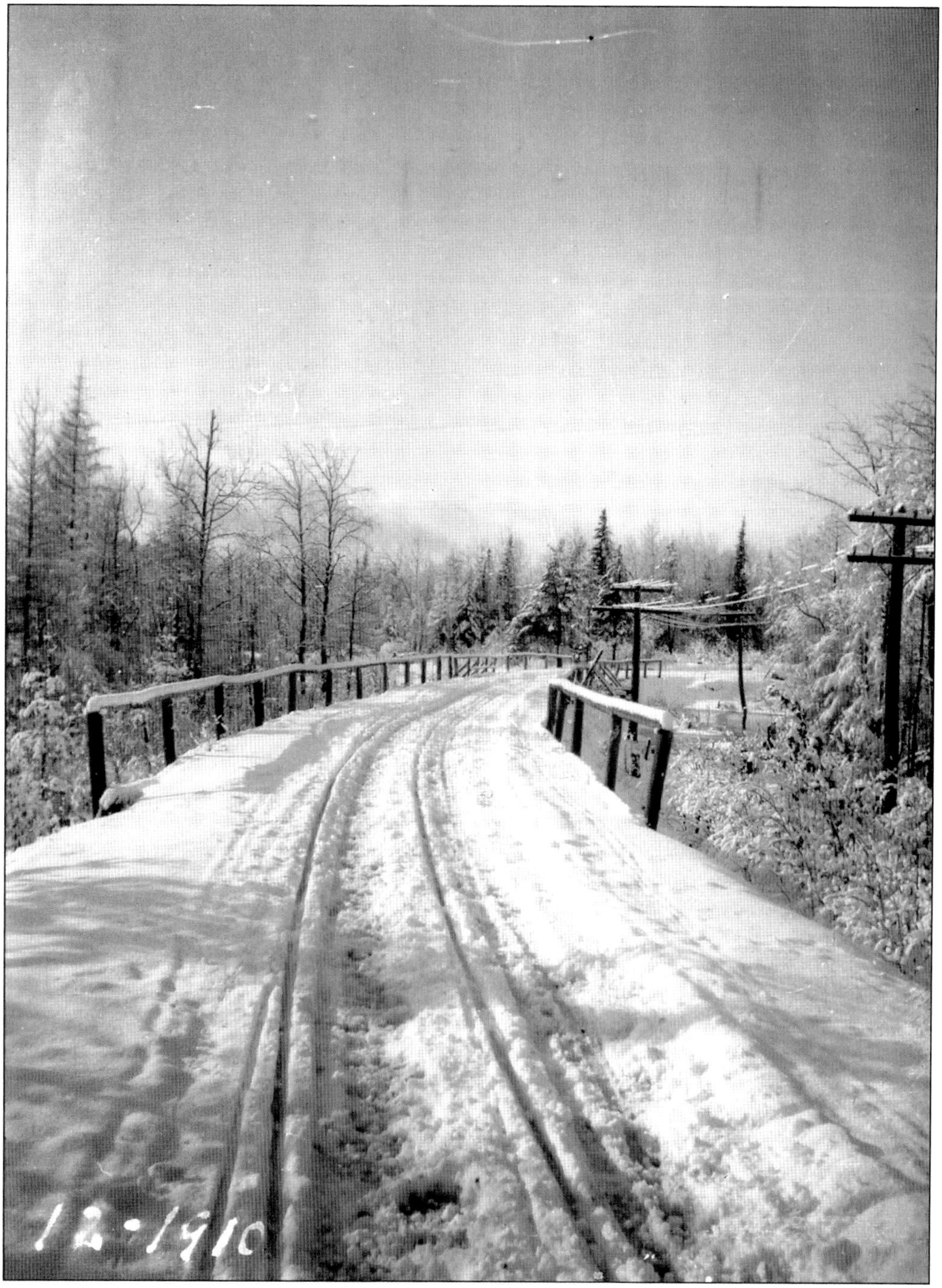

The date on this picture indicates it was taken in 1910 when the town was in its infancy. Millinocket has come a long way since the day of Thomas Fowler. The mill is still here, but the Great Northern Paper Company no longer exists. The mill has struggled over the years, but it still is turning out paper. The town will go on due to the strength and determination that came from its early ancestors. (Courtesy of Fred Fowler.)